Blueprint for PROJECT RECOVERY— A Project Management Guide

Blueprint for PROJECT RECOVERY— A Project Management Guide

The Complete Process for Getting Derailed Projects Back on Track

Ronald B. Cagle

AMACOM

American Management Association

New York • Atlanta • Brussels • Buenos Aires • Chicago • London • Mexico City

San Francisco • Shanghai • Tokyo • Toronto • Washington, D.C.

Special discounts on bulk quantities of AMACOM books are available to corporations, professional associations, and other organizations. For details, contact Special Sales Department, AMACOM, a division of American Management Association, 1601 Broadway, New York, NY 10019.
Tel.: 212-903-8316. Fax: 212-903-8083.
Web site: www.amacombooks.org

Library of Congress Cataloging-in-Publication Data

Cagle, Ronald B.
Blueprint for project recovery : a project management guide : the complete process for getting derailed projects back on track / Ronald B. Cagle.
p. cm.
Includes bibliographical references and index.
ISBN 0-8144-0766-8 (hardcover)
1. Project management. I. Title.

HD69.P75 C345 2003
658.4′04—dc21 *2002011733*

Printing number

10 9 8 7 6 5 4 3 2 1

TABLE OF CONTENTS

FIGURES

TABLES

PREFACE

Blueprint For Project Recovery—A Project Management Guide is a unique combination of text and interactive CD that provides:

- ❐ A tutorial for the aspiring project manager
- ❐ A text for the newly assigned project manager
- ❐ A checklist for the ongoing project manager
- ❐ A quick-response recovery tool for the project manager with a project in trouble

If you are part of a small business, this book provides insight into all levels of projects. It draws from the "best-of-the-best" to provide you with a consolidated view into what all businesses, large, small, government, and commercial, are doing.

If you are part of a large business or are associated with the federal, state, or local government as an employee or as a contractor, this book has special meaning for you. It uses many federal policies, plans, processes, and standards as references. It uses these references for two reasons: first, they are thorough, and second, you, as a taxpayer, have already paid for them—why not use them?

Projects and programs usually consist of three principal periods—planning, conducting, and concluding. The conducting period is divided into two parts that occur sporadically: normal and terrifying. The normal part consists of the day-to-day activities that are going according to plan. The terrifying part is when the project goes off track—roughly akin to a "near-miss" in an airplane. This book was written to take some of the terror out of the "near-miss."

While this book won't solve all your problems, it will give you a leg up on a lot of them. In addition, this book will provide techniques to tailor or customize the process to your way of doing business or for your specific business area or your specific technical problems.

Many companies reward project and program managers for jobs well done. These rewards come in a number of different forms. One of the rewards is in the category of recovery. It is a coveted award because any project or program manager who has been around for a while knows that it is considerably more difficult to restore a project or program than it is to start up or maintain one. Frequently, the recovery award is called the Phoenix Award. It is called the Phoenix Award because it relates to the mysterious phoenix—the bird that is the symbol of immortality, resurrection, life, and death. In ancient mythology, the phoenix was said to consume itself in flames and then, three days later arise from the ashes, allowing the cycle of life to continue. . . .

All too often, projects and programs are consumed in flames and turn to ashes. The purposes of this book are to recommend up-front planning, provide a checklist for ongoing projects, and, if you are really in a bind, effect the resurrection from the ashes and allow the project's cycle of life to continue.

Now, let's look at what is forthcoming in this book and how we are going to handle these elements.

The first part of the book consists of Chapters 1 through 5. Chapter 1 sets the stage with an overview of the project/program environment and the recovery process. Chapters 2 and 3 present checklists for programmatic and technical issues, together with the associated explanations that can be used as a checklist for planning a project or checking an ongoing project. Chapters 4 and 5 follow the same convention but, this time, offer a recovery approach for those issues that have, or may have, gone off track.

The second part of the book, Chapters 6 through 10, provides techniques and methodologies for expanding the provided database and tailoring it to your specific needs.

I recommend that you read the book from beginning to end and follow the process that is outlined. However, I recognize that you may not have time to do all that. For that reason, I have provided checklists to make the process easier and, if you have a problem that needs immediate attention, you can jump to Chapter 11 and use the interactive CD to help you solve the problem staring you in the face. If you take that approach, however, take some time to go back and read the whole book so you won't get in that bind again!

Ronald B. Cagle

ACKNOWLEDGMENTS

This book would never have come to print without the efforts of a number of people. First among these is Dr. Wallace G. Berger. Wally was instrumental in helping with some of the concepts and many of the technical details. He is the guru of architecture and metrics. We spent many hours in planning, and he spent a great deal of time reviewing the manuscript at all levels.

I want to offer special thanks to the following people:

To Mr. Robert Gray, an expert in software programs and in program rescue as well. He was a candidate for the coveted Phoenix Award several years ago. Bob is presently chief engineer for a transportation company in Canada. His reviews of content and contributions were extremely helpful.

To Mr. Larry Kile, an electrical engineer and program manager, and now a director of engineering for a large company in Atlanta.

To Mr. David Botto, a former engineering section head and programs director. He is now the president and CEO of his own airport implementation company.

To experts in contracts and subcontracts who participated in the peer review.

And to my wife, Judy, a schoolteacher who spent many, many hours reviewing the manuscripts and giving a great deal of helpful input regarding the impact and context of various word combinations. Not to mention putting up with my being at the computer day and night.

The contributions from each of you are sincerely appreciated.

Ronald B. Cagle

Blueprint for PROJECT RECOVERY— A Project Management Guide

CHAPTER 1

GETTING STARTED

Whether you are preplanning your project or your project is up and running and you want to conduct an in-process evaluation or whether you've experienced a failure in some part of your project, you are in the right place.

To begin, let's set the baseline by establishing some definitions. You may or may not agree with all the definitions, and that's okay as long as you understand how these terms are to be used in the book.

We'll start with the difference between a project and a program. Everybody has his own definition, so here's mine. A project is conducted for a customer who is internal to an enterprise. A program is conducted for a customer who is external to the enterprise; a program has legal ramifications between the enterprise and the customer. (See Figure 1-1.) The discriminator is the legal document or contract. Stated in another way, a program manager has Profit and Loss (P&L) and legal responsibility in addition to cost, schedule, and technical responsibilities. The project manager, on the other hand, has cost, schedule, and technical assignments. Thus, a program manager needs a slightly different skill

Figure 1-1 — Project/Program Environment

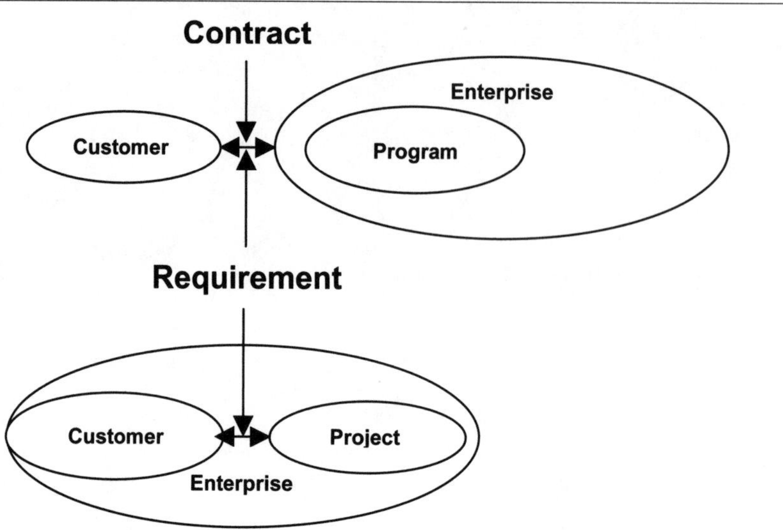

set than a project manager. Some people like to define a program as bigger than a project or as a collection of projects. While this can sometimes be true when a large program is subdivided into segments, or Sub Program Offices (SPOs), this makes projects appear to be less important than programs. They're not! Consider the enormity of the Manhattan Project, and I think you will understand why I have a lot of trouble with that definition.

For simplicity, I intend to use the term "project" throughout this book except in those cases where the term "program" is called for under this definition.

The second definition is the project and program environment. This consists of three elements: The customer (the one who creates the requirement), the enterprise (the company, corporation, or other legal entity), and the project or program itself. I visualize the program and project environments as shown in Figure 1-1.

The real difference is that the project is fully contained within the company, which is the creator of both the requirements and the home of the project. In the case of the program, however, the customer is outside the company. In this case, carefully note that the ensuing contract is between the customer and the company and not the customer and the program. The program is not a legal entity.

1.1 General

Figure 1-2 is a composite drawing that shows the relationships between several different parts of the overall project/program process.

The requirements (near the middle) are actually the beginning. The requirements drive the project/program implementation concept (up) and the project/program documentation and methodologies (down). On the upward leg, the requirements are converted into schedule and budget. On the downward leg, the requirements are decomposed into the Work Breakdown Structure (WBS).

The WBS is arguably the most important tool of the project planning process. The WBS shows the decomposed task to be accomplished by dividing the requirement into "chunks" that can be scheduled, costed, and controlled. Each of these chunks is then assigned to an appropriate operating organization for accomplishment. The majority of the WBS is product-oriented although it does contain some organizational and control aspects. Without these organizational and control aspects, the WBS is really a design tree, an equipment tree, or a product tree.

The requirements document (contract) and the WBS are the initial and major contributors to the all-important Requirements Traceability Matrix (see Attachment 7).

Finally, you add the methodologies of schedule, budget, and processes or procedures to control the cost, schedule, and quality of the product at the lowest level of the WBS, which is called the Work Package (WP). The Work Package appears in the WBS at the lowest level of the WBS at the intersect with the organizational element that will accomplish the task. Thus, the Work Package is really the heart of the WBS. The remainder of the structure is simply an organized way to get down to the Work Package by decomposing the requirement or a way to get back to a higher level by rolling up from the bottom.

Throughout the text of this book you will see references to a Work Breakdown Structure (WBS), a Requirements Traceability Matrix (RTM), a Requirements Flow-down Matrix (RFM), and a Work Package (WP). Each of these documents serves a vital role, and it is important to understand how each fits into the overall scheme of things. Figure 1-3 ties all these activities together in one diagram.

There are subtleties in Figure 1-3 that are worth mentioning. Notice first that the Customer Requirement, consisting of the Statement Of Work (SOW) and the Specification (Spec), drives the RTM to the left and the RFM to the right.

Figure 1-2 — Project/Program Requirements Control Relationships

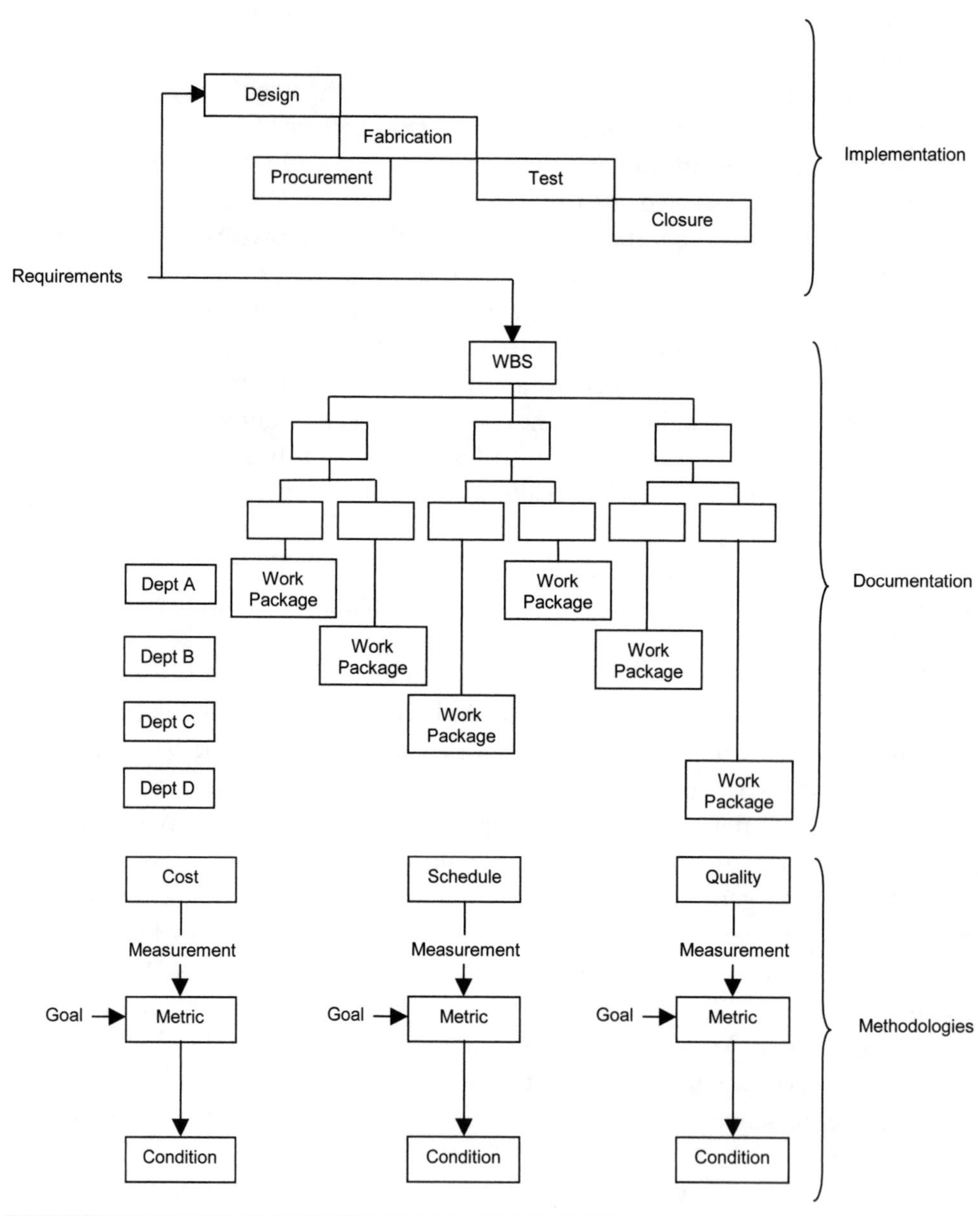

Figure 1-3 — Documentation Interrelationships

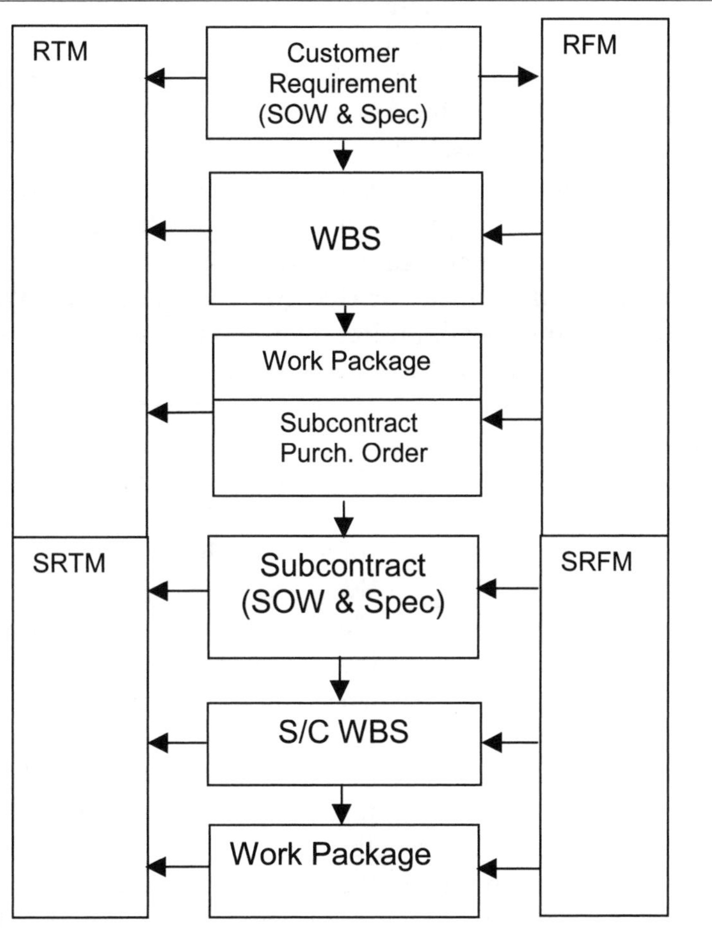

The RFM, in turn, drives all the remaining blocks in the diagram, including the Subcontract Requirements Flow-down Matrix (SRFM). The Customer Requirement (SOW and Spec) also drives the WBS terminating in the lowest level of the WBS, the Work Package. In this diagram, the Work Package is divided in half. That division represents an internal Work Package on top and a subcontract or purchased item on the bottom. This representation is for presentation purposes only. In a real WBS, Work Packages are physically separated from subcontract packages. All of these elements contribute to the overall product.

A subcontract and possibly a purchase order will continue to be divided down in the same manner as the prime contract structure. The RTM keeps track of everything that is going on throughout the project. The flow of the requirements and the documentation are downward. The work and product obviously flow in an upward direction.

Most projects or programs are planned by the Program Office from the top down. Cost and schedule are allocated to the organizational elements to make the project fit an overall cost/schedule envelope. Conversely, most projects are built from the bottom up by the operating organizations. The two approaches meet at the Work Package, and it is at this point where the shuffling and negotiation and, yes, "the weeping and gnashing of teeth," begin. At the Work Packages you can realize and calculate the risk level inherent in each Work Package and, by summary, in the overall project. As project manager, you may need to "task" (some call it "challenge") the Work Package Leaders to make the entire project fit into the proverbial five-pound bag. Tasking involves recognizing that the time or budget allocated (downward) is not what has been requested (upward). Whether or not it is sufficient is the basis of tasking. So, as project manager, you task the leader of the performing organization to accomplish the assigned task within the budget or schedule (or both) that you have allocated. It must be understood that tasking involves risk. Here is where your Risk Mitigation Plan (see Attachment 3) comes in, but how you handle this part of the project is pretty much up to you. The amount of work and negotiation that is necessary here will be, in great part, dependent on how this was handled during the Project Planning Phase.

This is, as they say, "where the rubber meets the road." All the schedule elements, the cost elements, and the quality factors must be applied to the Work Package. In order to determine whether the project is working properly, you must use measurements and apply them to goals in order to create metrics. Now you have a project or program that has the controls you need in order to make it work. If a Work Package is derailed, the project is derailed, so this is the point where you must not only monitor the project but the point at which you must control the project as well. Yes, the $500,000 project as well as the $500,000,000 program must be controlled at this level.

Accomplishment and reporting are assigned to an organizational element. Progress is monitored by the Program Office according to the metrics that have been established for each Work Package.

Using the tools shown above, you run and monitor the project throughout its lifecycle. There is periodic feedback from performance to requirement and frequent change from requirement to performance. With all of this going on, you can see how easily something can get derailed.

1.2 Requirements

In the last ten years or so, the absoluteness of requirements has been set aside. This is particularly true in the software world. The reasons requirements have softened are several. First, the demands of the marketplace have insisted that we bring a product to market before our competition—the mantra of the 1980s and 1990s was "greed and speed." This has meant eliminating the front end of many projects to try to get a jump on the competition. The pace of the marketplace demanded so-called "rapid prototyping" to get there first. Second, eliminating hard requirements allowed more latitude in developing new and different products. Products that were, in some cases, not even envisioned at the outset of the project evolved or appeared during the process. Finally, the culture of "generation X" created a "Leave me alone and let me do my own thing" attitude. The results? Some miraculous strides in progress, particularly software, and some colossal failures. The analysis? The less control, the greater the art, but the greater the risk. We are now at a point where we are trying to figure out how to lower the risk and still have the grand advances. I'm not sure we've figured all that out quite yet, but that's a big reason for this book. With all the failures we've suffered, we need some ways to try to prevent the failures and to recover when we do fail.

It appears a compromise is needed in the definition and how it is applied. For those projects you consider artful or creative in nature, how about at least establishing a charter at the outset to guide the project and establish some boundaries. If the project begins to falter, use the concepts of this book to back up and redefine those parts of the project that are going wrong. This will become an iterative process. It won't solve all the problems, but it will capture the best of each process and allow maximum advances. Whenever you go back, document the change, and update the charter to include your new findings. Tie these elements together and voilà! You have a crude requirements document. Now that you have more visibility, use the opportunity to try to extend to the next failing and shortstop it as well. This thing we have established as the charter now takes the place of the requirements document (contract), and you can read the following cause descriptions with that in mind.

1.3 The Search Methodology

Before we get to the Search Tables, let's look at the search methodology that is applicable to all the Search Tables in Chapters 2, 3, 4, and 5. The reason for this methodology will become clear when we get to "How To Use The Compact Disk (CD)." The purpose of Chapters 2 and 3 is to act as a checklist for planning and checking a project, and the purpose of Chapters 4 and 5 is to get a derailed project back on track.

In Chapters 2 and 3, read the assertions in order. If necessary, go to the page number shown under the "Explain" column to get a broader and deeper understanding of the assertion. If and when you can answer YES to the assertion, proceed to the next assertion. In this way you can evaluate the plans you have developed for your project either before the project is launched or while it is running. Be critical of each assertion.

In Chapters 4 and 5 again, read the assertions in numerical order. This time, however, you are looking for something that has failed on the project. In other words, you answer YES or NO to the assertion, as appropriate. If and when you can answer YES to the assertion, proceed to the next assertion. If your answer is NO, go to the page number listed in the Search Table under that assertion to find an explanation of the issue and a recovery plan to assist you in getting your project back on track.

There are eleven Categories of Causes containing thirty-nine assertions within the Programmatic Tables and twelve Categories of Causes containing forty-three assertions within the Technical Tables.

After a category of causes has been identified, the search changes to looking for the specific cause. The primary number of a cause is directly related to a category of causes. For instance Cause Group 1 relates to the SOW, and Cause Group 51 relates to the Architecture and so on. Each group is subdivided and identified by a letter.

Do not assume that, just because you are in the design phase, the problem itself is in the design phase. As you might suspect, problems that occur early in the project, such as misinterpreting the SOW or specification, do not show up until much later. Most problems or issues are not straightforward, and many require extensive digging and analysis. That's why you should always start at the beginning of each checklist, and that's why these checklists are so useful.

Now you should be ready to start using the Search Tables and, later, the interactive CD.

CHECKING PROGRAMMATIC PERFORMANCE

2.1 General

Checking programmatic performance is fundamental to a smooth-running project. The best time to accomplish this task, of course, is when you are planning the project; however, you can check your project performance at any time by using the checklist presented here.

2.2 Programmatic Performance Checklist

Table 2-1 is the Programmatic *Performance* Checklist. Use this table to check the content of your plans and processes when planning the project or to confirm the Project Plan when the project is running. The Programmatic *Recovery* Checklist is presented in Chapter 4 of this book.

With your project in mind and starting at 1a, read each assertion in the table. If you can answer YES to the assertion with respect to your project, check it off and proceed to the next one. If you need an explanation of the assertion, go to the page number listed under the "Explain" column for that assertion. If your answer is NO, you need to go to Chapter 4 and look in the Programmatic Recovery Tables using the same reference number.

2.3 Programmatic Explanations

Each assertion listed in the Programmatic Performance Checklist, shown in Table 2-1, is supported by a Cause Description. In the case of the Performance Checklist, the support is to broaden and deepen the understanding of the assertion. Following are explanations of the assertions found in the Programmatic Performance Checklist.

1 STATEMENT OF WORK (SOW)

1a The SOW was properly defined.

An SOW is properly defined when it fully describes the products or services to be delivered and states when and where they are to be delivered. Each product or service (sometimes called Contract Line Item Numbers or CLINs) must be separately listed. Additionally, the following documents should be referenced but are usually not included:

- ❒ Task Description
- ❒ Deliverable Documents List (sometimes called Contract Data Requirements List or CDRL)
- ❒ Period of Performance
- ❒ Schedule
- ❒ Reference Documents (referenced but not included)
- ❒ Modifying Factors (for example, the number of labor hours of specific disciplines that must be provided)
- ❒ Specification
- ❒ Financial Information (usually referenced but not included in SOW)

Any item in or referenced by the SOW is a legal part of the SOW. Therefore, each of these items must be understood. It is a good idea to search the entire

Table 2-1 — Programmatic Performance Checklist

1	STATEMENT OF WORK (SOW)	Explain	Yes
1a	The SOW was properly defined	10	
1b	The SOW is within our capabilties	12	
1c	The SOW was propertly interpreted	13	
1d	The SOW was properly negotiated	14	
1e	The SOW is properly monitored	15	
1f	The SOW is being properly performed	16	
2	SPECIFICATION	Explain	Yes
2a	The Specification was properly defined	17	
2b	The Specification is within our capabilities	18	
2c	The Specification was properly interpreted	20	
2d	The Specification was properly negotiated	20	
2e	The Specification was properly monitored	21	
2f	The Specification is being properly performed	22	
3	POLICIES, PLANS, AND PROCESSES	Explain	Yes
3a	There is a clear trail between standard policies and plans and the Project/Program Plan and Technical Plan	23	
3b	There is a clear trail between customer policies and plans and the Project/Program Plan and Technical Plan	23	
3c	There is a clear trail between enterprise policies and plans and the Project/Program Plan and Technical Plan	24	
4	ORGANIZATION	Explain	Yes
4a	The numbers of personnel assigned to each task are correct	25	
4b	The mix of personnel to accomplish the task is appropriate	26	
4c	The personnel are acting and reacting as a team	26	
5	TEAMING, ALLIANCES, AND SUBCONTRACTS	Explain	Yes
5a	The subcontracts were properly defined	26	
5b	The subcontract tasks are within the capabilities of each team member, partner, or subcontractor	28	
5c	The subcontracts were properly negotiated	28	
5d	The subcontracts are properly monitored	29	
5e	Team members, partners, and subcontractors are performing properly	29	
6	MATERIALS	Explain	Yes
6a	Purchase Orders were properly written	30	

(continues)

Table 2-1 — (Continued)

6b	All vendors are competent to perform their tasks	31	
6c	Purchase Orders are properly monitored	31	
6d	Vendors are performing properly	33	
7	**PERSONNEL**	**Explain**	**Yes**
7a	Each person is competent to perform the tasks assigned	33	
7b	Each person is available when needed	34	
7c	Salaries/wages are equal to or less than those bid	34	
7d	Interpersonal conflicts do not exist	34	
8	**TRAINING**	**Explain**	**Yes**
8a	All personnel have been adequately trained	35	
8b	The training program is economical	35	
9	**DATA MANAGEMENT**	**Explain**	**Yes**
9a	The proper amount of data is being delivered on time	35	
10	**QUALITY**	**Explain**	**Yes**
10a	The Quality Plan is thorough, complete, and authorized	36	
10b	Specific quality characteristics were identified that are important to the project	36	
10c	Quality is measured so that improvement or degradation is clear	36	
11	**FINAL DELIVERY**	**Explain**	**Yes**
11a	Final delivery was accepted by the customer without delay	36	
11b	Third-party or drop shipping is not involved	37	

SOW and find all the requirements and the modifiers and group them together for your own purposes.

A properly defined SOW will contain (either incorporated or appended) the findings of the requirements discussions (negotiations). These findings are as much a part of the requirements document (contract) as the initial document.

ADDITIONAL RESOURCES:

MIL-STD-245 (see glossary)

1b The SOW is within our capabilities.

You can make a quick assessment of your ability to perform the task by using the Experience Window in Table 2-2. Ask yourself the customer and product questions and then compare your answers to the answers and capabilities shown in the table.

Table 2-2 — Experience Window

Condition	Have Customer Experience	Have Product Experience	Capability to Perform
1	Yes	Yes	High
2	No	Yes	Moderate
3	Yes	No	Low
4	No	No	Unknown

That's not the end of it, however. Just having customer experience and product experience is not enough; it must be positive experience. If you have had experience with this customer, but it was not positive experience, you must neutralize the negative effects. If you do not do this, your ability to perform (or win) is in doubt. The same is true of product experience. If you have negative experience with a product, you are in the same boat. If either your customer experience or your product experience is negative, it is likely you will move downward at least two conditions on the chart. In other words, if you have good product experience but bad customer experience, you no longer have a high ability to perform. It is likely you now have a low to unknown ability to perform. Generally speaking, negative experience is worse than no experience.

In addition to satisfying the conditions of the table and the extra conditions, you must:

- ❒ Provide the personnel required to perform the task.
- ❒ Provide the facilities required by the task.
- ❒ Provide the finances required by the payment schedule to support the task.
- ❒ Perform the requirements of the Specification (as evaluated under Cause Description 2e).

1c The SOW was properly interpreted.

An SOW is properly interpreted when it is fully defined and when you fully understand the products or services to be delivered and the conditions surrounding the deliveries.

An SOW is properly defined when it fully describes the products or services to be delivered and when and where they are to be delivered. Each product or service (sometimes called Contract Line Item Numbers or CLINs) must be separately listed. Additionally, the following documents should be referenced, but are usually not included:

- ❐ Task Description
- ❐ Deliverable Documents List (sometimes called Contract Data Requirements List or CDRL)
- ❐ Period of Performance
- ❐ Schedule
- ❐ Reference Documents (referenced but not included)
- ❐ Modifying Factors (for example, the number of labor hours of specific disciplines that must be provided)
- ❐ Specification
- ❐ Financial Information (usually referenced but not included in the SOW)

Any item in or referenced by the SOW is a legal part of the SOW in a program and an ethical part of the SOW in both a program and a project. Therefore, each of these items must be understood. It is a good idea to search the entire SOW and find all the requirements and the modifiers and group them together for your own purposes.

To ensure you fully understand the SOW, you should:

- ❐ Meet with the customer and use the content listing above as a guide for your meeting. Ensure every item is covered.
- ❐ Go through each paragraph of the SOW that is or might be in question.
- ❐ Come to an understanding with the customer as to exactly what is wanted.
- ❐ Come to an understanding with the customer on how recovery can be made.

You should have the project manager and the technical manager on the proposal team and the requirements definition (negotiation) team.

1d The SOW was properly negotiated.

A properly negotiated SOW is one that has a balance between all its elements, is complete, and for which:

- ❒ The amount of money to be paid is adequate to complete the task.
- ❒ The time allowed is adequate to complete the task.
- ❒ The requirements definition (negotiation) minutes are documented and signed by both parties.

Again, follow the procedure outlined under Cause Description 1c above.

It is the responsibility of the requirements definition (negotiation) team to ensure that this balance exists and that minutes are taken and confirmed. One of the best ways to ensure balance is to require that the project manager be on the requirements definition (negotiation) team. The project manager will ensure there is a balance or will suffer the consequences.

And now, to be mugged by reality! Sometimes a strategic decision is made by the company to accept a task at a price less than it will actually cost; this is commonly called "buying in" (see glossary). In that event you must negotiate your position with your management to understand who will take the "hit." Get that understanding in writing!

1e The SOW is properly monitored.

The SOW is properly monitored when the work being performed is being monitored by lead technical and program personnel using accepted monitoring techniques such as:

- ❒ Schedule Reviews
- ❒ Budget Reviews
- ❒ Design Reviews
- ❒ Technical Interchange Meetings
- ❒ Team Meetings
- ❒ In-Process Reviews
- ❒ Project Reviews
- ❒ Customer Meetings

See the glossary for an expanded explanation of each of these meetings or reviews. Due to the variability of projects, the content of these meetings and reviews must be your own.

These interchanges must be conducted at frequent intervals. The lower the position in the hierarchy, the more frequent the interchange needs to be. In other words, Team Meetings should be held more often than Project Reviews, and Project Reviews should be held more often than Customer Meetings, and so forth.

Just because the SOW is being properly monitored does not necessarily mean the program is running properly; it only means that it is being monitored properly. The point is that if the program is not being monitored properly, you will not know it until it is too late.

These meetings and reviews pervade the entire process, as Table 2-3 shows.

Table 2-3 — Meetings and Reviews

Review or Meeting	Cause Description Appearance
Schedule Reviews	1f, 5e, 6d
Budget Reviews	1f, 5e
Design Reviews	11a, 51e, 52a, 53
Technical Interchange Meetings	1f, 5d, 5e, 6d
Subcontractor Meetings	5d, 5e
In-Process Reviews	5d
Customer Meetings	5d, 5e

The reviews must have metrics established to indicate if each event is in tolerance or out-of-tolerance. The content of each of the reviews must be appropriate for that review.

1f The SOW is being properly performed.

The SOW is being properly performed when the Design Reviews, the In-Process Reviews, the status meetings, the schedule, and the actual production of the product is on schedule, within budget, and is being produced in accordance with the Specification. These factors should be evident in such reviews as:

- ❒ Schedule Reviews
- ❒ Budget Reviews
- ❒ Design Reviews
- ❒ Technical Interchange Meetings
- ❒ Team Meetings

❒ In-Process Reviews
❒ Project Reviews

See the glossary for an expanded explanation of each of these meetings or reviews. Due to the variability of projects, the content of these meetings and reviews must be your own.

The reviews must have metrics established to indicate whether each event is in tolerance or out-of-tolerance.

2 SPECIFICATION

2a The Specification was properly defined.

The proof, as they say, is in the pudding. Can you understand exactly what the customer wants? Is it testable and is it provable? If you can answer YES to both those questions, the Specification is properly defined. A well-defined Specification contains at least the following topics:

❒ Scope of the Document
❒ Applicable Documents
❒ Requirements
❒ Item Definition
❒ Performance Characteristics
  - The performance requirements related to manning, operating, maintaining, and logistically supporting the prime item to the extent these requirements define or constrain design of the prime item and include response time, throughput rates, and exclusion times

❒ Physical Characteristics
  - The design constraints and standards necessary to assure compatibility of prime item components

❒ The electrical, mechanical, functional, and other interfaces between the principal item being specified and other items with which it must be compatible
❒ The major components of the principal item and the primary interfaces between such major components

- ❐ Qualification Requirements (for software) or Quality Assurance Provisions (for hardware)
- ❐ Process Requirements, if needed
- ❐ Materials Requirements, if needed

There are several types of Specifications. MIL-STD-490 has established and defined five different Specification (Spec) types as well as a number of subtypes. The standard provides a great deal of good information regarding the content and purpose of each Specification type. The Specification types are shown in Table 2-4.

Table 2-4 — Specification Types

Type	Specification
A	System/Subsystem/Segment
B	Development
B1	Prime Item
B2	Critical Item
B3	Noncomplex Item
B4	Facility of Ship
B5	Software
C	Product
C1a	Prime Item Function
C1b	Prime Item Fabrication
C2a	Critical Item Function
C2b	Critical Item Fabrication
C3	Noncomplex Item Fabrication
C4	Inventory Item
C5	Software
D	Process
E	Material

2b The Specification is within our capabilities.

A quick assessment can be made of your capabilities to perform by using the Experience Window in Table 2-5.

Table 2-5 — Experience Window

Condition	Have Customer Experience	Have Product Experience	Capability to Perform
1	Yes	Yes	High
2	No	Yes	Moderate
3	Yes	No	Low
4	No	No	Unknown

In addition to satisfying the conditions of the table above, you must:

❒ Provide the personnel required to perform the task.
❒ Provide the facilities required by the task.
❒ Provide the finances required by the payment schedule to support the task.
❒ Perform the requirements of the Specification.

The Specification is within your capabilities if you have previously established credentials in performing each requirement.

In order to fill in the "Have Product Experience" column in Table 2-5 properly, you may need to construct a matrix similar to the one shown in Table 2-6. The matrix lists all the requirements or tasks along the side and the programs (including Independent Research and Development (IR&D) programs) that the company has performed across the top. Every requirement or task should have an "X" at the intersection between the task and at least one program.

Table 2-6 — Task Qualification

	Project A	Project B	Project C	Project D	Project E
Task 1			X		
Task 2		X		X	
Task 3			X		
Task 4			X		
Task 5	X				X
Task 6					

If you do not have the requisite qualifications and thus cannot enter an "X" into the intersect, continue with the process to bring your capabilities up to the requirements of the Specification. Refer to Cause Description 2b (NO) for recovery.

2c The Specification was properly interpreted.

A Specification is properly interpreted when you fully understand the products or services to be delivered. Each product or service must be fully described in the Specification.

At a minimum, the Specification should contain:

- ❐ Scope of the Document
- ❐ Applicable Documents
- ❐ Requirements
- ❐ Item Definition
- ❐ Performance Characteristics
  - The performance requirements related to manning, operating, maintaining, and logistically supporting the prime item to the extent these requirements define or constrain design of the prime item and include response time, throughput rates, and exclusion times
- ❐ Physical Characteristics
  - The design constraints and standards necessary to assure compatibility of prime item components
- ❐ The electrical, mechanical, functional, and other interfaces between the principal item being specified and other items with which it must be compatible
- ❐ The major components of the principal item and the primary interfaces between such major components
- ❐ Qualification Requirements (for software) or Quality Assurance Provisions (for hardware)
- ❐ Process Requirements, if needed
- ❐ Materials Requirements, if needed

2d The Specification was properly negotiated.

The Specification was properly negotiated if there is a thorough understanding and agreement on the part of both parties as to what constitutes the scope, the schedule, and the budget. A well-defined Specification contains at least the following topics:

- ❒ Scope of the Document
- ❒ Applicable Documents
- ❒ Requirements
- ❒ Item Definition
- ❒ Performance Characteristics
  - The performance requirements related to manning, operating, maintaining, and logistically supporting the prime item to the extent these requirements define or constrain design of the prime item and include response time, throughput rates, and exclusion times
- ❒ Physical Characteristics
  - The design constraints and standards necessary to assure compatibility of prime item components
- ❒ The electrical, mechanical, functional, and other interfaces between the principal item being specified and other items with which it must be compatible.
- ❒ The major components of the principal item and the primary interfaces between such major components
- ❒ Qualification Requirements (for software) or Quality Assurance Provisions (for hardware)
- ❒ Process Requirements, if needed
- ❒ Materials Requirements, if needed

The negotiator must keep thorough and complete minutes regarding all changes to the Specification and these changes *must* be covered by both schedule and budget considerations. The minutes will have been signed by both parties of the negotiation. Later these minutes will be incorporated into the Specification as changes.

2e The Specification was properly monitored.

A Specification that is properly monitored is one that is under constant and complete control and has a change process that controls all changes made to the baseline.

One of the first things to be done in the Planning Phase is to develop a Requirements Traceability Matrix (RTM). You should have one RTM for the programmatics (SOW) and one for the product (Specification). Once you know where the requirement is being satisfied, it should be reasonably easy to assign a person to monitor the performance. The content of the RTM should follow a requirement from beginning to end. An example of such a document is shown in Table 2-7.

Table 2-7 — Requirements Traceability Matrix (RTM)

SOW/ Spec Para	Requirement	WBS Number	S/C SOW/ Spec Para	Unit Test Number	System Test Para	Monitor
SOW						
4.3.1	Security	06-03-02	N/A	T-0304	4.4.1	Smith
Spec						
3.2.1	System weight shall be less than 10,000 pounds	02-04-03	3.4.6	T-0045	3.4.1	Jones

In this case, an additional column should be added for the name of the monitor.

For additional information, see Attachment 7.

2f The Specification is being properly performed.

The Specification is being properly performed when the Design Reviews or Milestone Reviews are properly passed and accepted by the customer and the product is fabricated or produced in accordance with the design and accepted by the customer.

You can only answer YES to this assertion if you answered YES to assertions 2a, 2b, 2c, 2d, and 2e. If you answered NO to any of those assertions, you must rectify the situation before proceeding.

Ensure that every major milestone, such as the Preliminary Design Review (PDR) has inch stones leading up to it. Performance must be evaluated at every inch stone. Evaluate performance using the requirements of the major milestone and develop a "percent complete" chart for each inch stone and for the milestone.

3 POLICIES, PLANS, AND PROCESSES

3a There is a clear trail between standard policies and plans and the Project/Program Plan and Technical Plan.

The Project/Program and Technical Plans link to standard policies and plans through two avenues. One avenue is through enterprise policies and processes; the other is through the requirements document (contract). The requirements document (contract) references those standards through the Statement Of Work (SOW) and the Specification.

You should have a Standards Traceability Matrix (STM) similar to Table 2-8.

Table 2-8 — Standards Traceability Matrix (STM)

STANDARDS			APPEARANCE	
Industry	Customer	Enterprise	Project Plan	Technical Plan
ISO-9001	ISO-9001	Enterprise Quality Policy 09350	Para 4.6.8	Part I, Para 4.5.6
	MIL-STD-100	Enterprise Engineering Standards 06050	N/A	Part II, Para 1.2.3

The STM shown here is a multipurpose table in that the requirement source such as the contract paragraph, the company standard, and the standards documents are all included in one chart. You can use this technique to divide the three requirements into three separate charts. The STM is further explained in Attachment 13.

3b There is a clear trail between customer policies and plans and the Project/Program Plan and Technical Plan.

Customer policies and plans are linked to the Project/Program Plan through the requirements document (contract). The Statement Of Work (SOW) and the Specification should clearly spell out those customer policies, processes, and plans that are invoked as a part of the contract.

You should have an STM similar to Table 2-9.

Table 2-9 — Standards Traceability Matrix (STM)

STANDARDS			APPEARANCE	
Industry	**Customer**	**Enterprise**	**Project Plan**	**Technical Plan**
ISO-9001	ISO-9001	Enterprise Quality Policy 09350	Para 4.6.8	Part I, Para 4.5.6
	MIL-STD-100	Enterprise Engineering Standards 06050	N/A	Part II, Para 1.2.3

The STM shown here is a multipurpose table in that the requirement source such as the contract paragraph, the company standard, and the standards documents are all included in one chart. You can use this technique or separate the three requirements into three separate charts. The STM is further explained in Attachment 13.

3c There is a clear trail between enterprise policies and plans and the Project/Program Plan and Technical Plan.

A clear trail between enterprise policies and plans and the Project/Program Plan and Technical Plan exists when the Vision drives the Mission Statement, which, in turn, drives the Policies. The Policies are the foundation that sets standards for the Processes and Plans. The Project Plan and Technical Plan are a fundamental part of all the plans and should reflect the parts, sections, chapters, and paragraph upon which they are based.

The documentation of a corporation, company, or enterprise is near the top of the management "to do" list on how to run a company. The only things at higher rungs are the Strategic Plan, the Mission Statement, and the Vision. If the entity is ongoing and the documentation is at fault, it is not a good sign. If the documentation does not exist, it's even worse. If it is a new start, the entity should look upon the situation as a learning experience and fix the documentation. If the project documentation is lacking and the enterprise documentation is in order, it is an indication that there is a disconnect between the enterprise and the programs it runs. This can be overcome by using an "Executive Summary" that is agreed to by enterprise management and program management before the program is kicked off. The continuity is maintained by a Project

Advisory Council, a group of senior executives assigned to follow and advise each project.

You should have an STM similar to Table 2-10.

Table 2-10 — Standards Traceability Matrix

STANDARDS			APPEARANCE	
Industry	**Customer**	**Enterprise**	**Project Plan**	**Technical Plan**
ISO-9001	ISO-9001	Enterprise Quality Policy 09350	Para 4.6.8	Part I, Para 4.5.6
	MIL-STD-100	Enterprise Engineering Standards 06050	N/A	Part II, Para 1.2.3

The Standards Traceability Matrix shown here is a multipurpose table in that the requirement source such as the contract paragraph, the company standard, and the standards documents are all included in one chart. You can use this technique or separate the three requirements into three separate charts. The STM is further explained in Attachment 13.

4 ORGANIZATION

4a The numbers of personnel assigned to each task are correct.

When you first start your project, the organization chart and staffing table from the proposal will probably be your guides. As the project progresses, performance will be the rule. You must constantly ask yourself: "Is the job getting done?" Then, follow up with these questions: "Is the job getting done without working overtime?" "Is the morale of the team high?" If the answer to all those questions is YES, you're probably in good shape. You must however also ask yourself: "Do I have too many people?" The job could be getting done, you are not working overtime, and morale is high but you have too many people. Yes, that actually does happen on projects! Optimizing manpower is a constant task.

If your project is a large one that will last over a period of time, it is possible that the organization chart and manpower table will change. It is normal to have one organization and manpower table for design and another for test, production, and so forth. That's another reason you must ask yourself the opening question frequently.

4b The mix of personnel to accomplish the task is appropriate.

The mix of personnel to accomplish the task is appropriate if the job is getting done and the mix of personnel matches the mix shown on the organization chart and the staffing plan.

Mix, of course, means the different types of persons assigned, not just the numbers. The starting point is usually the proposal or the document that was the basis for providing the correct technical manpower and for costing the manpower for the project. The correct mix is absolutely essential. It is the basis for correctly accomplishing the task technically and for maintaining the budget.

It is important to keep the organization chart and the staffing plan up-to-date. Keep all staffing plans from the proposal on to show the transitions of personnel from time to time in the project. This will help when accounting for personnel changes and will provide an operational history for the next bid.

4c The personnel are acting and reacting as a team.

Just because a group of individuals are assigned to a project does not mean they are a team. In order to be a team, the individuals must act and react with regard to the team's goals. The group acts and reacts as a team when the responses to team goals are greater than the responses to individual goals.

While actions and reactions are the most important factor, there are other considerations that will help the group to continue to act as a team. First, and most important, is to have had team training using a facilitator qualified to conduct team training and an acceptable team training format. Second, which is usually a result of team training, is that the team has a Vision (see glossary) and a Mission Statement (see glossary).

5 TEAMING, ALLIANCES, AND SUBCONTRACTS

5a The subcontracts were properly defined.

The tasks of subcontractors, which include Teaming (see glossary) and Alliances (see glossary), are properly defined if there is a clear trail between the customer's requirement documents (SOW and Specification) to the subcontractor's requirements document (subcontract SOW and subcontract Specification) using a Requirements Flow-down Matrix (RFM) and from the subcontractor's requirements documents through the subcontractor's process using a Subcontract Requirements Traceability Matrix (SRTM).

An RFM with the characteristics shown in Table 2-11 should be used.

Additional information can be found in Attachment 8.

Additionally, the subcontractor should have an SRTM, such as that shown in Table 2-12.

The current industry standard is a family of products titled DOORS (for large and enterprise wide projects) and DOORSrequireIT (for smaller projects).

Table 2-11 — Requirements Flow-Down Matrix (RFM)

Spec Para	Company Reqt	WBS	Design Plan Para	S/C Plan Para	S/C A Para	S/C B Para
1.3.2		02-03-01	5.3.2	5.3.2	1.3.2	1.3.2
1.3.3		02-03-02	5.3.3	5.3.3	1.3.3	N/A
1.3.4		02-03-03	5.3.4	5.3.4	1.3.4	1.3.4
	QA Plan	04-01-01	8.2.6	8.2.6	4.3.6	4.3.6
	CM Plan	05-01-01	9.3.1	9.3.1	5.6.2	5.6.2

Table 2-12 — Subcontracts Requirements Traceability Matrix (SRTM)

SOW/ Spec Para	Requirement	WBS Number	S/C SOW/ Spec Para	Unit Test Number	System Test Para	Monitor
SOW						
4.3.1	Security	06-03-02	N/A	T-0304	4.4.1	Smith
Spec						
3.2.1	System weight shall be less than 10,000 pounds	02-04-03	3.4.6	T-0045	3.4.1	Jones

Both are commonly referred to as "Doors." Additional information on Doors can be found in Attachment 7.

5b The subcontract tasks are within the capabilities of each team member, partner, or subcontractor.

The subcontract tasks are within the capabilities of each team member, partner, or subcontractor if each has performed the same or a similar task before and no substantial changes have since occurred (i.e., critical personnel are still in place, and critical facilities are still available) or the subcontractor has some unique capability or capacity to perform the task. Such data should be maintained by the enterprise as a part of the Vendor/Subcontractor Database. If your enterprise does not keep such a database, a "quick fix," can be reached by constructing a matrix with the tasks along the side and a place for program entries across the top. The potential subcontractor then identifies the program where the same or a similar task has been performed.

If anything has changed (i.e., critical personnel are no longer available, critical facilities are not available, etc.) you should go to Chapter 4, Cause Description 5b (NO), Recovery section. If the subcontractor has a unique capability or capacity to perform that has not been tried before, this is the time to create a Risk Mitigation Plan (see Attachment 3).

As project manager, it is a good idea (in my opinion absolutely necessary) that you have written confirmation of this fact. Do not simply accept the statements of Marketing (who usually makes Teaming Agreements) or Management (who usually makes Alliances) that the company with whom you are aligned is qualified to perform the task. Teaming Agreements and Alliances are frequently made for political purposes. If you find such a situation exists, refer to Chapter 4, Cause Description 5b (NO) for recovery.

5c The subcontracts were properly negotiated.

The subcontracts were properly negotiated if they are fully understood by both parties and contain a balance between all the elements, and if:

- ❒ The amount of money to be paid is adequate to complete the task.
- ❒ The time allowed is adequate to complete the task.
- ❒ Both you and the subcontractor understand what is to be done and when.

It is the responsibility of the requirements definition (negotiation) team to ensure that this balance exists and that minutes are documented and signed.

One of the best ways to ensure balance is to require that the project manager be on the requirements definition (negotiation) team. The project manager will ensure there is a balance or will suffer the consequences.

5d The subcontracts are properly monitored.

The subcontract is properly monitored when the work being performed is being monitored by lead technical and project personnel using accepted monitoring techniques such as:

- ❒ Subcontract Progress Reviews—Subcontractor presents technical progress, budget status, schedule status, deliverables status, and data status
- ❒ Subcontractor Meetings—Special, single subject meetings as required
- ❒ Technical Interchange Meetings (TIMs)—Informal reviews of technical subjects
- ❒ Design Reviews—Formal reviews of designs. Subcontractor presents and defends the design and its support
- ❒ In-Process Reviews—Usually, informal reviews between milestones
- ❒ Pretest Meetings—Briefings to establish the basis for a test
- ❒ Posttest Reviews—Review of test data and issuance and formalization of action items and, if appropriate, sign-off

These reviews must be conducted at frequent and consistent intervals. The lower in the hierarchy (e.g., the project is lower in the hierarchy than company, etc.), the more frequent the review.

Simply conducting these meetings and reviews does not mean the subcontract is performing properly; it only means that the subcontract is being monitored properly. But, if the subcontract is not being monitored properly, you will not know if it is performing properly.

Within each of these must be monitoring points or metrics that indicate that an event is in tolerance or out-of-tolerance.

5e Team members, partners, and subcontractors are performing properly.

Team members, partners, and subcontractors are performing properly when all monitored events are being performed on schedule, within budget, and in a technically competent way. The method you use in determining this status is to conduct regular and frequent reviews at strategic points in the process to ensure that performance is proper. Such reviews are presented in detail in Cause Description 5d.

Monitored events are those events that are typical for a particular review. Usually, Schedule Reviews, Budget Reviews and Progress Reviews are held concurrently. Within each review there must be monitoring values and metrics to determine if the project is performing in tolerance. While projects vary infinitely in subject matter there are some values that must be monitored on all projects. Such meetings are frequently called Plans, Progress, and Problems Meetings. Such values and metrics are, at a minimum:

- ❒ Actual cost to date versus planned cost to date
- ❒ Actual performance to date versus planned performance to date
- ❒ Cost at completion
- ❒ Completion date
- ❒ Performed activities versus planned activities for last period
- ❒ Problems and recommended resolution
- ❒ Planned activities for next period

6 MATERIALS

6a Purchase Orders were properly written.

Each Purchase Order is complete and properly written when it contains: Reference Number, Order Date, Vendor, Contact Information, Name of Item, Stock (Catalog) Number, Number of Units, Price, Delivery Schedule, Delivery Location, Purchaser, and Authorizing Signature.

It is beneficial that the information contained in the Purchase Order be complete and properly written for a few reasons. For example, it conveys to the vendor exactly what is expected. Also, you must know exactly the status of each Purchase Order because of the impact it has on your schedule and your budget.

Most companies have preprinted Purchase Order forms. If yours does not, create your own. Even if your Purchase Order form is nothing more than a memo, at least it is documentation of what has been ordered and provides a basis for the schedule and for financial accountability. If your preprinted form does not contain all the information above, I suggest you add the information within the body of the Purchase Order.

6b All vendors are competent to perform their tasks.

All vendors are competent to perform their tasks if they have passed the criteria set forth in your enterprise standards. If you do not have enterprise standards, the following should be established as the criteria:

- ❐ Technical Performance
- ❐ Cost Performance
- ❐ Delivery Performance
- ❐ Management Performance
- ❐ Procurement Policies and Plans
- ❐ Quality Assurance Program (see Attachment 6 for Quality Assurance Plan)
- ❐ Cost of Quality Position (see glossary)

Figure 2-1 on the following page provides a framework for collecting this data.

6c Purchase Orders are properly monitored.

The Purchase Order is properly monitored when the work being performed is being monitored by the Materials Manager calling upon technical and program personnel as required and using accepted monitoring techniques such as:

- ❐ Vendor Progress Reports
- ❐ Vendor Meetings
- ❐ In-Process Reviews

The above include schedule and budget, if proper.

These reviews must be conducted at regular, frequent, and strategic intervals.

Simply conducting these meetings and reviews does not mean the vendor is performing properly; it only means that the Purchase Order is being monitored properly. But, if the Purchase Order is not being monitored properly, you will not know if the vendor is performing properly.

Figure 2-1 — Vendor Evaluation Sheet

VENDOR EVALUATION

Date	4-Jul-02
Program	High-Flyer
Subcontractor/Vendor	National Software
Equipment/Software	Analog Selction Algorithm
Evaluator	G. Smith
Scale Factor	0-5

Item	Consideration	Rating*
1	Organization	3
2	Management	4
3	Manpower	5
4	Access to Management	5
5	Processes	3
6	Procedures	2
7		
8		
9		
10		
	Subtotal**	22
	No. of items rated**	6
	Average of ratings (Subtotal/No of items)**	3.7

*An evaluated number within the Scale Factor.
**Calculated number.

M-M Form

Within each of these reviews there must be monitoring points or metrics that indicate that an event is in tolerance or out-of-tolerance.

If schedule is critical, the Purchase Order should include an incentive or liquidated damages clause that is invoked in the event the delivery time is not kept.

6d Vendors are performing properly.

Vendors are performing properly when all monitored events are being performed on schedule, within budget, and in a technically competent way. The method you use in determining this status is to conduct regular and frequent reviews at strategic points in the process to ensure that performance is proper. Such monitored events typically are:

- ❒ Vendor Meetings, including Schedule Reviews and Budget Reviews[1]
- ❒ Technical Interchange Meetings[2]
- ❒ In-Process Reviews

7 PERSONNEL

7a Each person is competent to perform the tasks assigned.

It should be apparent whether or not each person is competent to perform the tasks to which he or she is assigned. It is not usual to have job descriptions for project positions, so the personnel must learn what is expected of them in other ways. The best way is through team training, where each individual is apprised of the expectations of his position and the input the individual needs from others.

Knowing what is expected is one thing. Competency is quite another. The best way to establish competency is to interview each person before assigning individuals to the project. In a small company, you can usually rely on reputation and personal contact. In a large company, you may need to interview the individuals and read their background résumés. When the project is running, you judge competency by your observation, by MBWA (Management By Walking Around), and by asking questions of other team members.

Competency (a long-term characteristic) is not the same as reaction (a short-term characteristic). In other words, don't characterize a person based on a single sample of work or on his or her response on one day (the person may be having a bad day). Conversely, don't expect the "leopard to change its spots" based on a single day of responses.

Refer to Cause Description 7a (NO) for recovery.

7b Each person is available when needed.

If each person is available when needed, it will be self-evident. As project manager you will constantly be scanning the personnel and you can tell if anyone is missing. Watch the wording here carefully. As project manager, you must control the personnel. If you operate in a matrix organization, you must have an understanding with the functional manager that, once assigned, the personnel report to you. You must be a party to any planned absences.

No matter if you operate in a matrix or a projectized organization, you must keep up with your people and what they are doing from day to day.

7c Salaries/wages are equal to or less than those bid.

It should be clear by simply looking at the details supporting your budget that the individual salaries are equal to or less than those that were bid. You must use your judgment in this case. Use the bottom line of the budget as the guide—it is easier to achieve the bottom line than to achieve each and every line item. It may be to your benefit to have an individual of higher pay in a certain position and several of lower pay in other positions. You must make that judgment.

Take care if your program is longer than a few months and you use the matrix form of management. You may find that salaries fit the bid profile at the start of the program but some of your people get raises during the conduct of the program. People should be rewarded for good work and should have raises when they are due. Just make sure those raises are built into your budget.

7d Interpersonal conflicts do not exist.

Interpersonal conflicts do not exist when there is mutual respect between the members of the team.

If you have no interpersonal conflicts at all, one of two things is happening: You are the luckiest project manager alive, or you are not very close to the people part of your project. Even if you answered YES to this assertion, it might be a good idea to look at the Recovery association in Chapter 4, Cause Description 7d (NO) just to give the question a little more depth.

8 TRAINING

8a All personnel have been adequately trained.

All personnel have been adequately trained when they know their basic jobs thoroughly, when they know the mission of the team, when they know the product(s) to be produced, and when they know what part they play on the team and in developing the product(s).

It is advantageous to the project and the team and frequently to the individual that they be cross-trained. If it is not in your plan, it should be—unless it is against union rules or against some other rule over which you have no control.

8b The training program is economical.

The training program is economical when the dollar cost of the training program is equal to or less than the value derived from the training program. Further, in order to be economical, the value imparted to the individuals attending the training class must be worth the time employed in attending the program, for every person in attendance.

9 DATA MANAGEMENT

9a The proper amount of data is being delivered on time.

The proper amount of data is being delivered on time when the data deliveries match the data required in the Data Plan, and the Data Plan matches the requirements. Some documents are delivered once (i.e., System Test Results), and some require multiple deliveries (i.e., Monthly Status Reports).

Each line item of deliverable documentation in the requirement should contain a delivery date or schedule of dates, a format, a content requirement, and the name of the person responsible for generating the data. If it does not, you should create these requirements. All requirements are then included in the Data Plan.

Your deliveries may be formalized as they are in a government contract. In this case, you will have a Contract Data Requirements List (CDRL) that spells out what is to be delivered and numerous Data Item Descriptions (DIDs) that spell out the frequency of submission and the format of the submission.

Your Data Plan should specify in what form the data is to be delivered and to whom. Many projects have engineering deliver raw or refined reports to the Data Manager, who adds the boiler plate, coordinates the review, reproduces the number of copies necessary, and handles distribution. These same techniques, except for reproduction, can be used for electronic transmissions as well.

10 QUALITY

10a The Quality Plan is thorough, complete, and authorized.

The Quality Plan is thorough, complete, and authorized when it completely addresses and fills the requirements of the Quality Standards imposed by standard, customer, or your internal requirements document and it is authorized by the highest quality official of the enterprise. (See Attachment 6 for a Quality Assurance Plan outline complete with explanations and details.)

10b Specific quality characteristics were identified that are important to the project.

Specific quality characteristics were identified that are important to the project when these characteristics are documented and used as a checklist.

10c Quality is measured so that improvement or degradation is clear.

Quality is measured so that improvement or degradation is clear when each quality characteristic is measured and tracked via metrics.

Quality is measured so that improvement or degradation is clear when each quality characteristic shows clear improvement or degradation between the current reading and some standard or the last reading.

11 FINAL DELIVERY

11a Final delivery was accepted by the customer without delay.

It is expected that final delivery will be accepted by the customer without delay because it is one of the most important steps in the closure process. In order to ensure that this happens, the following must have been completed:

- ❒ Design Reviews or milestone reviews signed by customer
- ❒ All In-Process Documentation completed
- ❒ All Deliverable Documentation delivered
- ❒ All In-Process Tests accepted by the customer
- ❒ The final System Test accepted by the customer
- ❒ Product shipped to the point of delivery and in deliverable condition

11b Third-party or drop shipping is not involved.

Third-party or drop shipping is not involved whenever the product is shipped directly from your facilities to the customer's facilities.

If drop shipping is involved, you must have absolute control over shipping and receiving of the product. See 11b (NO).

Notes

1. Usually not for an FFP contract.

2. Unless the product is a commercially available commodity (i.e., a catalog item).

CHECKING TECHNICAL PERFORMANCE

3.1 General

Checking technical performance is fundamental to a smooth-running project. The best time to accomplish this task, of course, is when you are planning the project; however, you can check your project performance at any time by using the checklist provided here.

3.2 Technical Performance Checklist

Table 3-1 is the Technical *Performance* Checklist. Use this table to check the content of your plans and processes when planning the project or to confirm the Technical Plan when the project is running. The Technical *Recovery* Checklist is presented in Chapter 5 of this book.

Table 3-1 — Technical Performance Checklist

51	ARCHITECTURE	Explain	Yes
51a	All Critical Success Factors (CSFs) such as Mean Time To Repair (MTTR), Mean Time Between Failure (MTBF), etc., have been documented and understood	41	
51b	All modules/subsystems are well defined	41	
51c	All key functions such as time, length, weight, performance requirements, and interfaces, etc., listed in the requirements are appropriately covered	42	
51d	All major elements (physical and data) are described and justified	42	
51e	All key aspects of user interfaces are well defined	42	
51f	The Architecture hangs together conceptually	42	
52	**DESIGN**	**Explain**	**Yes**
52a	The design process is correct and traceable to enterprise, customer, and standard processes	42	
52b	The design is correct and traceable to the requirements	43	
52c	The design is efficient	43	
52d	The design adequately addresses issues that were identified and deferred to design at the architectural level	43	
52e	The design is partitioned into manageable segments	44	
52f	The design accounts for supportability, Life Cycle Cost (LCC), total cost of ownership, and future expansions	44	
52g	Technical Performance Measures (TPMs) such as data retrieval time, weight, error rate, etc., have been defined and accommodated	45	
53	**DESIGN REVIEWS**	**Explain**	**Yes**
53a	All Design Reviews were completed according to required processes	45	
53b	The customer approved each Design Review	45	
54	**IN-PROCESS REVIEWS**	**Explain**	**Yes**
54a	All required In-Process Reviews were conducted according to required processes	45	
54b	Each In-Process Review was approved by the appropriate authority	46	
55	**PROTOTYPES**	**Explain**	**Yes**
55a	The prototypes reflect the requirements	46	
55b	Prototypes were constructed incrementally	47	
55c	Prototype changes were incorporated into the design using the Change Control Process	47	
55d	Each prototype change was reviewed and accepted by the originator of the requirements	47	

(continues)

Table 3-1 — (Continued)

56	SUBCONTRACTS	Explain	Yes
56a	The sum of all subcontracts reflects all tasks allocated	48	
56b	Each subcontract contains all tasks allocated	48	
57	**PURCHASE ORDERS**	**Explain**	**Yes**
57a	The sum of all Purchase Orders reflects all purchases to be made	48	
57b	Each Purchase Order is complete	49	
58	**PRODUCTION/MANUFACTURING**	**Explain**	**Yes**
58a	All production/manufacturing processes are traceable to standard, customer, or enterprise processes	49	
58b	The line(s) were properly designed and set up for this (these) product(s)	50	
58c	Shop orders were correct and thorough	50	
58d	The materials were proper for the processes and the product(s) and do meet the requirements	50	
59	**UNIT TEST**	**Explain**	**Yes**
59a	Each Unit Test correctly reflects the requirement	51	
59b	Each design element that applies to the routine/module/subsystem has its own test case	51	
59c	Unit Test findings were reviewed for completeness and forwarded to be incorporated into Subsystem Tests and the System Test	51	
59d	All Problem Test Reports (PTRs) were captured, dispositioned (allocated for action), and worked off	52	
60	**SYSTEM TEST**	**Explain**	**Yes**
60a	The System Test Plan/Procedure was approved by the customer	52	
60b	The System Test is traceable to the requirements	52	
60c	The System Test tested all elements of the system concurrently	52	
60d	The System Test was performed under appropriate load(s)	53	
60e	The System Test was performed using the same kind of personnel that will be used by the customer	53	
60f	The System Test was properly documented and incorporated the test results of all prior-level tests	53	
61	**CONFIGURATION MANAGEMENT**	**Explain**	**Yes**
61a	The Configuration Management Plan (CMP) is thorough, complete, and authorized	53	
61b	Change requests were presented and approved by an appropriate level of the Review Board	54	
61c	Version controls are in place and are reflected on (in) the product	54	
62	**SYSTEM EFFECTIVENESS FACTORS**	**Explain**	**Yes**
62a	All required System Effectiveness Factors have been appropriately considered	54	

Starting at 51a, read each assertion in the table. If you can answer YES to the assertion, check it off and proceed to the next one. If you need an explanation of the assertion, go to the page number listed under the "Explain" column for that assertion.

3.3 Technical Explanations

Each assertion listed in the Technical Performance Checklist is supported by a Cause Description. In the case of the performance checklist, the support is to broaden and deepen the understanding of the assertion. Following are explanations of the assertions found in the Technical Performance Checklist.

51 ARCHITECTURE

51a All Critical Success Factors (CSFs) such as Mean Time To Repair (MTTR), Mean Time Between Failure (MTBF), etc., have been documented and understood.

All Critical Success Factors (CSFs) such as MTTR, MTBF, etc., must have been documented and fully understood as the same by both parties. When those CSFs are incorporated into the design, a clear trail must exist from each CSF to its incorporation into the design.

51b All modules/subsystems are well defined.

All modules/subsystems are well defined whenever all parameters that go into making up the module or subsystem are understood. While this statement can be somewhat subjective, it must be answered in objective terms. If there are parameters that are not understood, they must be defined. Look carefully at the old saw: "We know what we know and we know what we don't know, but our problems are evidenced when issues arise that we don't know we don't know." There is another old saw that states: "You certainly have a keen grasp of the obvious." The point is that all issues and considerations must be "thought through" in order to discover possibilities that are not mentioned. Whenever one of these possibilities is uncovered, it should be investigated and documented.

51c All key functions such as time, length, weight, performance requirements, and interfaces, etc., listed in the requirements are appropriately covered.

All key functions, performance requirements, and interfaces, etc., listed in the requirements are appropriately covered when all are listed on the ordinate (the "Y" axis—along the side) of the Requirements Traceability Matrix (RTM) (see Attachment 7) and the Requirements Flow-Down Matrix (RFM) (see Attachment 8), and the WBS locations are listed on the abscissa (the "X" axis—across the top or bottom). The requirements are appropriately covered when there is an "intersect" between all requirements and all the WBS locations showing dispositions.

51d All major elements (physical and data) are described and justified.

All major elements (physical and data) are described when they are understood equally by all parties involved. All major elements (physical and data) are justified when they contribute to the whole of the unit or system.

51e All key aspects of user interfaces are well defined.

All key aspects of user interfaces are well defined when they follow the accepted standards established for the industry such as IBM's User Access Guide[1] and/or Microsoft's Interface Guidelines[2] or other appropriate interface guidelines. Accepted psychological, physical, and human factors standards should be followed as well.

51f The Architecture hangs together conceptually.

The Architecture hangs together conceptually when the system specification describes the functional components of the system in terms of their behaviors and provides component-to-component interfaces resulting in a sum of the parts to make a whole.

52 DESIGN

52a The design process is correct and traceable to enterprise, customer, and standard processes.

The design process is correct and traceable to enterprise, customer, and standard processes whenever the required numbers and types of Design Reviews and the content of each Design Review are traceable to the standard, the customer, and the enterprise processes.

The design process is driven by enterprise, customer, and standard policies and processes. The links between these processes should appear on your Standards Traceability Matrix. The Standards Traceability Matrix is further explained in Attachment 13.

52b The design is correct and traceable to the requirements.

The design is correct and traceable to the requirements when every element of the produced product is directly traceable to a requirement. All the elements of the design process are brought into focus through the Requirements Traceability Matrix (RTM). The RTM will trace the requirement from the specification through the design process, through the qualification (preproduction) test process, through the manufacturing process, and through the final (operational) test to end with the final delivery to the customer. The RTM is an inherent part of the Technical Plan, which is attached to the Project Plan.

Let's take a moment to look at ethics. As you review the requirements that you will perform to, you must look at these requirements as a professional. After all, that's why you are being hired. If you find a requirement that you know is wrong or will not work, you have an obligation to advise your customer of that fact. If you "sandbag" this issue and try to make it up with a change later on, you are guilty of unethical conduct. Under some cases, you may be guilty of illegal conduct. To simply trace the requirement to its source is not sufficient. It must, to the best of your professional knowledge, be a valid requirement.

52c The design is efficient.

The design is efficient when it performs as the requirements document (contract) demands, has the inherent reliability, maintainability, and availability demanded by the requirements document (contract) or meets at least the same qualifications for these factors for competing products, and is economical in its design and production and throughout its life-cycle. Ensure that all CSFs (See Cause Description 51a) are incorporated as well.

52d The design adequately addresses issues that were identified and deferred to design at the architectural level.

The design adequately addresses issues that were identified and deferred to design at the architectural level when those architectural elements have been defined and are traceable to the design. Further, they must be addressed in the appropriate Design Review and clearly identified in the design.

52e The design is partitioned into manageable segments.

The design is partitioned into manageable segments when the segments are logical, can be defined, can be tested, can be scheduled, and can be costed. The purpose of this partitioning is to create groupings for the Work Breakdown Structure (WBS) that are manageable and consistent with the resources available (i.e., assigned internally or subcontracted, outsourced, or purchased as necessary).

52f The design accounts for supportability, Life Cycle Cost (LCC), total cost of ownership, and future expansions.

The design accounts for supportability, Life Cycle Cost (LCC), total cost of ownership, and future expansions whenever all these factors are taken into consideration in the design, production, implementation, and operations and maintenance alternatives.

The objective of an LCC analysis is to provide a basis for choosing the most cost-effective approach to the entire life cycle/total cost of ownership system, product, or unit within the available resources. Sometimes this can include planned or estimated future expansions as well. Pre Planned Product Improvement (P^3I) and the phasing in of those improvements should be a part of your up-front planning. The analysis must cover the entire lifespan of the system, product, or unit.

The LCC process provides a systematic methodology for evaluating and quantifying the cost impacts of alternative courses of action. It can be used to support trade-off analyses between several product design configurations or the sensitivity of a specific design to changes. The LCC can, and probably will, affect the distribution of costs between up-front design or production costs and field operation and maintenance costs. Care must be taken to involve the entire lifespan of the system, product, or unit. Frequently, only design or production costs are considered, leaving operation and maintenance costs to be added later. If the specification calls for a Design To Cost (DTC) approach, its result may well be different from the LCC. Be certain to check with the customer regarding intent. The customer could have intended LCC but said DTC or some similar term. The results will likely be different.

John C. Sterling provides an excellent comparison of LCC models at: www.nissd.com/sdes/papers/deslcc.htm.

52g Technical Performance Measures (TPMs) such as data retrieval time, weight, error rate, etc., have been defined and accommodated.

Technical Performance Measures (TPMs) such as data retrieval time, weight, error rate, etc., have been defined and accommodated whenever the TPMs are fully understood and appear in the related WBS sections and the related test procedures.

53 DESIGN REVIEWS

53a All Design Reviews were completed according to required processes.

All Design Reviews were completed according to required processes when the events of the Design Review are directly traceable to the requirements stipulated in standard processes, customer (contract and contract referenced) processes, and enterprise processes. In the event these processes are not available to you, see Cause Description 53a (NO).

53b The customer approved each Design Review.

The customer will have approved each Design Review if the customer has signed a sheet that confirms that the customer (through its representative, if necessary) agrees to the Design Review package, the Design Review, and the Design Review minutes, including Design Review action items.

54 IN-PROCESS REVIEWS

54a All required In-Process Reviews were conducted according to required processes.

All required In-Process Reviews were conducted according to required processes when the events of the In-Process Reviews are directly traceable to the requirements stipulated in standard processes, customer (contract and contract referenced) processes, and enterprise processes.

54b Each In-Process Review was approved by the appropriate authority.

The appropriate authority will have approved each In-Process Review if the appropriate authority has signed a sheet that confirms that the appropriate authority (through their representative, if necessary) agrees to the In-Process Review package, the In-Process Review, and the In-Process Review minutes, including In-Process Review action items.

55 PROTOTYPES

55a The prototypes reflect the requirements.

The prototypes reflect the requirements when the customer or client agrees that the prototype satisfies or demonstrates the requirements.

Prototyping is a technique for gathering and validating requirements through an early representation of the product. In prototyping, you gather preliminary requirements that you use to build a representation of the solution—a prototype. You review this with the customer, who may or may not give you additional or different requirements. You incorporate these changes and review them with the customer again. This repetitive process continues for an agreed number of iterations or until the product meets the customer's needs. The limitations are established by the contract, agreement, or understanding.

Gathering requirements can mean the difference between a project's success and its failure. Some developers tend to gather requirements forever and some do not gather them at all. Your project timeline must include the time required for gathering and developing a comprehensive list of requirements. Developers typically gather requirements in one-on-one interviews, but you can take advantage of a number of alternative techniques as well.

The most certain (and slowest) method of keeping up with prototype configuration or content is to follow the basic guidelines of any product development (requirement, baseline, change process, incorporation of change, etc.). As an alternative, it is generally agreed nowadays that the prototypes reflect the requirements if a physical inventory and/or functional test of the prototype(s) reflect the actual requirements at critical points.

Prototypes are not the end products; consequently, you should modify, truncate, or abbreviate the tests to expend the minimum amount of effort and resources consistent with proving the issue.

55b Prototypes were constructed incrementally.

For software projects, incremental construction is usually a necessity for complex programs. The purpose of incremental construction is to create modules that are in themselves testable and provable. This becomes a timesaver whenever you are testing a complex system, and the test fails somewhere along the line. Whenever a test fails, the system reverts back to the last increment that passed its tests. Whenever two tested modules are put together and the test fails, it is likely that the interfaces are incorrect. It is also possible that the specification for one or more of the modules is incorrect. All these conditions must be taken into consideration.

Incremental construction is generally less critical for hardware projects, but it follows the same general precepts as software projects.

55c Prototype changes were incorporated into the design using the Change Control Process.

Prototype changes were incorporated into the design using the Change Control Process (See Technical Cause Descriptions 61a, 61b, and 61c) when the changes are traceable through the product to the documentation that authorized the change.

Prototypes should be treated the same as First Articles in their development. This is particularly true if your process takes the prototype (or Breadboard or Brassboard) directly to development or production. Granted, many changes are devised during the prototype process and incorporated into the prototype to validate their efficacy. Indeed, that's what the prototype process is all about. However, if it is concluded that the in-process change should be a part of the prototype, its constituents must be incorporated at some point through the Change Control Process.

See Cause Description 55a. See the glossary for definitions of these terms.

55d Each prototype change was reviewed and accepted by the originator of the requirements.

Each prototype change was reviewed and accepted by the originator of the requirements whenever a clear trail exists from the requirement to the acceptance.

In the world of prototypes, this is the equivalent of a change process. Many times, prototype changes will be verbal from the originator. When you get a verbal requirement, stop and document the requirement, even if it's just a note. Otherwise, when you get to the end of the prototype, you will have no idea of its contents.

If you get a change to the prototype and it does not pan out, don't discard the documented requirement. It is a good way to keep up with resources such as computer time and labor hours that have been consumed and could be reimbursable.

56 SUBCONTRACTS

56a The sum of all subcontracts reflects all tasks allocated.

The sum of all subcontracts reflects all tasks allocated if the totality of all subcontracts and all work to be performed internally add up to the total requirements in the requirements document (contract).

The Requirements Traceability Matrix (RTM) is the tool that ties together the requirements from the requirements document (contract) to where and how the requirements are being performed. The Work Breakdown Structure (WBS) should follow the RTM directly with respect to specified equipment or modules and indirectly with respect to tasks or performance parameters. In the vernacular, this situation is referred to as the program or project having no holes or overlaps.

When evaluating subcontracts for holes and overlaps, consideration must be given to the fact that there will be some overlaps with respect to required processes. For instance, if a certain quality program is required of the overall program, it must be "flowed down" to each of the subcontractors. In this case, it might appear to be an overlap but it is not. It is, in fact, an appropriate allocation of requirements.

56b Each subcontract contains all tasks allocated.

Each subcontract contains all tasks allocated when the tasks contained in the subcontract are equal to the assigned tasks from the Requirements Flow-Down Matrix (RFM) and are reflected in the Requirements Traceability Matrix (RTM).

57 PURCHASE ORDERS

57a The sum of all Purchase Orders reflects all purchases to be made.

The sum of all Purchase Orders reflects all commercially available products to be purchased for the program or project.

The Requirements Traceability Matrix (RTM) is the tool that ties together the requirements from the requirements document (contract) to where and how the requirements are being performed. The RTM should follow the Work Breakdown Structure (WBS) directly with respect to specified equipment or modules. In the vernacular, this situation is referred to as the program or project having no holes or overlaps.

When evaluating Purchase Orders for holes and overlaps, consideration must be given to the fact that there will be some overlaps with respect to required processes. For instance, if the "Buy America" clause is required of the overall program, it must be "flowed down" to each of the Purchase Orders. In this case, it might appear to be an overlap but it is not. It is, in fact, an appropriate allocation of requirements.

57b Each Purchase Order is complete.

Each Purchase Order is complete and properly written when it contains: Reference Number, Order Date, Vendor, Contact Information, Name of Item, Stock (Catalog) Number, Number of Units, Price, Delivery Schedule, Delivery Location, Purchaser, and Authorizing Signature.

Most companies have preprinted Purchase Order forms. If yours does not, create your own. Even if your Purchase Order form is nothing more than a memo, at least it is documentation of what has been ordered and provides a basis for financial accountability.

58 PRODUCTION/MANUFACTURING

58a All production/manufacturing processes are traceable to standard, customer, or enterprise processes (see glossary).

All production/manufacturing processes are traceable to standard, customer, or enterprise processes when the heritage of the process is clearly referenced in the process.

Manufacturing processes are usually very involved and have tremendous effect on the final product. If the processes have been in effect for some time and neither the line nor materials have changed, chances are the processes are okay. Changing either the line (Cause Description 58b) or the materials (Cause Description 58d) can have an effect on the processes that was unanticipated.

58b The line(s) were properly designed and set up for this (these) product(s).

The line(s) were properly designed and set up for this (these) product(s) if the line produces the product according to the requirements.

If the line design, the processes, or the materials have not changed, chances are that the design of the line is okay. Changing either the processes (Cause Description 58a) or the materials (Cause Description 58d) can have an effect on production that was unanticipated. If the line design has changed, there has likely been an effect on the product that was unanticipated.

58c Shop orders were correct and thorough.

Shop orders were correct and thorough when the end product produced is the product that was specified by the customer.

Shop orders contain the need for an output product. Shop orders usually refer back to the specification (specified or derived) that the end product must meet. Obviously the specifications will be applicable to the end-product in measurement terms such as size, weight, functionality, etc. Usually, shop orders refer to the techniques or process, tools, raw products, etc., that must be used to produce the end product.

Many products require that a number of piece parts be provided to create the final end product. Shop orders control each step of the overall process to ensure that the final end product is the product specified. This process is true of either hardware or software.

Shop orders differ from work orders in that shop orders specify a product to be provided (e.g., rod, software module, etc.) whereas work orders specify a service to be provided (i.e., replace light bulb, etc.).

58d The materials were proper for the processes and the product(s) and do meet the requirements.

The materials were proper for the product(s) when the product meets the requirements. The materials must meet the requirements of the processes and/or materials list, and they must be the materials that were specified in the subcontract or Purchase Order.

59 UNIT TEST

59a Each Unit[3] Test correctly reflects the requirement.

Each Unit Test correctly reflects the requirement when each element of the Unit Test is directly traceable to each element of the unit requirement (specification) through the Requirements Traceability Matrix (RTM) or Subcontract Requirements Traceability Matrix (SRTM).

59b Each design element that applies to the routine/module/ subsystem has its own test case.

Each design element that applies to the routine/module/subsystem has its own test case when there is a direct correlation between the requirement and the elements tested in the unit, subsystem, or system test through the Requirements Traceability Matrix (RTM) or Subcontract Requirements Traceability Matrix (SRTM).

59c Unit Test findings were reviewed for completeness and forwarded to be incorporated into Subsystem Tests and the System Test.

Unit Test findings were reviewed for completeness and forwarded to be incorporated into Subsystem Tests and the System Test when the Unit Tests are traceable to the next level tests. When the Program Test Plan (PTP) is developed, it must include "stacking" the qualification and acceptance tests from the lowest level (Unit Tests) to the highest level (System Test). Care must be taken in the PTP to ensure that all units or subsystems placed under subcontract as well as units and subsystems you have developed adhere to this philosophy. This technique is sometimes called the "Test Flow Forward Technique."

When developing the PTP and the test requirements for the subcontracts, the Requirements Traceability Matrix (RTM) must be used to account for the requirements being "flowed down" into the PTP. The PTP must accommodate the "flow-down" and then, in turn, account for the "flow-up" of the product responses. The PTP should allow for building the system from the bottom up through the use of the test flow.

59d All Problem Test Reports (PTRs) were captured, dispositioned (allocated for action), and worked off.

All Problem Test Reports (PTRs) were captured, dispositioned, and worked off when there is complete accountability for every error that occurred during test conduct and every error was captured, dispositioned, corrected, and verified. The System Test, as written, must subsequently run without error.

60 SYSTEM TEST

60a The System Test Plan/Procedure was approved by the customer.

The System Test Plan/Procedure was approved by the customer when the System Test Plan/Procedure has been provided to the customer with lead time adequate for customer review, and the customer agrees with and approves the final content. The review/approval cycle may require iteration before approval is achieved.

60b The System Test is traceable to the requirements.

The System Test is traceable to the requirements when each requirement is forward traceable through the unit and the subsystem to the system via the Requirements Traceability Matrix (RTM). Each unit or subsystem requirement must be tested at least once at the appropriate level (i.e., at the unit level or at the subsystem level). System level requirements must be visible and backward traceable to the requirement through the RTM. The exceptions to this statement are those requirements that are only visible at the system level. Your RTM should reflect this particular situation by showing the requirement in the left-most column and the place where it is tested in the System Test. All columns in-between will have no entries or dashes.

60c The System Test tested all elements of the system concurrently.

System Test tested all elements of the system concurrently when all elements of the system are called into play as they will be whenever the system is operating in its normal mode.

60d The System Test was performed under appropriate load(s).[4]

The System Test was performed under appropriate load(s) when the loads on the system are the loads required by the specification.

60e The System Test was performed using the same kind of personnel that will be used by the customer.

The System Test was performed using the same kind of personnel that will be used by the customer with regard to training, education, experience, etc. To conduct with engineers a system test that was designed to be run by Level 1 technicians is an invalid test even when you follow all the other procedures of the test. Many times the customer will stipulate that the actual users must perform the System Test. In that case, there is no question. When you are planning your project, ensure you have set aside time to train or expose these persons to the system and its demands.

60f The System Test was properly documented and incorporated the test results of all prior-level tests.

The System Test was properly documented and incorporated the test results of all prior-level tests when the results of the Unit Level Tests and the Subsystem Level Tests are clearly visible in the construct and conduct of the System Test. The System Test should be an incremental test that relies upon the successful completion of all Unit and Subsystem Tests operating together under appropriate system loads.

61 CONFIGURATION MANAGEMENT

61a The Configuration Management Plan (CMP) is thorough, complete, and authorized.

The Configuration Management Plan (CMP) is thorough, complete, and authorized when it follows the format required by the customer and/or the enterprise and maintains the required content as specified in customer or enterprise configuration management policy. Further, the CMP must be signed by an authority that is authorized to sign such documents (usually the vice president or director of engineering, or an equivalent position).

The Configuration Management process could easily be looked upon as the

Janus process. Remember the Roman god Janus who looked both backward and forward? That's what the Configuration Management process does. It looks backward to the baseline, as established, and forward to the test process that will prove the viability of a change.

61b Change requests were presented and approved by an appropriate level of the Review Board.

Change requests were presented and approved by an appropriate level of the Review Board when the presentations and approvals followed the Configuration Management Plan (CMP). See Attachment 5 for more information.

61c Version controls are in place and are reflected on (in) the product.

Version controls are in place and are reflected on (in) the product when the affected product is appropriately marked with the version that describes it in the Version Description Document (VDD) (see glossary) and to which it has been tested.

62 SYSTEM EFFECTIVENESS FACTORS

62a All required System Effectiveness Factors[5] have been appropriately considered.

To say that all required System Effectiveness Factors have been appropriately considered, means that all the System Effectiveness Factors have been appropriately considered in both the product and the processes.

Notes

1. *Systems Application Architecture—Common User Access Guide to User Interface Design.* IBM Corporation, 1991 IBM Document Number SC34-4289 (available through IBM field offices).

2. *The Windows Interface Guidelines for Software Design.* Redmond, Wash.: Microsoft Press, 1995.

3. Defined as the smallest stand-alone component that produces a definable output from a definable input. The unit may be hardware or software. In the case of hardware, power can be external (i.e., a separate unit).

4. Loads are stresses placed upon a system. Loads are those stresses in units typical for the product such as pounds, watts, ergs, numbers of subsystems, etc.

5. The System Effectiveness Factors refer to Reliability, Availability, Maintainability, Supportability (including Logistics), Susceptability, Producibility, Human Engineering, Safety, and Security.

CHAPTER 4

RECOVERING FROM PROGRAMMATIC PROBLEMS

4.1 General

You will probably be alerted to having a programmatic problem by observing that one or more of your programmatic measurements or metrics is out of tolerance. Naturally, you will want to discover the cause of this condition, and that is where this chapter comes in. The Programmatic Recovery Checklist can be used at any time, not only for recovery but as an adjunct to planning or checking programmatic performance.

4.2 Programmatic Recovery Checklist

Table 4-1 is the Programmatic *Recovery* Checklist. Use this table to find and isolate a problem in the programmatic part of your project. The Programmatic *Performance* Checklist is presented in Chapter 2 of this book.

Table 4-1 — Programmatic Recovery Checklist

1	STATEMENT OF WORK (SOW)	Recovery	Yes
1a (NO)	The SOW was *not* properly defined	59	
1b (NO)	The SOW is *not* within our capabilities	60	
1c (NO)	The SOW was *not* properly interpreted	62	
1d (NO)	The SOW was *not* properly negotiated	64	
1e (NO)	The SOW is *not* being properly monitored	65	
1f (NO)	The SOW is *not* being performed properly	66	
2	**SPECIFICATION**	**Recovery**	**Yes**
2a (NO)	The Specification was *not* properly defined	67	
2b (NO)	The Specification is *not* within our capabilities	69	
2c (NO)	The Specification was *not* properly interpreted	70	
2d (NO)	The Specification was *not* properly negotiated	71	
2e (NO)	The Specification was *not* properly monitored	72	
2f (NO)	The specification is *not* being properly performed	73	
3	**POLICIES, PLANS, AND PROCESSES**	**Recovery**	**Yes**
3a (NO)	There is *not* a clear trail between standard policies and plans and Project/Program Plan and Technical Plan	74	
3b (NO)	There is *not* a clear trail between customer policies and plans and the Project/Program Plan and Technical Plan	75	
3c (NO)	There is *no* clear trail between enterprise policies and plans and the Project/Program Plan and Technical Plan	76	
4	**ORGANIZATION**	**Recovery**	**Yes**
4a (NO)	The numbers of personnel assigned to each task are *not* correct	77	
4b (NO)	The mix of personnel to accomplish the task is *not* appropriate	78	
4c (NO)	The personnel are *not* acting and reacting as a team	82	
5	**TEAMS, ALLIANCES, AND SUBCONTRACTS**	**Recovery**	**Yes**
5a (NO)	The subcontracts were *not* properly defined	83	
5b (NO)	The subcontract tasks are *not* within the capabilities of each team member, partner, or subcontractor	84	
5c (NO)	The subcontracts were *not* properly negotiated	87	
5d (NO)	The subcontracts are *not* properly monitored	88	
5e (NO)	Team members, partners, and subcontractors are *not* performing properly	89	
6	**MATERIALS**	**Recovery**	**Yes**
6a (NO)	Purchase Orders were *not* properly written	91	

(continues)

Table 4-1 — (Continued)

6b (NO)	All vendors are *not* competent to perform their tasks	91	
6c (NO)	Purchase Orders are *not* properly monitored	92	
6d (NO)	Vendors are *not* performing properly	95	
7	**PERSONNEL**	**Recovery**	**Yes**
7a (NO)	Each person is *not* competent to perform the tasks assigned	95	
7b (NO)	Each person is *not* available when needed	97	
7c (NO)	Salaries/wages are *not* equal to or less than those bid	98	
7d (NO)	Interpersonal conflicts *do* exist	99	
8	**TRAINING**	**Recovery**	**Yes**
8a (NO)	All personnel have *not* been adequately trained	101	
8b (NO)	The training program is *not* economical	102	
9	**DATA MANAGEMENT**	**Recovery**	**Yes**
9a (NO)	The proper amount of data is *not* being delivered on time	103	
10	**QUALITY**	**Recovery**	**Yes**
10a (NO)	The Quality Plan is *not* thorough, complete, and authorized	104	
10b (NO)	Specific quality characteristics that are important to the project were *not* identified	105	
10c (NO)	Quality is *not* measured so that improvement or degradation is *not* clear	105	
11	**FINAL DELIVERY**	**Recovery**	**Yes**
11a (NO)	Final delivery was *not* accepted by the customer without delay	106	
11b (NO)	Third-party or drop shipping *is* involved	107	

Starting at 1a, read each assertion in the table. If you can answer YES to the assertion, check it off and proceed to the next one. If you answer NO to the assertion, go to the page number listed under the "Recovery" column for that assertion.

4.3 Programmatic Recovery Cause Descriptions

Each assertion listed in the Programmatic Recovery Checklist, shown in Table 4-1, is supported by a Cause Description. In the case of the Programmatic Recovery Checklist, the support is to broaden and deepen the understanding of the assertion and to provide a recovery from the issue raised by your answer to the assertion. Following are explanations of the assertions found in the Programmatic Recovery Checklist.

1 STATEMENT OF WORK (SOW)

1a (NO) The SOW was *not* properly defined.

When an SOW is not properly defined, it can, and probably will, affect the budget, the schedule, and the quality of the product. But you need to be careful in claiming that the SOW is not properly written—it could be that you interpreted it incorrectly.

RECOVERY

Determine what the customer really wants. Discovery of this kind of situation probably means you bid the requirement(s) incorrectly and could be in for a lot of headaches. Further, you need to know why the requirements definition (negotiating) team made the interpretation it did so the problem won't happen again. If you have a good negotiator and a reasonable customer, you may be able to adjust the requirements document (contract) to incorporate the new interpretation as added scope. If not, and if the award has already been made and accepted, you'll have to absorb the cost.

To adjust the requirements, use the following process:

- ❒ Meet with the customer.
- ❒ Go through each paragraph of the SOW that is or might be in question.
- ❒ Come to an understanding with the customer as to exactly what he wants.
- ❒ Come to an understanding with the customer on how recovery can be made. This includes:
  - Schedule Recovery
  - Financial Recovery
  - Technical Recovery

Document all those findings and cosign the minutes of the meetings.

If the award has not been made, go through the same process. In this case you have more leverage because your obligation begins only after you accept the contract.

One way to ensure that this does not happen again is to have the project manager on the proposal team and the negotiation team. If it does happen again, maybe you need a new project manager!

If your project does not have an SOW, create one. If you do not have an outline for an SOW, use the following or consider the additional resources below:

- ❒ Task Description
- ❒ Deliverable Documents List
- ❒ Period of Performance
- ❒ Schedule
- ❒ Reference Documents
- ❒ Modifying Factors (for instance, the number of labor hours of specific disciplines that must be provided)
- ❒ Specification

Any item in or referenced by the SOW is a legal part of the SOW. Therefore, each of these items must be understood. It is a good idea to search the entire SOW and find all the requirements and the modifiers and group them together for your own purposes.

A properly defined SOW will contain (either incorporated or appended) the findings of the requirements discussions (negotiations). These findings are as much a part of the requirements document (contract) as the initial document.

Additional Resources:

MIL-STD-245

1b (NO) The SOW is *not* within our capabilities.

You can make a quick assessment of your ability to perform the task by using the Experience Window in Table 4-2. Ask yourself the customer and product questions and then compare your answers to the answers and capabilities shown in the table.

That's not the end of it, however. Just having customer experience and product experience is not enough; it must be positive experience. If you have had

Table 4-2 — Experience Window

Condition	Have Customer Experience	Have Product Experience	Capability to Perform
1	Yes	Yes	High
2	No	Yes	Moderate
3	Yes	No	Low
4	No	No	Unknown

experience with this customer, but it was not positive experience, you must neutralize the negative effects. If you do not do this, your ability to perform (or win) is in doubt. The same is true of product experience. If you have negative experience with a product, you are in the same boat. If either your customer experience or your product experience is negative, it is likely you will move downward at least two conditions on the chart. In other words, if you have good product experience but bad customer experience, you no longer have a high ability to perform. It is likely you now have a low to unknown ability to perform. Generally speaking, negative experience is worse than no experience.

In addition to satisfying the conditions of the table, you must:

- ❒ Provide the personnel required to perform the task.
- ❒ Provide the facilities required by the task.
- ❒ Provide the finances required by the payment schedule to support the task.
- ❒ Perform the requirements of the Specification (as evaluated under Cause Description 2f).

Risk increases as the condition numbers become greater. Chances are that you are here because your ability to perform is "moderate" or less. If it is "unknown," you probably should not have bid the task in the first place. Nevertheless, a problem exists that must be rectified.

RECOVERY

Create a matrix similar to the one shown in Table 4-3 and list all the requirements or tasks (this includes the contents of referenced documents as well as

Table 4-3 — Task Qualification

	Project A	Project B	Project C	Project D	Project E
Task 1			X		
Task 2		X		X	
Task 3			X		
Task 4			X		
Task 5	X				X
Task 6					

explicitly included documents) as rows and the projects (including IR&D programs) that the enterprise has performed as columns. Every requirement or task should have an "X" at the intersection between the requirement and at least one program. If not, continue with the process to try to bring the SOW within your capabilities.

To try to bring the SOW within your capabilities, you must create a Risk Mitigation Plan and determine how the risk can be neutralized. (Note that Task 6 in the table has no entries and therefore must be brought within your capabilities). If the SOW is truly not within your capabilities, you have two alternatives, neither of which is usually within the purview of the project manager but must be defined and then taken to management for approval or action.

If the task is within the state of the art, you may be able to buy resolution by teaming or creating an alliance with another company. Sometimes, simply hiring one or several individuals with the requisite knowledge will solve the problem.

If it is not within the state of the art and you have not already bid the project then no-bid. If it is not within the state of the art and you have already bid the project, then ethics requires that you must immediately meet with the customer and discuss the issue. Of course, you are at the mercy of the customer and his lawyers at this point, and you may well end up repaying whatever reparations are necessary (i.e., you committed and expanded funds but did not perform). This is the point where we ask ourselves the perennial 2 A.M. wake-up question: "Why did we bid this thing in the first place?"

1c (NO) The SOW was *not* properly interpreted.

When an SOW is not properly interpreted, it can, and probably will, affect the budget, the schedule, and the quality of the product. In order to be properly interpreted, it must obviously contain all the pertinent information that needs to be interpreted.

Discovery of this kind of situation probably means you bid the task or scope incorrectly and could be in for a lot of headaches. Further, you need to know why the requirements definition (negotiating) team made the interpretation they did so it won't happen again. If you have a good negotiator and a reasonable customer, you may be able to adjust the contract to incorporate the new interpretation as added scope. If not, you'll have to absorb the costs.

In order to be properly interpreted, an SOW must be properly defined. An SOW is properly defined when it fully describes the products or services to be delivered and states when and where they are to be delivered. Each product or service (sometimes called Contract Line Item Numbers or CLINs) must be separately listed. Additionally, the following documents should be referenced, but are usually not included:

- ❒ Task Description
- ❒ Deliverable Documents List (sometimes called Contract Data Requirements List or CDRL)
- ❒ Period of Performance
- ❒ Schedule
- ❒ Reference Documents (referenced but not included)
- ❒ Modifying Factors (for example, the number of labor hours of specific disciplines that must be provided)
- ❒ Specification
- ❒ Financial Information (usually referenced but not included in the SOW)

Any item in or referenced by the SOW is a legal part of the SOW in a program and an ethical part of the SOW in both a program and a project. Therefore, each of these items must be understood. It is a good idea to search the entire SOW and find all the requirements and the modifiers and group them together for your own purposes.

RECOVERY

Meet with the customer, and use the content listing above as a guide for your meeting. Ensure that every item is covered. Go through each paragraph of the

SOW that is or might be in question. Come to an understanding with the customer as to exactly what the customer wants. Come to an understanding with the customer on how recovery can be made. This includes:

- ❒ Schedule Recovery
- ❒ Financial Recovery
- ❒ Technical Recovery

Document all the understandings. It may be advisable to reverse contract (see glossary) the customer and, when approved, include those understandings in the requirements document (contract) as an official change. Be careful—some customers take a dim view of this action.

One way to ensure that this does not happen again is to have the project manager and the technical manager on the proposal team and the negotiation team. Then, if it happens again, maybe you need a new project manager!

Additional Resources:

MIL-STD-245

1d (NO) The SOW was *not* properly negotiated.

Very simply, a poorly negotiated SOW is one in which there is either a misunderstanding of the task or a lack of balance between the scope of work to be accomplished, the amount of money to be paid, and the time allowed to complete the task. Usually, the performer of the work is concerned only if the scope of work exceeds the budget or the schedule. But the other side of the equation should also be true. Every negotiation should be a win-win negotiation. Otherwise, the aggrieved party will attempt to "get even."

RECOVERY

Determine what the customer really wants. Then determine what you are willing to do. If you can resolve any of the issues so that they are within scope, you're in luck. If not, stand by for an overrun. Your enterprise policies should call for complete minutes of the negotiation, signed by both parties. If they don't, establish your own policy that does. Establish a standard checklist for your discussions. If you do not have such a checklist, please refer to Attachment 17.

- ❐ Meet with the customer.
- ❐ Go through each paragraph of the SOW that is or might be in question.
- ❐ Come to an understanding with the customer as to exactly what he wants.
- ❐ Come to an understanding with the customer on how recovery can be made. This includes:
  - Schedule Recovery
  - Financial Recovery
  - Technical Recovery

One way to ensure this does not happen again is to have the project manager and the technical manager on the proposal team and the negotiation team. If it happens again, maybe you need a new project manager!

1e (NO) The SOW is *not* being properly monitored.

The SOW is *not* properly monitored when the work being performed is *not* being monitored by lead technical and program personnel using accepted monitoring techniques.

RECOVERY

Establish appropriate meetings and reviews to monitor all aspects of your project. Table 4-4 shows the most common meetings and reviews usually established for a project.

Because of the variability of projects, the content of these meetings and reviews must be your own.

These interchanges must be conducted at frequent intervals. The lower the position in the hierarchy, the more frequent the interchange. In other words, Schedule Reviews should be held more often than Customer Reviews.

Just because the SOW is being properly monitored does not necessarily mean the program is running properly; it only means that it is being monitored properly. The point is that if the program is not being monitored properly, you will not know it until it is too late.

The reviews must have metrics established to indicate if each event is in

Table 4-4 — Meetings and Reviews

Review or Meeting	Cause Description Appearance
Schedule Reviews	1f, 5e, 6d
Budget Reviews	1f, 5e
Design Reviews	11a, 51e, 52a, 53
Technical Interchange Meetings	1f, 5d, 5e, 6d
Subcontractor Meetings	5d, 5e
In-Process Reviews	5d
Customer Meetings	5d, 5e

tolerance or out-of-tolerance. The content of each of the reviews must be appropriate for that review.

1f (NO) The SOW is *not* being performed properly.

The SOW is *not* being properly performed when any review shows that performance is out-of-tolerance in such elements as:

- ❒ Schedule
- ❒ Budget
- ❒ Design

RECOVERY

First, schedule the necessary meetings. Since you are having problems, the meetings should be more frequent than normal at first. The frequency can be decreased as the program progresses.

Second, review the measurements and metrics and determine which are out-of-tolerance and which are in tolerance. For those that are out-of-tolerance, you need to make a tactical decision as to how to handle each one. Some may be allowed to run normally and, with increased scrutiny, will in time be brought back into tolerance. For instance, there may be times when an event is behind schedule today or this week but will be back on schedule by next month. That is frequently a problem with the plan. If this is the case, let it run and return to schedule later. Don't fool yourself, however. Ensure that the event will be back in tolerance shortly. Make a note of the situation so the plan can be changed for the next project. Others may require a Tiger Team (a group formed to resolve this specific issue) to bring them back into tolerance. You must make that judgment on-site.

Third, when all the measurements and metrics are back in tolerance, monitor all events closely and regularly. Because elements of the project have been out-of-tolerance and, as a consequence, additional effort has been expended, it may be advisable to replan the project. If this is necessary, refer to the "Recovery" section presented in Cause Description 2d.

2 SPECIFICATION

2a (NO) The Specification was *not* properly defined.

If you do not thoroughly understand the Specification, it is not properly defined. Granted, the problem may be your fault but, if you don't understand it, it makes no difference. You must understand the Specification before proceeding further. A Specification that is *not* properly defined is one that is either not understandable or not testable.

It is the responsibility of the requirements definition (negotiating) team to ensure that these conditions are satisfied. One of the best ways to ensure this is to require that the technical manager be on the requirements definition (negotiating) team. The technical manager will ensure that there is full understanding and that the result is testable or will suffer the consequences.

RECOVERY

Understand the Specification. Read it and dissect it if necessary. Use a checklist to evaluate the Specification. If you don't have a checklist, use the following:

- ❒ Scope of the Document
- ❒ Applicable documents
- ❒ Requirements

- ❐ Item Definition
- ❐ Performance Characteristics
  - The performance requirements related to manning, operating, maintaining, and logistically supporting the prime item to the extent these requirements define or constrain design of the prime item and include response time, throughput rates, and exclusion times
- ❐ Physical Characteristics
  - The design constraints and standards necessary to assure compatibility of prime item components
- ❐ Interfaces between the principal item being specified and other items with which it must be compatible
- ❐ The major components of the principal item and the primary interfaces between such major components
- ❐ Qualification Requirements (for software) or Quality Assurance Provisions (for hardware)

If a particular issue is not addressed in the Specification, it needs to be discussed. Minutes must be taken, and both parties need to agree to and sign the minutes. You may be able to get some events to be considered out-of-scope and get them funded. Even if you don't get this concession, at least you'll know "how big the bear is." You may well need to replan your program around this new understanding.

If you are dealing with a government Specification, there is an application developed by NASA that can help with the Requirements Traceability chore. That product is called *SpecsIntact,* meaning "Specifications kept intact." The product was developed and is used primarily for facility projects but can be used for others as well. Information can be requested from:

SpecsIntact

Kennedy Space Center, FL 32899

Technical Support line – 321-867-8800

Fax:	321-867-1444
E-mail:	specsintact@ksc.nasa.gov
Web site:	http://si.ksc.nasa.gov/specsintact/index.asp

Additional Resources:

MIL-STD-490

2b (NO) The Specification is *not* within our capabilities.

If the Specification is *not* within your capabilities, you must either determine what will bring it within your capabilities or walk away from it. If you have not bid the task or if the contract has not been awarded, you have the alternative of simply no-bidding or stopping your proposal effort. If you have already been awarded the program, it's a different story.

RECOVERY

First, you must establish your strengths and weaknesses; that is, where you have experience and can perform and where you do not have the ability to perform.

Based on the assumption that "if you've done it before you can do it again," a quick assessment can be made of the task by using the Task Qualification Matrix shown in Table 4-5.

The Task Qualification Matrix lists all the requirements or tasks in the left-most column and the projects (including IR&D programs) that the enterprise has performed across the top. Every requirement or task should have an "X" at the intersect with at least one project. If not, continue with the process to try to bring the Specification to within your capabilities.

To bring your capabilities up to the requirements of the Specification, you

Table 4-5 — Task Qualification

	Project A	Project B	Project C	Project D	Project E
Task 1			X		
Task 2		X		X	
Task 3			X		
Task 4			X		
Task 5	X				X
Task 6					

first need to create a Risk Mitigation Plan and determine how the risks (such as Task 6 in the table above) can be neutralized.

It's no fun to have a "tiger by the tail." If this situation occurs, you could have a real problem.

If the Specification is truly not within your capabilities, you have two alternatives, neither of which is usually within the purview of the project manager but must be defined and then taken to management for approval or action.

If the task is beyond your capabilities but within the state of the art, you may be able to buy resolution by teaming or creating an alliance with another company. Sometimes, simply hiring one or several individuals with the requisite knowledge will solve the problem.

If the task is beyond your capabilities and is not within the state of the art and you have not already bid the project, then no-bid. If you have already bid the project, you must immediately sit down with the customer and lay out the problem and the answers that have been tried and that failed to work. What you are trying to do here is expand the content of the diversity attacking the problem. All these steps must be undertaken as rapidly as possible. If you have a failure and know you have a failure with no recourse, you must notify your customer at the earliest possible time. It may hurt and hurt severely, but that's the only ethical thing to do.

2c (NO) The Specification was *not* properly interpreted.

When a Specification is not properly interpreted, it can, and probably will, affect the budget, the schedule, and the quality of the product.

RECOVERY

Determine what the customer really wants. Discovery of this kind of situation probably means you bid the requirement(s) incorrectly and could be in for a lot of headaches. Further, you need to know why the requirements definition (negotiating) team made the interpretation they did so it won't happen again. If you have a good negotiator and a reasonable customer, you may be able to adjust the requirement to incorporate the new interpretation as added scope. If not, you'll have to absorb the costs. Use the following process:

- ❒ Meet with the customer.
- ❒ Go through each paragraph of the Specification that is or might be in question (I really recommend that you don't skip any).

- ❒ Come to an understanding with the customer as to exactly what is wanted.
- ❒ Come to an understanding with the customer on how recovery can be made. This includes:
  - Schedule Recovery
  - Financial Recovery
  - Technical Recovery

One way to ensure this does not happen again is to have the project manager and the technical manager on the proposal team and the requirements definition (negotiation) team. If it happens again, maybe you need a new project manager.

Additional Resources:

MIL-STD-245

2d (NO) The Specification was *not* properly negotiated.

If the Specification was not properly negotiated, you may or may not have an opportunity to renegotiate. If you do not have an opportunity to renegotiate, you are likely looking into an overrun. A Specification is not properly negotiated if there is a difference of opinion between the customer and the contractor as to the meaning or content of any element of the Specification.

RECOVERY

If you have an opportunity to renegotiate, use the following outline or one of your own. The point is to use a control mechanism. See Attachment 17.

- ❒ Scope of the Document
- ❒ Applicable Documents
- ❒ Requirements
- ❒ Item Definition
- ❒ Performance Characteristics
  - The performance requirements related to manning, operating, maintaining, and logistically supporting the prime item to the extent these

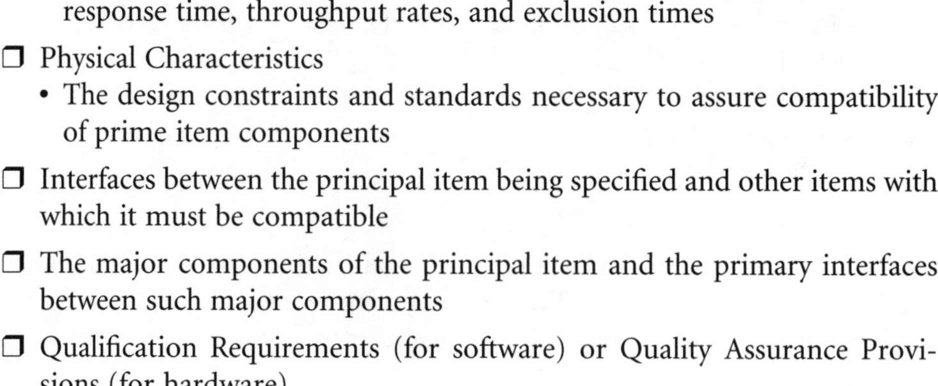

requirements define or constrain design of the prime item and include response time, throughput rates, and exclusion times

- ❒ Physical Characteristics
  - The design constraints and standards necessary to assure compatibility of prime item components
- ❒ Interfaces between the principal item being specified and other items with which it must be compatible
- ❒ The major components of the principal item and the primary interfaces between such major components
- ❒ Qualification Requirements (for software) or Quality Assurance Provisions (for hardware)

If you do not have an opportunity to renegotiate (this is the norm), you will need to replan your program. Replanning will include attempting to achieve a balance between the three items scope, schedule, and budget. The issue will be that scope exceeds schedule or budget or both. How do you do that?

First, establish any of these variables as fixed; the other two can be the variables to be renegotiated. If schedule is king, the scope can be reduced or funding increased. If the budget is absolute, scope can be reduced or time expanded.

A primary rule of thumb is that the longer a program runs, the more it will cost. On a hardware program, you will get more return from compressing the existing schedule than from trying to reduce labor. On a software program, compressing the schedule without a concomitant reduction in scope will likely increase defects and, consequently, cost. Look for operations that will increase the efficiency of the operation and thus reduce the time it takes to perform the operation. There are many ways to accomplish this, but any of them could have a legal impact on the contract (for instance, working unpaid overtime). Use the problem-solving processes discussed in Chapter 6 of this book and select the options that are right for you, your team, and your contract.

Don't overlook minimizing labor, but make it a lower priority than optimizing the schedule.

2e (NO) The Specification was *not* properly monitored.

If the requirement is valid and monitoring responsibility has been assigned but has gone out of control without your knowledge, the fault lies in one place and one place alone, with the monitor. If monitoring responsibility was not assigned, it's your fault.

You must insist on a Requirements Traceability Matrix (RTM) and an appropriately assigned monitor.

RECOVERY

Start back with the Specification and develop a Requirements Traceability Matrix (see Attachment 7) similar to Table 4-6 below. Add a column for the monitor's name.

Cover every requirement, assign monitoring responsibility for every requirement, and establish a schedule for frequent reporting from the monitor to the project leadership.

Table 4-6 — Requirements Traceability Matrix (RTM)

SOW/ Spec Para	Requirement	WBS Number	S/C SOW/ Spec Para	Unit Test Number	System Test Para	Monitor
SOW						
4.3.1	Security	06-03-02	N/A	T-0304	4.4.1	Smith
Spec						
3.2.1	System weight shall be less than 10,000 pounds	02-04-03	3.4.6	T-0045	3.4.1	Jones

2f (NO) The Specification is *not* being properly performed.

The Specification is not being properly performed when the in-process reviews or the design reviews were not passed properly or were not accepted by the customer or when the product was not fabricated or produced in accordance with the design or was not accepted by the customer.

The problem must be that the requirements are not being satisfied. You had to state that the Specification was properly defined (1a), within your capabilities (1b), properly interpreted (1c), and properly negotiated (1d) in order to get here in the first place. Therefore, you must proceed with the understanding that the requirements are not being satisfied.

RECOVERY

Return to the Specification and cross-check the Specification with the Requirements Traceability Matrix (RTM). Determine which of the requirements are not being met using Table 4-7 as a start.

Table 4-7 — Problem Cross-Reference Table

Does the problem lie in:	Go to Cause Description
Architecture	51a, 51b, 51c, 51d, 51e, 51f
Design	52a, 52b, 52c, 52d, 52e, 52f, 52g
Design Reviews	53a, 53b
In-Process Reviews	54a, 54b
Prototypes	55a, 55b, 55c, 55d
Subcontracts	56a, 56b
Purchase Orders	57a, 57b
Production/Manufacturing	58a, 58b, 58c, 58d
Unit Test	59a, 59b, 59c, 59d
System Test	60a, 60b, 60c, 60d, 60e, 60f

If the first time you know the Specification is not being properly performed is when it misses or fails a major milestone, you are not on top of your project. Every requirement in the RTM should have a monitor, and every major milestone should have inch stones leading up to it.

As soon as you recover from the immediate problem, go back and establish the requisite monitor for each requirement still to be performed and establish inch stones for each milestone yet to be accomplished.

3 POLICIES, PLANS, AND PROCESSES

3a (NO) There is *not* a clear trail between standard policies and plans and the Project/Program Plan and Technical Plan.

The Project/Program Plan and Technical Plan *must* link to standard policies and plans through two avenues. One of those is through enterprise policies and processes; the other is through the requirements document (contract). The requirements document (contract) references those standards through the Statement Of Work (SOW) and the Specification.

You should have an STM similar to Table 4-8 shown below. The STM is explained in Attachment 13.

RECOVERY

Create an STM similar to Table 4-8 with your data inserted.

Table 4-8 — Standards Traceability Matrix

STANDARDS			APPEARANCE	
Industry	**Customer**	**Enterprise**	**Project Plan**	**Technical Plan**
ISO-9001	ISO-9001	Enterprise Quality Policy 09350	Para 4.6.8	Part I, Para 4.5.6
	MIL-STD-100	Enterprise Engineering Standards 06050	N/A	Part II, Para 1.2.3

Table 4-8 is a multipurpose table in that the industry, customer, and enterprise standards documents are all included in one chart. You can use this technique, or you can separate the documents into three separate charts. The advantage of using three charts is that industry and enterprise charts will probably remain constant for most, if not all, projects, and only the customer chart needs to be researched. The advantage of using the multipurpose chart is that the relationships between all elements—and there will be many—are clearly presented.

You must start with the requirement and not the appearance. Starting with the appearance will give you a false sense of accomplishment.

Refer to Attachment 13 for more detail.

3b (NO) There is *not* a clear trail between customer policies and plans and the Project/Program Plan and Technical Plan.

The Project/Program Plan and Technical Plan *must* link to customer policies and plans through two avenues. One of those is through enterprise policies and processes; the other is through the requirements document (contract). The requirements document (contract) references those standards through the Statement Of Work (SOW) and the Specification.

You should have an STM similar to Table 4-9. The STM is explained in Attachment 13.

RECOVERY

Create an STM similar to Table 4-9 with your data inserted.

Table 4-9 — Standards Traceability Matrix

STANDARDS			APPEARANCE	
Industry	Customer	Enterprise	Project Plan	Technical Plan
ISO-9001	ISO-9001	Enterprise Quality Policy 09350	Para 4.6.8	Part I, Para 4.5.6
	MIL-STD-100	Enterprise Engineering Standards 06050	N/A	Part II, Para 1.2.3

Table 4-9 is a multipurpose table in that the industry, customer, and enterprise standards documents are all included in one chart. You can use this technique or separate them into three separate charts. The advantage of using three charts is that industry and enterprise charts will probably remain constant for most, if not all, projects and only the customer chart needs to be researched. The advantage of using the multipurpose chart is that the relationships between all elements, and there will be many, are clearly presented.

You must start with the requirement and not the appearance. Starting with the appearance will give you a false sense of accomplishment.

Refer to Attachment 13 for more detail.

3c (NO) There is *no* clear trail between enterprise policies and plans and the Project/Program Plan and Technical Plan.

The Project/Program Plan and Technical Plan *must* link to enterprise policies and plans through two avenues. One of those is through enterprise policies and processes; the other is through the requirements document (contract). The requirements document (contract) references those standards through the Statement Of Work (SOW) and the Specification.

You should have an STM similar to Table 4-10. The STM is explained in Attachment 13.

RECOVERY

Create an STM similar to Table 4-10 with your data inserted.

Table 4-10 — Standards Traceability Matrix

STANDARDS			APPEARANCE	
Industry	**Customer**	**Enterprise**	**Project Plan**	**Technical Plan**
ISO-9001	ISO-9001	Enterprise Quality Policy 09350	Para 4.6.8	Part I, Para 4.5.6
	MIL-STD-100	Enterprise Engineering Standards 06050	N/A	Part II, Para 1.2.3

Table 4-10 is a multipurpose table in that the industry, customer, and enterprise standards documents are all included in one chart. You can use this technique or divide them into three separate charts. The advantage of using three charts is that industry and enterprise charts will probably remain constant for most, if not all, projects and only the customer chart needs to be researched. The advantage of using the multipurpose chart is that the relationships between all elements, and there will be many, are clearly presented.

Refer to Attachment 13 for more detail.

4 ORGANIZATION

4a (NO) The numbers of personnel assigned to each task are *not* correct.

The numbers of personnel must be contributing to a problem or you probably would not be looking at this particular issue at this time. It could be that you simply reviewed the organization chart and found that there were more or fewer people than called for by the organization chart and manpower table. A big part of your job is to constantly optimize the organization.

You must constantly ask yourself: "Is the job getting done?" Then, follow up with the questions: "Is the job getting done without working overtime?" and "Is the morale of the team high?" If the answer to all those questions is YES, you're probably in good shape. You must however also ask yourself: "Do I have too many people?" The job could be getting done, you are not working overtime, and morale is high, but you have too many people. Do you have too many people or too few?

RECOVERY

If the manpower numbers do not match the organization chart, one of two things is wrong: The number of people is wrong or the organization chart is wrong. What a keen grasp of the obvious!

If you don't have enough people, even if you are getting the job done, you need to review the tasks and task distribution. If you are running under the manpower projected, you could be saving money. Conversely, you could be driving the people to the point where major mistakes will be made. You are the best judge of the answer to that question. Don't just let this situation ride. Evaluate it carefully and be certain of your decision. How do you get more people? That's a question that will be unique to your organization. No matter the final answer, you will need to perform a workload analysis and show that you need more people. You may be able to simply request more people or go out and hire more people or you may simply be shut off from increasing your manpower. The answer depends on your organization and the organization and task type (i.e., government versus commercial, fixed price contract versus cost plus contract, not-for-profit, volunteer, etc.). Each will have a different answer. More people will cost more money and, if you have P&L responsibility, it will be a large part of your cost equation.

If you have too many people, it is likely that you are headed for an overrun. If not, it possibly means that the people are not the same level as those that were bid. If this is the case, the project manpower must be reevaluated. Don't limit your investigation to numbers alone. Refer to Cause Descriptions 4b (NO), 7a (NO), 7b (NO), and 7c (NO).

4b (NO) The mix of personnel to accomplish the task is *not* appropriate.

The mix of personnel to accomplish the task is *not* appropriate if the job is *not* getting done or the mix of personnel does *not* match the mix shown on the organization chart. The first is much more important than the second.

If the mix of personnel is not appropriate, it means there is a disconnect between what was bid and how the program is manned. It is possible that the job is getting done just fine with an improper mix of personnel; however, if that is the case, the staffing plan is incorrect, which means you probably bid incorrectly. If the mix, on average, is lower than what was bid, you will probably save some money. In this case, it makes sense to change the staffing mix. If the mix is higher than what was bid, it will probably cost you money. In this case, you need to change the real mix to what was bid. There is a fine line between mix and numbers. For instance, you could have fewer people of higher levels who are getting the job done, and the end result is the same dollars as were bid. The opposite is true as well. The bottom line is to match the dollars being spent to the task being done.

RECOVERY

The primary task is to get the job done on or ahead of time, within or under budget, and with technical compliance.

When the task is kicked off, you may be in a personnel situation that is different now from what it was at the time the program was bid. There are a number of situations that can occur and that require different action.

Following are sets of budget and schedule situations and the particular action required for each one:

On Budget/On Schedule. Stay the course!

On Budget/Ahead of Schedule. Build a reasonable schedule reserve for use later on, particularly during integration and test.

Over Budget/On Schedule. Reassess the organization mix and personnel qualifications. Can they be changed and still get the job done? Can you reduce the staffing to get back on budget? Change mix or numbers of personnel.

Over Budget/Ahead of Schedule. Reduce the staffing on the project.

Over Budget/Behind Schedule. Problem. First, don't let it get any worse. Reevaluate the staffing mix. Can you get by with fewer people who are more efficient? If you can't fix this problem as soon as it occurs, it is the beginning of a "death spiral." If all attempts fail, try to get the scope, schedule, or cost changed.

Reassess the organization mix and personnel qualifications. Is this a temporary condition or reflective of the program in the long-term? If short-term, and you have a cost type contract, increase personnel (with the customer's concurrence). If you have a fixed price type contract, consider replanning and/or bringing on temporary personnel or change the mix to get you back on schedule. If long-term, and you have a cost type contract, replan and increase personnel or increase schedule (with the customer's concurrence). If you have a fixed price type contract, replan.

Here we are talking about the organization mix which means personnel. Our options are to leave alone, add, decrease, or change the mix. There are also other options, such as "fast-tracking" and conducting parallel activities, that may well need to be considered.

There is a price to pay for each change made. If your mix is different from the organization chart, and if the job is getting done but the people are being overworked, even if the job were on budget, you could change the mix so the work balance is proper. Now, as Project Manager, you may like the short-term results (on schedule, under budget) but the long-term ramifications may bite you. Just when you need your people the most, at the end of the program, they will be exhausted and you may lose everything you have gained and then some.

If your mix is different from the organization chart and the job is not getting done regardless of whether or not the job is on budget, change the mix of personnel to be the same as the organization chart.

Many times there are simply not enough people available in an organization to go around. There are three ways to get around this problem. The first is the most obvious—hire more people. This may or may not be the right answer. If you hire more people, it will cost more money. Can you afford it and will management allow it? Even though that may solve your problem, management may take a dim view of hiring more people because, when your project ends, the company is stuck with these additional people. Even if you are projectized (meaning all necessary personnel are assigned directly to the project), employees are hired by the enterprise and allocated to the program so they are company employees (i.e., not program employees). There is an approach to management that says: "If you hold down the number of people on a project, the people already assigned to the project will rise to do the work required." This may or may not work. Sometimes it does work and the result on a fixed price contract is more profit. However, if it continues for more than a short time, the usual result is a loss of morale and employee turnover. The second way is to work overtime (meaning paid overtime as opposed to the above technique of forced and unpaid overtime). This is the right technique if you need to increase manpower by less than about 30 percent (the actual amount depends on your accounting procedures) or need to increase manpower for a short period of time. Overtime costs only the direct time worked and, perhaps, a premium. It carries *higher* loadings (based on a percentage system) but *not additional* loadings of G&A (General and Administrative) and overhead. The third way is to increase the efficiency of the people available. There are three ways to do this. One is to "swap out" one person for another. Sometimes, even swapping out for a higher-paid person is more efficient than hiring another person, assuming the higher-paid person is more efficient than the lower-paid person. Next, you can train, and thus upgrade, the person whose efficiency you need to improve. That, of course, assumes training will do it. Finally, you can outsource some of the effort or use contract employees. These are all popular options. Use care here if you have a union contract. You need to do the math as it applies to your program to decide which of these techniques to use.

There is another factor that must be considered with regard to personnel and organization if you use the matrix form of management and personnel allocation. If you proposed enough personnel and *time* for those personnel in the proposal and now find that there is not enough time being applied to your program, it may be the fault of the matrix method rather than of the personnel. What happens is that there is a loss of efficiency when changing from program to program and even in transit from program to program. If you are lucky, you may get 80 percent of the time bid by a functional manager for a person's time. Someone has to pay for the inefficiency of the changeovers and the transit time. The result? The program pays for it! You might try to negotiate the "lost 20 percent" from the Functional Manager as a part of his overhead. Before you laugh your head off, this has worked. It depends on the importance of the project to the company and/or the foresight of the Functional Manager. Care must be taken here because under some conditions (federal contracts, for instance) this could be an unacceptable and even illegal practice.

Under Budget/On Schedule. Nice position to be in. So long as you are not stressing your people, you could continue and build a budget reserve.

However, you should reassess the organization mix and personnel qualifications. If you have a cost type contract, reduce personnel (with the customer's concurrence). If you have a fixed price type contract, consider building a schedule by keeping the people and getting ahead of schedule or create a budget reserve by reducing the personnel. Extreme care and caution need to be exercised here. If you have complete budget control, this is a good move. However, if you start to build a reserve, and management consumes that reserve as current profit, you could be in trouble downstream if you have any problems. Once it is declared as profit it is not available to you as "free" money.

Under Budget/Ahead of Schedule. Congratulations. This is great for a Project Manager, but be sure you are not riding a wave that will crash soon. Project your present staffing and schedule and ensure that there is not a "black hole" somewhere.

Under Budget/Behind Schedule. This is typically a staffing issue. That is, you have not staffed up to get the job done. The first thing to do is to get back on schedule, then worry about cost.

Additional Resources:

"Program Management—Turning Many Projects into Few Priorities with TOC." This article was originally presented at the National Project Management Institute Symposium (Philadelphia, October, 1999) by Francis S. "Frank" Patrick.

4c (NO) The personnel are *not* acting and reacting as a team.

In order to be a team, the individuals must act and react with regard to the team's goals. The group acts and reacts as a team when the responses to team goals are greater than the responses to individual goals.

If the individuals are not acting and reacting as a team, it could be caused by one or several reasons: First, there may be individuals in the group that decline (refuse) to be a part of the team. Second, team training was not thorough or was inappropriate. Third, there was no team training at all.

RECOVERY

If there are individuals in the group that decline (refuse) to be a part of the team, it is likely an individual rather than a team problem. Refer to Cause Description "7d (NO) Interpersonal conflicts *do* exist." If the responsible person is replaced, you may need to recap that part of the team training package that has to do with interfaces and responsibilities of individuals. The balance could change by changing individuals on the team.

If team training was not thorough or was inappropriate, the actions or reactions may be subtle or profound. Recovery is a matter of degree and team training needs to be changed by some amount. If the response is subtle, chances are that the team training package can be changed slightly. In this case, identify the shortfall and have the training coordinator rework that part of the package. That change can then be given by you or by the training department, depending on the size and nature of the change. If the change is profound, it is clear the training department must revise and re-present the package. Re-presenting the package will be subject to the same timing constraints as in the following paragraph.

If there was no training presented before the project was started, you are confronted with a real problem. Now, the value of preproject training becomes obvious. A training package must be developed or purchased and presented to the group. These are the problems of those responsible for training. Your problem will be how to stop work long enough to have your people attend the training course. Most team training courses are presented in one- to three-day sessions. You may be able to divide the course into segments to be given after hours, or you could have the course given in a long weekend or two weekends. These options could be impacted by the work schedule already in progress (i.e., the people are already overworked) or union rules that may prohibit such action. Finally, you could stop the project and conduct the training course. Before you start laughing, consider just how bad the situation is. This could be the most cost-effective approach. You must be the judge.

5 TEAMS, ALLIANCES, AND SUBCONTRACTS

5a (NO) The subcontracts were *not* properly defined.

The tasks of subcontractors, which includes team members and alliances, are *not* properly defined unless they have a clear trail between the subcontract Statement Of Work and the requirements document (contract) through the Requirements Flow-down Matrix (RFM), and a clear trail between the subcontract Specification and the requirements document (contract) Specification through the Requirements Traceability Matrix (RTM).

RECOVERY

Begin with your customer's requirement that defines your Statement Of Work (SOW) and the Specification (Spec) for the product that you are to produce. Decompose the SOW and the Spec using the Work Breakdown Structure (WBS), the RTM, and the RFM. Establish a clear link between the requirement and how and by whom it will be accomplished. The best way to accomplish this task is to establish an RTM that reflects the requirement from your customer through your organization. At that point, part of the requirement will be allocated to one or more subcontractors. The best way to keep up with this trail is by using a Subcontract Requirement Flow-down Matrix (SRFM). Require your subcontractor(s) to provide a Subcontract Requirement Traceability Matrix (SRTM) to complete the link through his processes.

If you do not have an RFM or SFRM, you can use Table 4-11 as a start.

Additional information can be found in Attachment 8.

If you do not have an RTM or SRTM, you can use Table 4-12 as a start.

Additional information can be found in Attachment 7.

Table 4-11 — Requirements Flow-Down Matrix (RFM)

Spec Para	Company Reqt	WBS	Design Plan Para	S/C Plan Para	S/C A Para	S/C B Para
1.3.2		02-03-01	5.3.2	5.3.2	1.3.2	1.3.2
1.3.3		02-03-02	5.3.3	5.3.3	1.3.3	N/A
1.3.4		02-03-03	5.3.4	5.3.4	1.3.4	1.3.4
	QA Plan	04-01-01	8.2.6	8.2.6	4.3.6	4.3.6
	CM Plan	05-01-01	9.3.1	9.3.1	5.6.2	5.6.2

Table 4-12 — Requirements Traceability Matrix (RTM)

SOW/ Spec Para	Requirement	WBS Number	S/C SOW/ Spec Para	Unit Test Number	System Test Para	Monitor
SOW						
4.3.1	Security	06-03-02	N/A	T-0304	4.4.1	Smith
Spec						
3.2.1	System weight shall be less than 10,000 pounds	02-04-03	3.4.6	T-0045	3.4.1	Jones

Additional Resources:

US Army Field Manual (FM) 770-78

5b (NO) The subcontract tasks are *not* within the capabilities of each team member, partner, or subcontractor.

The subcontract tasks are not within the capabilities of each team member, partner, or subcontractor if each has not performed the same or a similar task before. The method by which this decision is reached is to construct a matrix with the tasks along the side and a place for project entries across the top. The potential subcontractor then identifies the project where the same or a similar task has been performed. Where there are no intersects of tasks and projects, the subcontractor has no proven ability to perform this task. Hopefully, this exercise is being performed before the subcontract is awarded. The answer here is simple: Do not award this subcontract to this subcontractor.

RECOVERY

If the subcontract has already been awarded to a subcontractor who cannot perform the task, you have two options. The first is to terminate the subcontractor for cause and recompete the subcontract. The second is to attempt to assist the subcontractor to recover. Once again, the initial steps are to create a matrix and evaluate the subcontractor's weaknesses. Create a matrix with the tasks along the side and a place for project entries across the top. The subcontractor then identifies the project where the same or a similar task has been performed. Where there are no intersects of tasks and projects, the subcontractor has no proven ability to perform this task. For each intersect that is not marked (identified as having that ability) a recovery plan must be created.

If a subcontract is beyond the capabilities of your subcontractor, the selection should not have been made in the first place. Please refer to Cause Description 2d (NO), above for more ideas of how to resolve this event.

It is not unusual to assume that a partner "knows what he is doing" and doesn't need a detailed Statement Of Work, etc., to do his job. . . . Wrong! That may work for a few months but, I assure you, in the long run it is the wrong answer. You should have a standard, and all-inclusive, program or process for all subcontracts. That statement applies to team members and alliances as well as the usual run of subcontractors. If you do not have such a standard, you can use the format in Table 4-13 as a start.

To try to bring the shortfall within your subcontractor's capabilities, the first action must be to create a Risk Mitigation Plan and determine how the risk (such as the shortfall shown for Task 6 in Table 4-13) can be neutralized.

To confirm your position, it is a good idea to perform the vendor selection process, at least to the evaluation level, by filling in the Vendor Evaluation Sheets for each discipline as described in Attachment 14 and shown in Figure A14-1 there. You may need this confirmation later on.

If the Specification is truly not within your subcontractor's capabilities, you have two alternatives depending on whether the task is within the state of the art:

If it is, you may be able to buy resolution by teaming or creating an alliance

Table 4-13 — Task Qualification

	Project A	Project B	Project C	Project D	Project E
Task 1			X		
Task 2		X		X	
Task 3			X		
Task 4			X		
Task 5	X				X
Task 6					

or subcontracting with another company. Sometimes, simply hiring one or several individuals with the requisite knowledge will solve the problem. Agreement with the subcontractor will be necessary to determine whether the subcontractor buys the ability or you do. Make sure funding follows function. The determining factor usually is whether or not the task is reasonably separable from the other tasks.

If it is not, you must immediately sit down with the subcontractor and discuss the issue in earnest. Is there any recovery possible from this situation? Can it be parsed and part of it salvaged without destroying the project? Can it be redefined and accomplish the same ends?

Next, you must sit down with marketing (in the case of a teaming) or management (in the case of an alliance) or both and lay out the situation. Teaming and alliances are frequently made for political purposes, and you need to be very careful before making any major changes. If there are political conditions involved, it is advisable to get a release of responsibility from management for the nonperformance of the subcontractor. This may be difficult and even political suicide to initiate. Be careful and use your best judgment for your particular situation

If you have a failure and know you have a failure with either no recourse or an alternative that is not part of the Specification, you must notify your customer at the earliest possible time. This action is absolutely required under some contract conditions (federal contracts, for instance) and may or may not be required under other circumstances, but it's the ethical thing to do. It will require sitting down with the customer, laying out the problem and the answers that have been tried and that failed to work, and reviewing the alternatives that could be used. All these steps must be undertaken as rapidly as possible.

5c (NO) The subcontracts were *not* properly negotiated.

Very simply, a poorly negotiated subcontract is one in which there is a misunderstanding of the task by either party or in which a balance between the scope of work to be accomplished, the amount of money to be paid, *or* the time allowed to complete the task is lacking.

RECOVERY

Determine exactly what the problem is. Was the problem yours? That is, did you incorrectly state the task to be accomplished, the schedule, or the budget? Is the problem attributable to the subcontractor? That is, did he incorrectly interpret the task, the schedule, or the budget?

- ❒ Meet with the subcontractor.
- ❒ Go through each paragraph of the subcontract that is or might be in question.
- ❒ Come to an understanding with the subcontractor as to exactly what the baseline is.
- ❒ Determine exactly who is at fault.
- ❒ Come to an understanding with the subcontractor on how recovery can be made. This includes:
  - Schedule Recovery
  - Financial Recovery
  - Technical Recovery

Based on the answer to the question regarding fault, come to an understanding of exactly how correction will be made.

If the fault is yours, negotiate what you must to get the program back on the road again. Otherwise, you may be looking at a legal situation.

If the fault is with the subcontractor, instruct them as to what must be done to get the program back on the road again in a Show Cause letter. Consider the resulting proposal. If the subcontractor agrees, restructure the subcontract and reinstitute the metrics to ensure proper monitoring. If the subcontractor does not agree, you have two choices:

1. Restructure the subcontract until agreement can be achieved. This can include subdividing the overall task, changing the numbers, adjusting the schedule, changing the design, or many other things.
2. Terminate the subcontract for cause and either perform the work yourself or search for another subcontractor.

Make every attempt to resolve the issues. I don't advocate "caving in" to a poorly performing subcontractor, but you must make a judgment that will be the best solution for the project. Don't let your ego get in the way. This is a good time to call for advice.

If this issue turns political, as it sometimes can when teaming or alliances are involved, make sure you protect yourself by documenting the facts surrounding the situation. If possible, get relief from that part of the program so that you will not be held responsible for the shortcomings of a politically selected, non-performing subcontractor. This is dangerous ground because you just might be held responsible at that point anyway. This issue is sticky and will change with the personalities involved.

Going to court is the solution of last resort. Remember, the project schedule clock is still running!

5d (NO) The subcontracts are *not* properly monitored.

Simply stated, a subcontract is not properly monitored if an event, positive or negative, occurs and you are not aware of its happening.

RECOVERY

Implement regular and frequent reviews at strategic points in the process to ensure that performance is proper. Such reviews include:

- ❐ Subcontract Progress Reviews—Subcontractor presents technical progress, budget status, schedule status, deliverables status, and data status
- ❐ Subcontractor Meetings—Special, single-subject meetings as required
- ❐ Subcontractor Technical Interchange Meetings (TIMs)—Informal reviews of technical subjects
- ❐ Subcontractor Design Reviews—Subcontractor presents and defends the design and its support in a formal environment

- ❒ Subcontractor In-Process Reviews—Informal reviews between milestones
- ❒ Subcontractor Pretest Meetings—Briefings to establish the basis for a test
- ❒ Subcontractor Posttest Reviews—Review of test data and issuance and formalization of action items

These reviews must be conducted at frequent and consistent intervals. The lower in the hierarchy (viz. project is lower in the hierarchy than company, etc.) the more frequent the review.

Within each of these meetings or reviews, measurements or metrics must be established and monitored to determine if an event is in tolerance or out-of-tolerance.

5e (NO) Team members, partners, and subcontractors are *not* performing properly.

Team members, partners, and subcontractors are *not* performing properly when monitored events are *not* being performed on schedule, are *not* within budget, *or* are *not* technically competent. The methods you use in determining this status is by monitoring established measurements or metrics within the meetings and reviews discussed in Cause Description 5d (NO).

RECOVERY

Ensure that the metrics supplied and examined at these meetings and reviews address the critical areas. If fiscal problems have arisen, reassess the fiscal metrics being presented and select a set of metrics that give the needed visibility into project progress. If schedule problems have arisen, reassess the scheduled event or events that are directly and indirectly involved with this problem (i.e., predecessor and successor events). If technical problems have surfaced, it is usually best to convene a Technical Interchange Meeting (TIM).

Monitored events are those events that are typical for a particular review. Usually, Schedule Reviews, Budget Reviews, and Progress Reviews are elements of a Project Review except when they are single-subject meetings. Within each review there must be monitoring values and metrics to determine if the project is performing in tolerance. Although projects vary infinitely in subject matter, there are some values that must be monitored on all projects. Such meetings are frequently called Plans, Progress, and Problems meetings. Such values are, at a minimum:

- ❒ Actual cost to date versus planned cost to date
- ❒ Actual performance to date versus planned performance to date
- ❒ Cost at completion
- ❒ Completion date
- ❒ Performed activities versus planned activities for last period
- ❒ Problems and recommended resolution
- ❒ Planned activities for next period

Because you may have only noted that something is wrong with this Cause Description, you may need to refer to other Cause Descriptions to get to the actual source of the problem. Table 4-14 will refer you to alternative Cause Descriptions.

Each performance review must have some sort of Earned Value Measurement System (EVMS) as a basis for the review. An EVMS is not a single measurement system but rather, a process. While there are books written on the subject, the books tend to describe a single approach to EVMS; essentially, that is actual performance versus planned performance. For an exhaustive list of articles on different EVMSs, see the Web site of Dr. David S. Christensen. of Southern Utah University at: www.suu.edu/faculty/christensend/public.html.

Each design review and in-process review must be conducted to some standard. For the contents of a typical design review or in-process review, see MIL-STD-1521.

Table 4-14 — Meetings and Reviews

Review or Meeting	Cause Description Appearance
Schedule Reviews	1f, 5e, 6d
Budget Reviews	1f, 5e
Design Reviews	11a, 51e, 52a, 53
Technical Interchange Meetings	1f, 5d, 5e, 6d
Subcontractor Meetings	5d, 5e
In-Process Reviews	5d
Customer Meetings	5d, 5e

6 MATERIALS

6a (NO) Purchase Orders were *not* properly written.

When a Purchase Order is not properly written, it can, and probably will, affect the budget, the schedule, and the quality of the product.

RECOVERY

Initiate or reinitiate the Purchase Order. Ensure that there is a clear trail to the requirements document (contract) backward through the Requirements Flow-down Matrix (see Attachment 8) and the Requirements Traceability Matrix (see Attachment 7).

Ensure that the Purchase Order fully describes the products or services to be delivered. Each product or service must be separately listed.

Each Purchase Order is complete and properly written when it contains: Reference Number, Order Date, Vendor, Contact Information, Name of Item, Stock (Catalog) Number, Number of Units, Price, Delivery Schedule, Delivery Location, Purchaser, and Authorizing Signature.

It is beneficial that the information contained in the Purchase Order be complete and properly written for a few reasons. For example, it conveys to the vendor exactly what is expected. Also, you must know exactly the status of each Purchase Order because of the impact it has on your schedule and your budget.

Most companies have preprinted Purchase Order forms. If yours does not, create your own. Even if your Purchase Order form is nothing more than a memo, at least it is documentation of what has been ordered and provides a basis for the schedule and for financial accountability. If your preprinted form does not contain all the information above, I suggest you add the information within the body of the Purchase Order.

6b (NO) All vendors are *not* competent to perform their tasks.

Vendors are *not* competent to perform their tasks if they have *not* passed the criteria set forth in your enterprise standards. If you do not have enterprise standards, the following should be established as the criteria:

- ❒ Technical Performance
- ❒ Cost Performance
- ❒ Delivery Performance
- ❒ Management Performance
- ❒ Procurement Policies and Plans
- ❒ Quality Assurance Program (see Attachment 6 for Quality Assurance Plan)
- ❒ Cost of Quality Position (see glossary)

Each criterion must meet the levels established by the enterprise or, in the instance that there are no enterprise standards, by your project. The vendors should have been graded against these criteria before each subcontract was awarded.

RECOVERY

Each vendor that has been shown to be not competent should be reevaluated using the format similar to that shown in Figure 4-1 on the following page.

The results of this evaluation will isolate the vendor's problem area. If you already know what that problem area is, fine. In that case, this exercise will document the situation for any future activity found necessary such as a Show Cause letter, etc.

Once you have isolated the problem area, you can set about determining the cause of the problem and eliminate or change it.

6c (NO) Purchase Orders are *not* properly monitored.

Simply stated, a Purchase Order (PO) is *not* properly monitored if an event, positive or negative, occurs and you are not aware of its happening.

The PO can be considered to be properly monitored when the vendor's work is monitored by an assigned project person (usually the Materials Manager calling upon technical and program personnel as required) using monitoring techniques such as:

Figure 4-1 — Vendor Evaluation Sheet

VENDOR EVALUATION

Date	4-Jul-02
Program	High-Flyer
Subcontractor/Vendor	National Software
Equipment/Software	Analog Selction Algorithm
Evaluator	G. Smith
Scale Factor	0-5

Item	Consideration	Rating*
1	Organization	3
2	Management	4
3	Manpower	5
4	Access to Management	5
5	Processes	3
6	Procedures	2
7		
8		
9		
10		
	Subtotal**	22
	No. of items rated**	6
	Average of ratings (Subtotal/No of items)**	3.7

*An evaluated number within the Scale Factor.
**Calculated number.

M-M Form

- ❒ Vendor Progress Reports
- ❒ Vendor Meetings
- ❒ In-Process Reviews

The above include Schedule and, if proper, Budget Reviews.

These reviews must be conducted at regular, frequent, and strategic intervals.

Simply conducting these meetings and reviews does not mean the subcontract is performing properly; it only means that the subcontract is being monitored properly. But, if the subcontract is not being monitored properly, you will not know if it is performing properly.

Within each of these must be monitoring points or metrics that indicate that an event is in tolerance or out-of-tolerance.

If schedule is critical, the PO should include an incentive or liquidated damages clause (see glossary) that is invoked in the event the delivery time is not kept.

RECOVERY

POs present a particular problem. Because they are generally of relatively low economic value, they are frequently issued then left alone. A problem is not in evidence until the item is not shipped, and then it's too late. Consequently, you must monitor a PO as you would a subcontract.

Establish reports, reviews, and meetings such as:

- ❒ Vendor Progress Reports
- ❒ Vendor Meetings
- ❒ In-Process Reviews

These reports, meetings and reviews include schedule progress and, if proper, budget.[1]

These reviews must be conducted at regular, frequent, and strategic intervals.

Within each of these must be monitoring points or metrics that indicate that an event is in tolerance or out-of-tolerance. When an out-of-tolerance condition occurs, it must be rectified immediately. Most POs are issued for short-turn-around items, and time is critical.

The most common problem with POs is that the item purchased is "bumped out" of its planned place in the production cycle by some other, higher priority project. If this happens, you must ensure that the item is reinstated on the production line in time to make your schedule. If schedule is critical, it is a good idea to have an incentive or liquidated damages clause in the PO that puts a dollar value on delivery time.

6d (NO) Vendors are *not* performing properly.

Vendors are *not* performing properly when all monitored events are *not* being performed on schedule, within budget, *or* are *not* technically competent. The method you use in determining this status is to conduct regular and frequent reviews at strategic points in the process to ensure that performance is proper.

RECOVERY

Implement regular and frequent reviews at strategic points in the process to ensure that performance is proper. Such reviews include:

- ❒ Vendor Meetings, including
  - Schedule Reviews
  - Budget Reviews[2]
  - Technical Interchange Meetings (TIMs)[3]
- ❒ In-Process Reviews

Because you are only noting that something is wrong with this Cause Description, you may need to refer to other Cause Descriptions to get to the actual source of the problem. Table 4-15 on the following page will refer you to alternative Cause Descriptions.

7 PERSONNEL

7a (NO) Each person is *not* competent to perform the tasks assigned.

What happened to the people we proposed to perform this job in the first place? To win the job, the best people in the company are usually bid and their resumes are placed in the proposal. Unfortunately, every other program wants

Table 4-15 — Meetings and Reviews

Review or Meeting	Cause Description Appearance
Schedule Reviews	1f, 5e, 6d
Budget Reviews	1f, 5e
Design Reviews	11a, 51e, 52a, 53
Technical Interchange Meetings	1f, 5d, 5e, 6d
Subcontractor Meetings	5d, 5e
In-Process Reviews	5d
Customer Meetings	5d, 5e

these people too, and another project got there first! Some customers have recognized this trait and insist that at least 80 percent of the people bid must be assigned to the job. This is probably the number one problem with a large company bidding and running many programs simultaneously using the matrix management system.

This situation can usually be seen during the Planning Phase and can be used to predict a problem in the future but how do you rectify this situation? There are three ways.

RECOVERY

First, the best way I know of to get the right people is to have the most exciting project in the company. The right people will be clamoring to be a part of it. Or you could be the best project manager in the company, and the right people will come knocking at your door to be on your project. These are absolutely the best ways to man a project. If either of these conditions is beyond reality, show management how much will be lost if the right people are not assigned to this project, and either get the right people assigned from the company or hire the right people.

Second, training existing people is a good answer, but it is second best. There's certainly nothing wrong with training—it's just the cost of training. Someone has to pay for training in money or time or both. How is training paid for in your company? Does the company pay for the training and the trainer's time and for the student's time or does the program pay for any or all or some of these? The answers to these questions will have a bearing on how you proceed. Remember, even if the company pays for all the elements, you will not have the people to perform program tasks while they are in training.

If your company uses the matrix form of personnel assignment, then you must resolve the competency issue with the functional manager. The chances are that the reason you have the person assigned is that you are getting what's left over. Refer back to Cause Description 7a and use the same techniques to help you resolve this issue here. If your project personnel are assigned directly as they are in a projectized organization, then the issue must be resolved with the human resources department or your own people. Who interviewed this person in the first place? These kinds of mistakes are often made and leave the project and the company with people who are constantly being transferred around rather than resolving the personnel issues. This issue really should have been solved during the hiring process! If you have already hired this person or if there are no other persons available from the function, training is the only real alternative. To double up or offer unanticipated On the Job Training (OJT) will likely drive your budget "off-scale-high."

Third, you could fire this person (if company policies allow such action) and hire another person in his place. Just remember, the firing-hiring process in a large company usually takes a long time and there are frequently legal issues involved with firing a person in any size company.

7b (NO) Each person is *not* available when needed.

If each person is not available when needed, it means that you have lost control of the personnel situation. Occasionally, this will happen when a flu epidemic comes roaring through and you are caught in the middle of it. Technically, that's not necessarily lack of control, but you must nevertheless recover the time and the work.

Some of your people may be on vacation or on leave. If you are aware of that situation and have accommodated their absences, you have control. If you are not aware that one or more of your people are on leave, you have lost control. This situation occurs most often when the matrix form of management is used and the individual coordinates absence with his or her functional supervisor but you are not aware of the situation. This is bad news.

RECOVERY

Establish an understanding with both the people assigned to your project and with the functional managers that you must be a part of the coordination loop before anyone takes off on vacation, leave, etc.

Occasionally, a person will encounter a sudden illness or bereavement.

There's not much you can do about these situations except to try to cover them. The best way to cover these situations is to look at each position when you are not under pressure and consider what you will do if this person or that person is absent for one, two, or three days or even weeks. In one case you may be able to double up. In another case you may be able to defer the task of the person missing. In another case you will need a temporary person to fill in. Consider making up a matrix with the names along the side and the conditions across the top. At the intersects, enter the action to take. This approach takes a lot of trauma out of the situation when it occurs, but takes a lot of time on the front end, and situations may change as the program progresses through design, implementation, test, etc. This technique is worth its weight in gold when your personnel are represented by a union and there is the possibility of a strike.

7c (NO) Salaries/wages are *not* equal to or less than those bid.

I don't think I need to say too much about this event except to say it happens all the time in the matrix form of management. One of the major reasons it happens is that, once again, you get a different person than the one that was bid, or the person that was bid gets a raise (that you didn't know about) before being assigned to your project. This person may be a senior person whom you would love to have, but just can't afford because his salary is over what was bid.

RECOVERY

There are several ways to approach this issue. First, you can change the mix of personnel to accommodate this person or these persons. I recommend that you pursue this avenue first, even if you want to get relief in other ways. This is the first question the functional manager or management will ask you. Second, you can approach the functional manager to assign someone else. After all, the functional manager was the one who bid this labor rate in the proposal and then gave you something else. Third, you can attempt to convince the functional manager to subsidize the delta salary of the individual within the functional manager's overhead (care must be taken here, especially on government contracts, which may not allow this action). Finally, you can request profit or cost relief from management to the extent that this person or these persons are impacting your budget. Don't be surprised if you get turned down though.

7d (NO) Interpersonal conflicts *do* exist.

Interpersonal conflicts *do* exist when tension, personal problems, or downright animosity is exhibited between members of the team.

RECOVERY

Interpersonal conflicts are a behavior exhibited for a number of reasons. Among them are:

1. Personality conflict between individuals
2. Personality issue of an individual
3. Difficult personal (outside) environment
4. Difficult work environment
5. Lack of understanding of one's role
6. Rejection of one's role

This book is not and does not intend to be a treatise on psychological issues and human behavior. However, there are some layman's observations and actions that can be taken by the project manager to preserve the objectives of the project team. These observations and actions follow the numbering scheme above. Before employing any of these approaches, you may want to attempt to rectify the situation yourself. That's fine if it is just a squabble. If it's a real problem, however, don't get any more involved than letting the people concerned know that you are aware of the situation and that if they don't fix it themselves, you will fix it. Sometimes that solves the problem and sometimes it moves the problem underground. Know your team members and use good judgment. You personally should not go too much further with these situations. If possible, turn the problem over to the personnel (HR) office or other professionals in the company who are equipped and chartered to handle these kinds of situations. Your job is that of project manager.

1. *Personality conflict between individuals.* Personality conflicts between individuals occur for many reasons, most of which are not fully understood. You can recover from this situation in one of two ways. First, you can choose the person who is most useful to the team and transfer the other one. Second,

you can determine the most likely fomenter of the problem and transfer or fire (if you have the authority) that individual.

2. *Personality issue of an individual.* Individual personality issues occur in a lot of people. Sometimes you just have to put up with them. There are some people who are critical to the project and they know it and use that position to their advantage. How you handle this one is a measure of how you handle all the personnel issues. The only suggestions I can offer is to take this person to lunch and try to get next to him. Or, if you have political power, use it. Or, just put up with him. Or transfer him. Just remember that the good of the project is the most important factor in your decision.
3. *Difficult personal environment.* When a difficult personal environment exists, it sometimes takes a long time to recognize. The situation can manifest itself in a number of ways—the individual's work begins to suffer or the individual becomes cranky or both. The ways to handle these situations can vary widely. Part of the solution could depend on your company. Does the company have an Employee Assistance Program (EAP) that could help this individual and relieve the situation? If so, get the person enrolled. Another approach is to get the person transferred to a staff position somewhere so that the problems do not affect others. Still another approach is to fire or have the person fired. This is very difficult in a large company these days. It requires a lot of record keeping and consulting and a lot of time on your part. Use the option that benefits the project the most (i.e., produces the least impact).
4. *Difficult work environment.* This situation is more in your ballpark than the employee's. Why is the work environment difficult? Is the source of the problem the customer, the company, policies and procedures, the facility itself (e.g., a smelly building), the schedule, the budget, or something else? Only after you determine and analyze the source of the problem can you begin to take action. The answers to these questions could easily fill another book. The only suggestion I can make here is to recognize and fix the situation if at all possible because it will deeply affect your project. On the other hand, you may not be able to rectify the situation at all and simply have to live with it. This is tough and is one of the main reasons people quit projects and companies. If you can't solve this problem directly, try to offer an offsetting positive that is greater than the negative offered by the problem (i.e., offer a premium such as more money or a cruise or a vacation, etc., for working this project). Even if you can't get the problem solved, it needs to be documented and forwarded. Certainly it needs to be a part of the "Lessons Learned" paper you will generate at the end of the project. **A word of cau-**

tion here. If the "smelly building" is the result of an environmental situation that could harm your team members (and you), you must take action to remove the people, and perhaps the equipment, from that environment. To do otherwise is both foolish and possibly criminal. If you have personal knowledge of a hazardous condition and choose to ignore it, you could be legally and morally responsible for the harm done to your people or the equipment. This is not legal advice—it is common sense.

5. *Lack of understanding of one's role.* A true lack of understanding of one's role resolves to only two possibilities. First, the individual has not been properly apprised of what is expected of him and possibly of what he should expect of those around him. Both these issues can be overcome with training. True team training covers both these issues and is a valuable asset to any project. Second, the individual has been apprised of his role and still does not understand it. Try to apprise this person once again. If that fails, neither of us can resolve the issue—send the person back to his functional manager.
6. *Rejection of one's role.* If this occurs, you have a real problem! This is classically known as a standoff. Who is going to win this one? The first thing for you to do is to make sure that the role you are asking this individual to perform is the correct one. Is this what the project needs in order to be successful? Or was a mistake made when this role was defined? Was a mistake made in assigning this individual to this role? If you made the mistake, then you need to reconsider. The mistake could be that the individual's talents were not fully considered. How about adjusting the roles to make the project run smoothly? Can you do that and make the project work properly and solve the individual's problem? If you can, do it. If the other side of this situation is the problem—that is, this individual will reject the role no matter what, you have only one choice—one of you has to go. Which one is up to you.

8 TRAINING

8a (NO) All personnel have *not* been adequately trained.

Insufficient training is a sad set of affairs. Usually the reason for not providing training is that it's expensive or that time has not been scheduled for it. If you think training is expensive or time consuming, wait until you see the bill for not training or not training properly. It will not only affect this task but will show your customer base that you don't have the trained people to do this kind of work.

RECOVERY

First, you must discover what training is lacking. Is it basic training—the individual does not know how to perform the basic job assigned? Is it specific training—the individual does not know how to perform the team-specific task? The answer is to provide the proper training needed.

If the answer is basic training, you have a personnel competency issue and need to return to Cause Description 7a and 7a (NO). If the answer is specific team training, you must provide or arrange to have provided team orientation or training.

Even though you won't have the program people you need while they are being trained, at least they will be trained when they get back. If you are in the Implementation Phase of your task and just find out you need some special training, you will find that training can be performed after normal duty hours or on weekends, or you may be able to bring in others who are trained to mentor your people on an OJT basis. Where there is a will, there is a way.

For the project, nothing could be worse in the world of training than having attended the wrong training. Time will have been used that will have to be made up, and new training will need to be added, which will itself use up even more time and money. The worst kind of wrong training is the training course that gives out wrong information that leads to people making the wrong decisions or taking the wrong actions. Carefully evaluate the content of the courses your people will attend.

8b (NO) The training program is *not* economical.

The training program could be too expensive in dollars or in time consumed. Even if the company pays for training, the project loses the time of its personnel in attendance. This is particularly true if you are beyond the Implementation Phase in your project. Look very carefully at training and the real need for it once the project has started. It could be very expensive indeed. By the way, a training course may well be too expensive. Usually the training department, usually a part of human resources, has evaluated the training course before it is presented, but occasionally something slips through. I have had personal experience with this situation. It ended up costing three days of the time of two dozen of the highest paid and most needed persons in the company. Carefully evaluate the need and the cost of training courses.

RECOVERY

First, make yourself aware of the training programs available in the company and in the marketplace. Concern yourself with project-oriented training courses and team-oriented training courses. There are many of them available.

Second, if someone else has proposed training for your task team, carefully evaluate the need for and the cost of the proposed training program. Sometimes the training department comes up with programs they are fully convinced are great but are actually a waste of your time and the time of your team members.

Third, if you find that you have attended a training program that is indeed too expensive, either in dollar or time terms, there is not too much you can do to recover on your program. Instead, report the findings to HR (training) and to management and, if possible, seek relief from the cost burden. Be sure to list this situation in your "Lessons Learned" paper (see glossary).

9 DATA MANAGEMENT

9a (NO) The proper amount of data is *not* being delivered on time.

The proper amount of data is *not* being delivered on time when the data deliveries *do not* match the data stipulated in the requirements document (contract). Some documents are delivered once (i.e., System Test results) and some require multiple deliveries (i.e., Monthly Status Reports).

Each line item of deliverable documentation in the requirements document (contract) should contain a delivery date or schedule of dates, a format, and a content requirement. If it does not, you should create these requirements. All requirements are then included in the Data Plan.

RECOVERY

Create a Data Plan using a spreadsheet program or a Relational Data Base (RDB) program with a report similar to Table 4-16.

Usually the first Data Plan is created with delta dates (i.e., dates relative to award). Soon after award, the actual dates are used. By using this format and by using a spreadsheet application, the sort function is of great value.

Ensure that proper resources are allocated to implement the Data Plan and that the customer's expectations regarding the scope, content, detail, and format of the deliveries are clearly understood.

It is usual for data to be created in one part of the organization (engineering,

Table 4-16 — Data Delivery Matrix

Doc No	Title	Resp.	Format	First Del	Frequency
A-0001	Monthly Progress Report	Jones	DID 1234	30 days ARO[1]	Monthly
T-0001	System Test Package	Smith	DID 2345	System Test minus 30 days	One time
T-0002	System Test Results	Harris	DID 4567	System Test plus 30 days	One time

[1]ARO: After Receipt of Order.

for instance) and forwarded to the Data Manager for formatting and disposition. Ensure that each person understands what data is expected. This is equally true for electronic transmissions.

Except in the smallest projects, the person who generates the data is not usually the person who sends the data to the customer. Without Project Office review, cognizance, coordination, and control, the practice of individuals sending data directly to the customer is guaranteed to give you heartache.

10 QUALITY

10a (NO) The Quality Plan is *not* thorough, complete, and authorized.

The Quality Plan is *not* thorough, complete, and authorized when it does not completely address and fill the requirements stipulated for the project or when it has not been authorized by the proper authority.

RECOVERY

Review the requirements stipulated by the requirements document (contract) or by enterprise policies and fulfill the requirements. You should have completed this issue before the project started. It is of little value to write a Quality Plan after the fact.

Refer to Attachment 6 for a Quality Assurance Plan Outline and a Quality Control Plan Outline.

Additional References:

MIL-STD- 9858
MIL-STD- 2167
MIL-STD- 2168
ISO-9000

10b (NO) Specific quality characteristics that are important to the project were *not* identified.

Specific quality characteristics that are important to the project were *not* identified when these characteristics are *not* documented and used as a checklist.

RECOVERY

There must be documented characteristics of the item being developed whether that item is a system or a unit or a module. The best place to derive these characteristics is from the Specification. If you do not have such a list, use the following characteristics as a starter and look into the Specification for similar items that may be used to characterize the quality of the item in question.

- ❒ General
  - Primary purpose of the item
  - Interfaces of the item
  - Common language within the item
  - Life-cycle objectives
  - Operations and maintenance plan
- ❒ Specific
  - MTTR/MTBF
  - Availability
  - Other specific characteristics from Spec

10c (NO) Quality is *not* measured so that improvement or degradation is *not* clear.

Quality is *not* measured so that improvement or degradation is *not* clear when each quality characteristic is *not* measured and *not* tracked via metrics.

RECOVERY

Return to Cause Description 10b and ensure that each quality factor is recognized and documented. Create a two-column list and enter the quality factors in the left column. Evaluate each factor and assign or develop a measurement or metric for each factor that will not only show success or failure but will show general "health" as well (i.e., an analog that shows direction of quality and can be compared to a standard or the last reading).

11 FINAL DELIVERY

11a (NO) Final delivery was *not* accepted by the customer without delay.

It is expected that final delivery will be accepted by the customer without delay because it is one of the most important steps in the closure process. Occasionally, the customer will not accept the product for one reason or another. There can be only three reasons that the customer will not accept the product at final delivery. These are:

1. You have not completed all the requirements stipulated in the requirements document (contract).
2. There are circumstances beyond the control of the customer.
3. The customer simply does not want to accept the product.

RECOVERY

In the first situation, ask the customer why the product is not being accepted. What requirements have not been met? Next, you need to outline the requirements and lay out the Requirements Traceability Matrix (RTM), then double-check the requirements and results. If necessary, make the changes required. Then call the customer for a conference and make your presentation and show you have completed all requirements.

In the second case, you still ask the customer the same questions. There are three possible reasons that the customer cannot accept delivery. These are: force majeure, an Act of God, or some reason the product honestly cannot be accepted, such as the fact that transportation services or storage facilities are not available. Check your contract to determine if the first two are exceptions to the contract. If they are, inventory the product, work with the customer to secure the product, and relieve the team. If the third issue is the reason, inventory the product, work with the customer to secure the product, and relieve the team. Go through all closure steps that you can. If the first two factors are not invoked or if the third factor is the issue and you have completed all requirements for delivery, you likely have a claim. You must advise the customer of this situation. Go through all closure steps that you can to minimize additional costs to the customer.

In the third case, you likely have a political situation on your hands. First, ensure that you have an open communication channel with the customer. Ensure that you have completed all requirements necessary for delivery. If at all possible, negotiate with the customer to make final delivery. Sometimes a customer will use acceptance as a bludgeon to get something he wants. And sometimes it is cheaper in the long run to cave in and give customers what they want. But, if the wants are expensive and if you are clean and can prove it, and if you have exhausted all reasonable remedies, inventory the product. Advise management, turn the issue over to legal, and advise the customer of the situation in writing.

11b (NO) Third-party or drop shipping *is* involved.

Third-party or drop shipping *is* involved whenever the product is *not* shipped directly from your facilities to the customer's facilities.

This may appear to be a strange way to end up the checklist but it is a situation that can contribute greatly to finalizing a contract or delivery. Drop shipping (shipping from an associate or subcontractor) can be a useful and sometimes economical methodology. Just as often however, it can end up being uneconomical and get you into trouble in that you are depending on another contractor who does not have the responsibility you have.

RECOVERY

Short of not using third-party or drop shipping, I suggest you add an incentive clause to the subcontract with the associate or subcontractor. Such an incentive clause would have the effect of more than neutralizing any liability you might incur for late or bad delivery. The reason I say "more than" is because your reputation is on the line. You could have run a wonderful program for a long time and lose it all at the last moment. You need to make the penalty so severe that the event does not happen. By the way, if you use penalties, it is a good idea (and sometimes required) that you use positive incentives as well. In other words, if you penalize a subcontractor for being late, give a bonus for being early or even on time. There are situations when you want the product to arrive *exactly* on time, not sooner, not later. Each of these situations requires analysis and judgments—it is not possible to develop a checklist to cover all these situations. Instead, as always, use your good sense.

Notes

1. Most Purchase Orders are issued against a catalog number and a catalog price; therefore a budget review is not called for. However, if there is an add-on or modification using your money, Budget Reviews are proper.

2. Most Purchase Orders are issued against a catalog number and a catalog price; therefore, a budget review is not called for. However, if there is an add-on or modification using your money, Budget Reviews are proper.

3. You can usually hold TIMs only when there is a change in the standard purchased product.

RECOVERING FROM TECHNICAL PROBLEMS

5.1 General

You will probably be alerted to having a technical problem by observing that one or more of your technical measurements or metrics is out-of-tolerance. Naturally, you will want to discover the cause of this condition, and that is where this chapter comes in. The Technical Recovery Checklist can be used at any time, not only for recovery but as an adjunct to planning or checking technical performance.

5.2 Technical Search Tables

Table 5-1 is the Technical *Recovery* Checklist. Use this table to find and isolate a problem in the technical part of your project. The Technical *Performance* Checklist is presented in Chapter 3 of this book.

Table 5-1 — Technical Recovery Checklist

51	ARCHITECTURE	Recovery	Yes
51a (NO)	All Critical Success Factors (CSFs) such as Mean Time To Repair (MTTR), Mean Time Between Failure (MTBF), etc., have *not* been documented and understood	112	
51b (NO)	All modules/subsystems are *not* well defined	113	
51c (NO)	All key functions such as time, length, weight, performance requirements, and interfaces, etc., listed in the requirements are *not* appropriately covered	114	
51d (NO)	All major elements (physical and data) are *not* described and/or *not* justified	115	
51e (NO)	All key aspects of user interfaces are *not* well defined	116	
51f (NO)	The Architecture does *not* hang together conceptually	117	
52	**DESIGN**	**Recovery**	**Yes**
52a (NO)	The design process is *not* correct and/or traceable to enterprise, customer, and standard processes	117	
52b (NO)	The design is *not* correct and *not* traceable to the requirements	119	
52c (NO)	The design is *not* efficient	120	
52d (NO)	The design does *not* adequately address issues that were identified and deferred to design at the architectural level	122	
52e (NO)	The design is *not* partitioned into manageable segments	122	
52f (NO)	The design does *not* account for supportability, Life Cycle cost/total cost of ownership, and future expansions	123	
52g (NO)	Technical Performance Measures (TPMs) such as data retrieval time, weight, error rate, etc., have *not* been defined *or* accommodated	124	
53	**DESIGN REVIEWS**	**Recovery**	**Yes**
53a (NO)	All Design Reviews were *not* completed according to required processes	125	
53b (NO)	The customer has *not* approved each Design Review	127	
54	**IN-PROCESS REVIEWS**	**Recovery**	**Yes**
54a (NO)	All required In-Process Reviews were *not* conducted according to required processes	127	
54b (NO)	The appropriate authority has *not* approved each In-Process Review	129	
55	**PROTOTYPES**	**Recovery**	**Yes**
55a (NO)	The prototypes do *not* reflect the requirements	130	
55b (NO)	Prototypes were *not* constructed incrementally	132	
55c (NO)	Prototype changes were *not* incorporated into the design using the Change Control Process	133	
55d (NO)	Each prototype change was *not* reviewed and accepted by the originator of the requirements	133	

56	SUBCONTRACTS	Recovery	Yes
56a (NO)	The sum of all subcontracts does *not* reflect all tasks allocated	133	
56b (NO)	Each subcontract does *not* contain all tasks allocated	134	
57	**PURCHASE ORDERS**	**Recovery**	**Yes**
57a (NO)	The sum of all Purchase Orders does *not* reflect all purchases to be made	135	
57b (NO)	Each Purchase Order is *not* complete	136	
58	**PRODUCTION/MANUFACTURING**	**Recovery**	**Yes**
58a (NO)	All production/manufacturing processes are *not* traceable to standard, customer, or enterprise processes	138	
58b (NO)	The line(s) were *not* properly designed and set up for this (these) product(s)	139	
58c (NO)	Shop Orders were *not* correct or thorough	139	
58d (NO)	The materials were *not* proper for the processes and the product(s) and/or did *not* meet the requirements	140	
59	**UNIT TEST**	**Recovery**	**Yes**
59a (NO)	Each Unit Test does *not* correctly reflect the requirement	141	
59b (NO)	Each design element that applies to the routine/module/subsystem does *not* have its own test case	143	
59c (NO)	Unit Test findings were *not* reviewed for completeness and *not* forwarded to be incorporated into Subsystem Tests and the System Test	144	
59d (NO)	All Problem Test Reports (PTRs) were *not* captured, dispositioned, or worked off	144	
60	**SYSTEM TEST**	**Recovery**	**Yes**
60a (NO)	The System Test Plan/Procedure was *not* approved by the customer	146	
60b (NO)	The System Test is *not* traceable to the requirements	147	
60c (NO)	The System Test has *not* tested all elements of the system concurrently	148	
60d (NO)	The System Test was *not* performed under appropriate load(s)	149	
60e (NO)	The System Test was *not* performed using the same kind of personnel that will be used by the customer	149	
60f (NO)	The System Test was *not* properly documented and did *not* incorporate the test results of all prior-level tests	150	
61	**CONFIGURATION MANAGEMENT**	**Recovery**	**Yes**
61a (NO)	The Configuration Management Plan (CMP) is *not* thorough, complete, *or* authorized	150	
61b (NO)	Change requests were *not* presented and approved by an appropriate level of the Review Board	152	
61c (NO)	Version controls are *not* in place and are *not* reflected on (in) the product	153	
62	**SYSTEM EFFECTIVENESS FACTORS**	**Recovery**	**Yes**
62a (NO)	All required System Effectiveness Factors have *not* been appropriately considered	154	

Starting at 51a, read each assertion in the table. If you can answer YES to the assertion, check it off and proceed to the next one. If you answer NO to the assertion, go to the page number listed under the "Recovery" column for that assertion.

5.3 Technical Recovery Cause Descriptions

Each assertion listed in the Technical Recovery Checklist is supported by a Cause Description. Each Cause Description broadens and deepens the understanding of the checklist assertion and provides a recovery from the issue raised by the assertion. Following are explanations of the assertions found in the Technical Recovery Checklist.

51 ARCHITECTURE

51a (NO) All Critical Success Factors (CSFs) such as Mean Time To Repair (MTTR), Mean Time Between Failure (MTBF), etc., have *not* been documented and understood.

All Critical Success Factors (CSFs) such as MTTR, MTBF, etc., have *not* been documented and understood if they have *not* been incorporated into the design and a clear trail does *not* exist from each CSF to its incorporation into the design.

RECOVERY

The first step in this process is to create a CSF Checklist. Begin by creating a matrix as shown in Table 5-2. Notice that the requirement is in the far left column and the final proof is in the far right column. Scour the requirements document (contract) for requirement inputs and complete that column first.

Table 5-2 — Critical Success Factor (CSF) Matrix

CSF	Unit A	Unit B	Unit C	Unit D	Final Proof
MTTR 0.5 hrs	0.5 hrs	0.5 hrs	0.5 hrs	0.5 hrs	RMA Analysis Para 3.2.1
MTBF 30,000 hrs	30,000 hrs	30,000 hrs	30,000 hrs	30,000 hrs	RMA Analysis Para 3.2.2

Consider using the "shalls" list created in Attachment 7 to assist in your requirement inputs.

The second step is to follow the requirement through the WBS and make a columnar entry in the matrix to reflect each product-related Work Package (i.e., Work Packages such as Project Management, etc., would not be included). Enter the paragraph number at each point where the requirement intersects a Work Package.

Finally, trace the CSF to its final proof whether that proof is in a physical test or arrived at by analysis. Reflect the paragraph number of the Test Plan and how each CSF will be proved.

51b (NO) All modules/subsystems are *not* well defined.

All modules/subsystems are *not* well defined whenever all parameters that go into making up the module or subsystem are *not* understood. While this statement can be somewhat subjective, it must be answered in objective terms. If there are parameters that are not understood, they must be defined. All issues and considerations must be thought through in order to discover possibilities that are not mentioned. Whenever one of these possibilities is uncovered, it should be investigated and documented.

RECOVERY

You will often need to use multiple information-gathering techniques to get a complete picture of the system you're working on. Here are some techniques you can use as you set out to gather the requirements:

Before the project is formalized:

1. Conduct interviews and discussions with the performing organizations and stakeholders to determine their interpretations of the objective requirements and their inferences of any undocumented potential requirements. These discussions can be held on an individual basis, as a collective group, or as a group using a facilitator. Using group inputs results in a better product but takes a lot more time.
2. Document the issues discovered during Step 1 above and discuss them with the customer. Validate as "requirement" or no "requirement." Conduct further interviews and discussions with the customer to determine the customer's intent. If new requirements or definitions of existing requirements occur,

document each issue and get a full reading to determine its validity and whether it has been properly defined. Qualify each requirement as mandatory, highly desirable, desirable, or nice to have. Keep very careful notes (minutes) of these sessions with the customer. Turn these notes into Change Notices and formalize them with the customer. Even if the changes are denied, you have a basis for change if the issue arises later on.

After the project is formalized:

1. This means that you have already signed up to the requirement as it exists and is documented. Consequently, it may be more difficult to get the requirement incorporated into the SOW or Spec and considered "in-scope." This is particularly true if you are operating under a fixed price contract. Use the same techniques as above. If you are working on a project instead of a program, you shouldn't have to worry about the contractual issues. In either event, it is best to understand the requirements to the fullest extent possible as early as possible. The nature of a Research and Development (R&D) project or program is that it will probably be under constant change. The same rules apply, however, and the baseline must be updated constantly.
2. Another technique that can be used after the job has started is to interview or simply walk through with the people who are performing the job. Sometimes these results are surprising because the performing people are not in a formal mode or mood and you learn what the real issues are. You should be performing In-Process Reviews, as described in Cause Description Family 54, In-Process Reviews.

51c (NO) All key functions such as time, length, weight, performance requirements, and interfaces, etc., listed in the requirements are *not* appropriately covered.

All key functions, performance requirements, and interfaces listed in the requirements are *not* appropriately covered when all are *not* listed on the ordinate (the "Y" axis—up the side) of the Requirements Traceability Matrix (RTM) (see Attachment 7) and the Requirements Flow-Down Matrix (RFM) (see Attachment 8) *or* the WBS locations are *not* listed on the abscissa (the "X" axis—across the top or bottom). The requirements are *only* appropriately covered when there is an intersect between all requirements and all the WBS locations showing dispositions.

RECOVERY

Quite clearly, what is needed is to list the requirements and the WBS elements and ascertain the intersects. If you do not have an RTM or an RFM, use the references shown above (Attachments 7 and 8) and create the necessary documentation.

Immediately after you have created the matrix, assess the actions and resources necessary to accomplish the requirements in the matrix. It is one thing to list the requirements and quite another to find the resources to get them done.

Key functions are usually easy to handle. They are explicit in the specification and lend themselves nicely to the RTM, RFM approach.

Performance requirements are not usually quite so straightforward in that there are frequently different ways and methods to reach a given performance. Nevertheless, performance requirements are objective and can be treated squarely with objective methods. If performance is to be distributed to more than one WBS element, the usual method of allocating and accounting for performance requirements is through the use of budgets. A budget allocates part of the performance requirement to one WBS element and part of the performance requirement to another WBS element and so on until the entire budget is satisfied. Those responsible for each WBS element must meet the budget allocation as if it were the entire specification.

Frequently, interfaces are not covered in a specification but must be inferred or created. This is particularly true if you have the option of decomposing the system into your own segments or software modules. In this case, you should define the interface and all the parameters of the interface and document them. Usually, these parameters and characteristics are documented into an Interface Control Document (ICD). ICDs vary by the interface they portray, and each is usually different. What must be covered in the ICD is a complete characterization of both sides of the interface or the interface each side must meet. Such characterizations might include voltage levels, accepted interfaces (such as RS-232, etc.) the segment or module must meet. As you can see, this can go on ad infinitum. Just ensure that the interface is adequately characterized and documented.

51d (NO) All major elements (physical and data) are *not* described and/or *not* justified.

All major elements (physical and data) are *not* described and/or *not* justified when the system does not hang together or when there are obvious gaps in or between components of the system or when the functions or physical attributes of subelements are not clear.

Do not confuse this assertion with having a system "A" Spec (see Cause Description 2a) which will only characterize the system at a functional level.

RECOVERY

You must meet with the customer to determine the customer's intent for any element that is not characterized, no matter whether it is a subsystem or a module. You must be cautious in this regard. If the customer tells you to characterize it yourself, you can do that. But, do that just once. If you characterize the elements and take them to the customer and the customer says, "No, that's not quite what I wanted, go back and recharacterize," you are in a process called "Bring me a rock." In other words, the creator of the requirement does not know what is really wanted and will tell you to "Bring me another rock" until the right rock is evidenced. This process will consume you and your team.

You must insist that the customer either characterize the elements and their interfaces or give you complete latitude to do it, in writing.

51e (NO) All key aspects of user interfaces are *not* well defined.

All key aspects of user interfaces are *not* well defined when they *do not* follow the accepted standards established for the industry.

RECOVERY

If you are at this point, you probably did not get direction from your customer (generator of the requirements) regarding what standards to follow. Here, we are talking about color, size, look and feel, data rates, protocols, location, and, to some degree, content.

The first step is to identify the user interfaces. The second step is to apply the standards accepted by the industry for those interfaces. Probably 98 percent of the characteristics of all known user interfaces have been defined in standards of some sort.

Additionally, to ensure that the interface is thoroughly understood, each side should simulate the other side of the interface for internal testing before integration. This should illuminate incompletely specified aspects of the interface. Both sides are likely to interpret ambiguous parts of the specification in different ways, so comparison will bring to light any problems in the interface definitions.

Once all these steps have been accomplished, it is wise to sit down with the customer and get agreement regarding the interfaces. The agreements should then be documented and incorporated into the design requirements, reviewed at the Design Reviews, and demonstrated and tested at every applicable level. See also Cause Description 51d.

51f (NO) The Architecture does *not* hang together conceptually.

The Architecture *does not* hang together conceptually when the system specification fails to describe the functional components of the system in terms of their behaviors or to provide component-to-component interfaces.

RECOVERY

Architecture recovery is an iterative and interactive process, accomplished in four steps:

The first step is the discovery or definition of a set of views that represent the system's fundamental structural and behavioral elements.

The second step is a fusion of the extracted views.

The third step is the development of attribute-based relationships among the system's components.

The fourth step is revisiting the previous steps with a view to architectural conformance and targets for reengineering.

52 DESIGN

52a (NO) The design process is *not* correct and/or traceable to enterprise, customer, and standard processes.

Here we are talking about the *design process,* not the design. To be sure, incorrect design processes can, and probably will, lead to incorrect design. Whenever an incorrect design surfaces and is recognized, the design must be changed. The question though is: "Why was the design incorrect in the first place?" That cause is pursued in Cause Description 52c. So, chances are, we got here by going through Cause Description 52c. Incorrect design processes are determined by eliminating the other causes.

The design process is *not* correct and/or traceable to enterprise, customer, and standard processes whenever the required numbers and types of Design Reviews and the content of each Design Review are *not* traceable to the standard, the customer, and the enterprise processes.

The design process is frequently defined by the customer in the Statement Of Work. The customer will require that this particular program have a Preliminary Design Review (PDR), a Critical Design Review (CDR), an In-Process Review (IPR), or any number of other Design Reviews. In the supporting or standard documents, the customer will define the content of those reviews. This is the usual mode of operation. When an enterprise works with a customer or set of customers, the enterprise generally incorporates the usual customer requirements into the enterprise policies, plans, and processes. Probably the best example of this is contractors who work with the federal government.

RECOVERY

Lay out the appropriate enterprise requirements (see glossary), the customer requirements (from the requirements document), and the standard requirements (see glossary) for the design process. Interrelate all the requirements and summarize and organize them into a checklist that will drive the design process paragraphs of the program plan. Retain that information to solidify all data trails. You should end up with a general matrix that will boil down to an outline similar to the one below. If it is not possible to accommodate the above steps, go directly to the outline below and use and update it as necessary.

Paragraph	Title
1.0	Organization
1.1	Objectives
1.2	Responsibilities
1.3	Authority
2.0	Decision and Control Process
3.0	Configuration Management
3.1	Hardware
3.2	Software
3.3	Documentation
4.0	Review Process
4.1	Design Reviews
4.2	Subcontractor Reviews
4.3	Design Approval and Certification

5.0	Continuous Acquisition and Logistic Support (CALS)
6.0	System Test Planning
7.0	Technical Performance Management
8.0	Communication Plan
9.0	Action Item Process
10.0	Conflict Resolution process
11.0	Requirement Management Process
12.0	Development Process (including trades)

52b (NO) The design is *not* correct and *not* traceable to the requirements.

It is possible, but not likely, that a design is correct and yet not traceable to the requirements. The primary ingredient in that process is luck. It is not a desirable position in which to be. It is assumed that if you cannot trace the design to the requirements, you do not have a Requirements Traceability Matrix (RTM) or, if you do, the RTM is wrong or the design is wrong.

RECOVERY

The first step in this process is to create an RTM. If you do not have an RTM, use Table 5-3 as a start. Modify the RTM for your own needs. Just be sure not to change the concepts of content and flow.

Table 5-3 — Requirements Traceability Matrix (RTM)

SOW/ Spec Para	Requirement	WBS Number	S/C SOW/ Spec Para	Unit Test Number	System Test Para	Monitor
SOW						
4.3.1	Security	06-03-02	N/A	T-0304	4.4.1	Smith
Spec						
3.2.1	System weight shall be less than 10,000 pounds	02-04-03	3.4.6	T-0045	3.4.1	Jones

Once you have concluded that the design is incorrect, you must determine why it is incorrect. There are four possibilities:

1. The requirement was misinterpreted, resulting in an incorrect design. In this case, you need to go back to Cause Factor 2a/2a (NO) and find out why the requirement was misinterpreted and reconcile the requirement.
2. There are customer requirements or expectations (implicit requirements) that were not previously revealed.
3. The designer was (is) incompetent. In this case, you need to go to Cause Factor 7a/7a (NO) and work the problem from there.
4. The Design Review processes were not followed. In this case, you need to go to Cause Factor 52a/52a (NO) and work the problem from there.

Finally, you need to ensure that the necessary design tasks are included in the project schedule and are properly monitored and performed.

52c (NO) The design is *not* efficient.

The design is *not* efficient when it *does not* perform as the requirements document (contract) demands, *or does not have* the inherent reliability, maintainability, *or* availability demanded by the requirements document (contract), or *does not* meet at least the same qualifications for these factors for competing products and is *not* economical in its design, production, *or* throughout its life cycle.

Notice the use of the conjunction *or*. If your product does not meet *all* the requirements *and* conditions, it is not efficient. This does not mean that trade-offs cannot be performed. But, if a trade is made, it must be agreed to by the customer and documented in the requirements. If the product is a competitive product being designed to the assumed requirements of the marketplace, management, as well as the departments of marketing, sales, production, customer relations, maintenance, and quality must be involved and must accept the trade. Usually the trade involves cost at the expense of some other factor set such as reduced maintainability to gain faster production (e.g., using rivets instead of screws) resulting in lower cost.

RECOVERY

The first step in this process is to create an RTM. If you do not have an RTM, use Table 5-4 as a start. Modify the RTM for your own needs. Just be sure not to change the concepts of content and flow.

Table 5-4 — Requirements Traceability Matrix (RTM)

SOW/ Spec Para	Requirement	WBS Number	S/C SOW/ Spec Para	Unit Test Number	System Test Para	Monitor
SOW						
4.3.1	Security	06-03-02	N/A	T-0304	4.4.1	Smith
Spec						
3.2.1	System weight shall be less than 10,000 pounds	02-04-03	3.4.6	T-0045	3.4.1	Jones

Ensure that the RTM contains those factors associated with efficiency. Or, if this is a subjective evaluation, list those factors that are in question along with their counterparts. Increasing or decreasing one factor will have a direct impact on at least one other factor.

Immediately after you have created the matrix, assess the actions and resources necessary to accomplish the requirements in the matrix. It is one thing to list the requirements and quite another to find the resources to get them done.

It must be understood that efficiency requirements in one regime or discipline or product will not be the same as the efficiency requirements in another. For example, the reliability required for a component of a lawn tractor may not necessarily be the same as the reliability required for a component of the space shuttle.

It is a good idea to conduct a Failure Mode Effect Analysis (FMEA also referred to as FMECA-Failure Mode and Criticality Analysis—see paragraph 8.2.3 in Chapter 8) for components that are expected or required to have a high reliability, availability, or similar stringent requirement.

Additional Resources:

MIL-STD-1629; automotive standards such the SAE, AIAG or Ford Motor Company.

Relex V x.x; from Relex Software
540 Pellis Road, Greensburg, PA 15601

Phone: 724-836-8800
info@relexsoftware.com

52d (NO) The design does *not* adequately address issues that were identified and deferred to design at the architectural level.

The design does *not* adequately address issues that were identified and deferred to design at the architectural level when those architectural elements have *not* been defined *or* are *not* traceable to the design. Further, they are *not* addressed in the appropriate Design Review *or* clearly identified in the design.

RECOVERY

In order for the system to be complete, all the requirements must be incorporated into the architecture and the design, and the "data trail" must be identifiable. Frequently, at the architectural level, issues appear that are too complex to be addressed at that level or are not defined enough to create an architecture to drive them. This is particularly true in R&D programs. As the design unfolds, these deferred items must be kept up with and referred back to the architecture element from which they were deferred in the first place. Making additions to the RTM, in reverse order, is a good way to accomplish this task.

52e (NO) The design is *not* partitioned into manageable segments.

The design is *not* partitioned into manageable segments when the segments are either *not* logical, *cannot* be defined, *cannot* be tested, *cannot* be scheduled, or *cannot* be costed. The purpose in partitioning is to create groupings for the Work Breakdown Structure (WBS) and thus distribute the workload among the resources available. If this cannot be accomplished, the task cannot be efficiently worked—if it can be worked at all.

RECOVERY

Decompose the requirements into logical groupings. The groupings can be by subsystem, physical grouping, functional grouping, time ordering, data flow, control flow, or some other criterion. Grouping forced by resources available can be used but should be the last item on the list, not the driving factor. Remember that the next step will be the allocation of requirements into the groupings you have established. In some cases, the groupings may need to be adjusted to make all the requirements fit as in Figure 5-1.

Figure 5-1 — Requirements Allocation

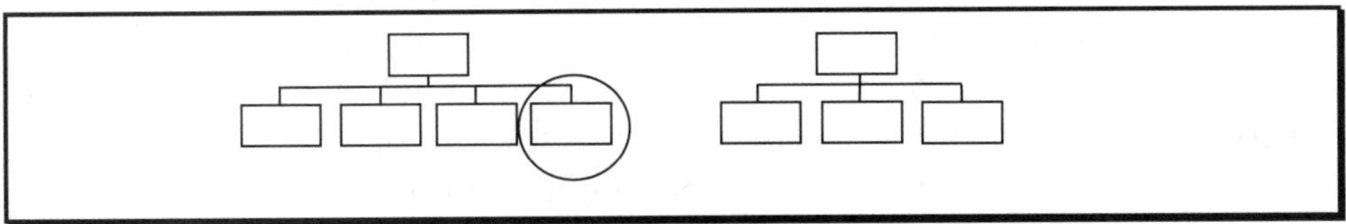

A major rule for partitioning is to minimize interfaces across partition elements. These interfaces are the most challenging technical issues on most projects. Does this box belong in this tree or the other tree? You must answer this question by establishing a "clean" line of division between both the grouping criterion and the allocation of requirements. Don't distribute part of a grouping in one WBS box and the remainder in another box. Try not to distribute part of a requirement in one WBS box and the remainder in another. If you must do this, you must create a "budget" to allocate those parts and to document where you put them. Even when the lines are clean, you may well still need to interface one element with another. In this case, ensure that a reasonable and usable Interface Control Document (ICD) exists or is created. See Cause Description 51c/51c (NO) for more detail regarding ICDs.

52f (NO) The design does *not* account for supportability, Life Cycle cost/total cost of ownership, and future expansions.

The design *does not* account for supportability, Life Cycle Cost (LCC), total cost of ownership, and future expansions whenever all these factors are *not* taken into consideration in the design, production, implementation and operations, and maintenance alternatives.

RECOVERY

If you are at or near the very beginning of your project, you are in a position to achieve the objectives of LCC, that is: Choosing the most cost-effective approach to the entire life cycle/total cost of ownership system, product, or unit within the available resources. Sometimes this can include planned or estimated future expansions as well. The analysis must cover the entire lifespan of the system, product, or unit. The LCC process provides a systematic methodology for evaluating and quantifying the cost impacts of alternative courses of action.

It can be used to support trade-off analyses between several product design configurations, or the sensitivity of a specific design to changes. The LCC can, and probably will, affect the distribution of costs between up-front design or production costs and field operation and maintenance costs. Care must be taken to involve the entire life span of the system, product, or unit. Frequently, only design or production costs are considered, leaving operation and maintenance costs to be added later. If the specification calls for a Design To Cost approach, its result may well be different than the Life Cycle Cost. Be certain to check with the customer regarding intent. The customer could have intended Life Cycle Cost but said Design To Cost or some similar term. The results will probably be different.

If you are at a point other than the very beginning of your project and are confronted with LCC issues, you are starting a long uphill battle. The LCC program should be started before design is begun, indeed, before parsing of the system has begun. Usually, LCC begins with trade-off analyses first on various designs, then on various production methods and techniques, and finally on the planned operations and maintenance approaches.

Nevertheless, you are here and must make the best of what you have. If you are in the design phase, you could stop and conduct trade-offs and then reenter the design phase. If you are beyond the design phase and into the production phase, chances are that it will be too expensive to go back. At this point, it is probably prudent to stop the project and to concentrate on the production phase and beyond. Consider alternatives that not only make production more efficient and less expensive but alternatives that make operations and maintenance more efficient. This is the point at which you need to consider spare parts. It is much more efficient to turn out spare parts during the production phase than to retool at a later time and gear up to produce those parts. Remember the $800.00 hammer? That's what happened. The proper alternative is to provide Pre Planned Product Improvements (P^3I) during the planning cycle and phase these improvements in over time.

If you are beyond production, the only alternatives you have are installation, operation, and maintenance. Here, you simply look at trade-offs for those aspects of the project.

52g (NO) Technical Performance Measures (TPMs) such as data retrieval time, weight, error rate, etc., have *not* been defined *or* accommodated.

Technical Performance Measures (TPMs) such as data retrieval time, weight, error rate, etc., have *not* been defined *or* accommodated whenever the TPMs are *not* fully understood *or do not* appear in the related WBS sections *or* the related test procedures.

RECOVERY

It will probably be necessary to start with definitions of the TPMs. Likely, you will need to decompose the TPM into its constituents and define each of them. Most TPMs are metrics; that is, they have a measurement (or measurements) related to a goal or are expressed as a goal. For instance, an error rate of less than 10^{-6} bits. In this case, you will need to define the number of bits in a total transmission and then define the number of errors of transmission. You will then need to define a method of measurement that will verify the TPM—an error rate counter, for instance.

This process goes on and on, but I think you see the point—decompose the TPM into its constituents, define them, and measure them.

53 DESIGN REVIEWS

53a (NO) All Design Reviews were *not* completed according to required processes.

All Design Reviews were *not* completed according to required processes when the events of the Design Review are *not* directly traceable to the requirements stipulated in standard processes, customer (contract and contract-referenced) processes, or enterprise processes.

RECOVERY

Lay out the enterprise requirements, the customer requirements, and the standard requirements for Design Reviews. Interrelate all the requirements and summarize and organize them into a checklist that will drive the Design Reviews part of the Program Plan. Retain that information to solidify all data trails. You should end up with a general matrix that will boil down to an outline similar to the one below. If it is not possible to accommodate the above steps, go directly to the outline below and use and update it as necessary.

Design Review Package Content and Review Outline:

- ❒ Mission and Requirements Analysis
- ❒ ConOps (Concept of Operations)

- ❒ Functional Flow Analysis
- ❒ Use Cases
- ❒ Preliminary Requirements Allocation
- ❒ System/Cost Effectiveness Analysis
- ❒ Trade Studies (e.g. addressing system functions in mission and support hardware/firmware/software)
- ❒ Synthesis
- ❒ Logistics Support Analysis

Specialty Discipline Studies (i.e., hardware and software reliability analysis, maintainability analysis, armament integration, electromagnetic compatibility, survivability/vulnerability (including nuclear), inspection methods/techniques analysis, energy management, environmental considerations):

- ❒ System Interface Studies
- ❒ Generation of Specification
- ❒ Program Risk Analysis
- ❒ Integrated Test Planning
- ❒ Producibility Analysis Plans
- ❒ Technical Performance Measurement Planning
- ❒ Engineering Integration
- ❒ Data Management Plans
- ❒ Configuration Management Plans
- ❒ System Safety
- ❒ Human Factors Analysis
- ❒ Value Engineering Studies
- ❒ Life Cycle Cost Analysis
- ❒ Preliminary Manufacturing Plans
- ❒ Manpower Requirements/Personnel Analysis
- ❒ Milestone Schedules
- ❒ Communications Plan

- ❐ Training Plan
- ❐ Security (Threat) Analysis

The source for the above list is MIL-STD-1521, Paragraph 10.3, plus embellishment. Because it is a governmental (DOD) standard, it may well be overly complex. But it's a lot easier to eliminate a line item than to create one. Modify the list for your specific needs.

Additional Resources:

MIL-STD-1521

53b (NO) The customer has *not* approved each Design Review.

The customer will *not* have approved each Design Review unless the customer has signed a sheet that confirms that the customer (through a representative, if necessary) agrees to the Design Review package, the Design Review, and the Design Review minutes, including Design Review action items. *Note: Any exceptions taken should be included in the Action Items and thus achievable.*

RECOVERY

Create and use a Design Review Approval Sheet containing information similar to Figure 5-2 on the following page.

Details regarding the Design Review Approval Form can be found in Attachment 15.

54 IN-PROCESS REVIEWS

54a (NO) All required In-Process Reviews were *not* conducted according to required processes.

All required In-Process Reviews were *not* conducted according to required processes when the events of the In-Process Reviews are *not* directly traceable to the requirements stipulated in standard processes, customer (contract and contract referenced) processes, and enterprise processes.

Figure 5-2 — Design Review Approval Form

DESIGN REVIEW APPROVAL

The ________(1)_____________ Design Review Minutes

containing the ______(1)_________Design Review Package

labeled ________(2)_____________

and dated ______(3)_________

and

The _________(1)___________Design Review

conducted on ______(3)__________ together with the Design Review Action Items are

hereby approved

and

__________(4)____________________ is hereby directed to proceed to the next stage

of the program.

Signed _____(5)________ of __________(6)______________ Date ________________

RECOVERY

Lay out the enterprise requirements (see glossary), the customer requirements (from the requirements document), and the standard requirements (see glossary) for In-Process Reviews. Consolidate all the requirements and summarize and organize into a checklist that will drive the In-Process Reviews part of the Program Plan. Retain that information to solidify all data trails. If it is not possible to accommodate the above steps, use the following topics to guide your In-Process Reviews.

In-Process Review Process

In-Process Reviews should be used to inspect individual products during the product (hardware and/or software) development life cycle. A record of each review must be maintained and presented at the end of the review.

In-Process Review Team

In-Process Review Teams normally consist of three to five members. One member should be designated as team leader or moderator. The remaining team members conduct the inspection.

Schedule

An In-Process Review should be conducted at the completion of each designated phase or subphase of the product life cycle.

Agenda

All internal reviews must be conducted to an agenda that has been distributed in advance of the review meeting. The agenda should call for a briefing, the inspection, notes preparation, and a debriefing.

Review Participants

Qualified participants from process control, quality assurance, representatives from the preceding phase and from the subsequent phase as well as representatives from other appropriate organizations should take part in the review.

Documentation

The In-Process Review should be documented in an In-Process Review Approval Form similar to that provided in Attachment 16.

54b (NO) The appropriate authority has *not* approved each In-Process Review.

The appropriate authority will *not* have approved each In-Process Review unless the appropriate authority has signed a sheet that confirms that the appropriate authority (through their representative, if necessary) agrees to the In-Process Review package, the In-Process Review and the In-Process Review minutes, including In-Process Review action items. *Note: Any exceptions taken should be included in the action items and thus achievable.*

RECOVERY

Create and use an In-process Review Approval sheet containing information similar to Figure 5-3.

Figure 5-3 — In-Process Review Approval Form

IN-PROCESS REVIEW APPROVAL FORM

The ___(1)____ In-Process Review Minutes containing

the __(1)_____In-Process Review Package

labeled ___(2)_______ and

dated ____(3)_______

and

The __(1)___In-Process Review

conducted on ___(3)_______ together with the In-Process Review Action Items are

hereby approved

therefore

____(4)____ is hereby directed to proceed to the next stage of the program.

Signed ___(5)_____ of ______(6)________ Date _______________

55 PROTOTYPES

55a (NO) The prototypes do *not* reflect the requirements.

The prototypes *do not* reflect the requirements when the customer or client *does not* agree that the prototype satisfies or demonstrates the requirements.

This is perhaps subjective, but is the nature of prototyping. It is common in the prototyping process that the customers have new or added requirements or have changed their minds. This is fundamental to the prototyping process. When this happens, the product and the requirement must be compared and if they do not agree, the product must be reworked until they do agree or the contractual agreement must be modified.

The best way to eliminate subjectivity is to conduct a physical or functional audit. For a detailed description of functional configuration audits and physical configuration audits, see MIL-STD-1521. These audits are essentially physical and functional inventories against the requirements.

There is a dichotomy inherent in the prototyping process. While it is a quick way to get a technical result and customer feedback, it is fraught with programmatic problems. This is due to the fact that technical people are talking to technical people, both wanting to solve the issue technically, usually without regard to the programmatic issues. The differences lie in what you (your project) have agreed to provide. It is not uncommon for a project to start with a general set of technical requirements and agree to provide X number of man-hours to achieve that result. Even though the technical requirement may not have been met, the contractual requirement may be met.

RECOVERY

The first step is to define the issue. Have the technical requirements been met? Have the contractual requirements been met? Likely not, so let's separate the issues into logical pairs, as in Table 5-5, and recover from there.

Table 5-5 — Issue Pairs and Recoveries

Technical	Contractual	Recovery
Not Met	Not Met	Continue until one or the other is met then proceed as shown below
Met	Not Met	If you have met the technical objectives but not met the contractual objectives, it usually means you are in an overrun condition. If you have a cost plus contract, you should be able to adjust the manpower or schedule to fit the actual profile. If you have a fixed price contract, you may well have to absorb the costs. The general rule-of-thumb is that you do not take an R&D task on a fixed price basis.
Not Met	Met	One of three alternatives: 1) Change the technical requirement, 2) Change the contractual conditions, 3) Quit.*
Met	Met	No issue

*Assumes neither Alternative (1) nor (2) will work and there is common agreement with the customer.

Additional Resources:

Guides to physical inventory can be found in:

IEEE Std 610.12-1990
MIL-STD-973, 1521, 2167, and 498
DID DD-1423
MIL-STD-1521

Guides to functional inventory can be found in:

MIL-STD-973
DID DD-1423
ISO-9000-3:1991(E)
MIL-STD-1521

55b (NO) Prototypes were *not* constructed incrementally.

If prototypes are *not* constructed incrementally and two or more modules are put together and fail testing, you will likely have no idea where the problems lie. Prototypes can be constructed incrementally either vertically or horizontally. A vertical increment means that modules are constructed serially and the subsequent modules are added on to existing modules. A horizontal increment means that increments are constructed concurrently then integrated one by one to form another module, a subsystem, or a system.

RECOVERY

In order to recover properly, you must go all the way back to the original input requirement and then follow the "decomposition" process into the various WBS elements (see Cause Description 51c). The next step is to go through the composition and unit testing of the modules (see Cause Description Family 59) and the interface requirements of the modules. You are looking for specific inconsistencies, so this document cannot possibly address the questions, much less the answers, to these issues.

55c (NO) Prototype changes were *not* incorporated into the design using the Change Control Process.

Prototype changes were *not* incorporated into the design using the Change Control Process (see Technical Cause Descriptions 61a, 61b, and 61c) when the changes are *not* traceable through the product to the documentation that authorized the change.

RECOVERY

Prototypes must be treated the same as First Articles in their development. This is particularly true if your process takes the prototype (or Breadboard or Brassboard) directly to development or production. Granted, many changes are devised during the prototype process and incorporated into the prototype to validate their efficacy. Indeed, that's what the prototype process is all about. However, if it is concluded that the in-process change should be a part of the prototype, the changes must be incorporated through the Change Control process.

See the glossary for definitions of all these terms.

55d (NO) Each prototype change was *not* reviewed and accepted by the originator of the requirements.

Each prototype change was *not* reviewed and accepted by the originator of the requirements whenever an acceptance of the change is not documented and made a part of the project documentation.

RECOVERY

When you get a verbal requirement, stop and document the requirement, even if it's just a note. You can use that documentation as a basis for sign-off by the originator of the requirements.

56 SUBCONTRACTS

56a (NO) The sum of all subcontracts does *not* reflect all tasks allocated.

The sum of all subcontracts *does not* reflect all tasks allocated if the totality of all subcontracts and all work to be performed internally *do not* add up to the total requirements in the requirements document (contract).

RECOVERY

This situation results in either a duplicity of effort (overlaps) or a shortfall of effort (holes). Neither is acceptable. However, when evaluating subcontracts for holes and overlaps, consideration must be given to the fact that there will be some perceived overlaps with respect to required processes. For instance, if a certain quality program is required of the overall program, it must be flowed down to each of the subcontractors. In this case, it might appear to be an overlap, but it is not. It is, in fact, an appropriate allocation of requirements.

Obviously, the first thing to be done is to identify the holes and the overlaps. You must have some idea that there are holes or overlaps or you wouldn't be here in the first place. Once again, create or review the Requirements Traceability Matrix (RTM) and the Requirements Flow-Down Plan.

If you do not have an RTM, you can use Table 5-6 as a start. Modify the table for your own needs. Just be sure not to change the concepts of content and flow.

Table 5-6 — Requirements Traceability Matrix (RTM)

SOW/ Spec Para	Requirement	WBS Number	S/C SOW/ Spec Para	Unit Test Number	System Test Para	Monitor
SOW						
4.3.1	Security	06-03-02	N/A	T-0304	4.4.1	Smith
Spec						
3.2.1	System weight shall be less than 10,000 pounds	02-04-03	3.4.6	T-0045	3.4.1	Jones

If you do not have an RFM, you can use the following table as a start. Modify Table 5-7 on the following page for your own needs. Just be sure not to change the concepts of content and flow.

56b (NO) Each subcontract does *not* contain all tasks allocated.

Each subcontract *does not* contain all tasks allocated when the tasks contained in the subcontract are *not* equal to the assigned tasks from the Flow-Down Matrix and/or the assigned tasks from the Requirements Traceability Matrix (RTM).

Table 5-7 — Requirements Flow-Down Matrix (RFM)

Spec Para	Company Reqt	WBS	Design Plan Para	S/C Plan Para	S/C A Para	S/C B Para
1.3.2		02-03-01	5.3.2	5.3.2	1.3.2	1.3.2
1.3.3		02-03-02	5.3.3	5.3.3	1.3.3	N/A
1.3.4		02-03-03	5.3.4	5.3.4	1.3.4	1.3.4
	QA Plan	04-01-01	8.2.6	8.2.6	4.3.6	4.3.6
	CM Plan	05-01-01	9.3.1	9.3.1	5.6.2	5.6.2

RECOVERY

If you do not have an RFM you can use the following table as a start. Modify Table 5-8 below for your own needs. Just be sure not to change the concepts of content and flow.

Table 5-8 — Requirements Flow-Down Matrix (RFM)

Spec Para	Company Reqt	WBS	Design Plan Para	S/C Plan Para	S/C A Para	S/C B Para
1.3.2		02-03-01	5.3.2	5.3.2	1.3.2	1.3.2
1.3.3		02-03-02	5.3.3	5.3.3	1.3.3	N/A
1.3.4		02-03-03	5.3.4	5.3.4	1.3.4	1.3.4
	QA Plan	04-01-01	8.2.6	8.2.6	4.3.6	4.3.6
	CM Plan	05-01-01	9.3.1	9.3.1	5.6.2	5.6.2

If you do not have an RTM, you can use Table 5-9 on the following page as a start. Modify the table for your own needs. Just be sure not to change the concepts of content and flow.

57 PURCHASE ORDERS

57a (NO) The sum of all Purchase Orders does *not* reflect all purchases to be made.

The sum of all Purchase Orders *does not* reflect all tasks allocated if the totality of all Purchase Orders *does not* add up to the total requirements to be purchased in the requirements document (contract) and in the Design Plan.

Table 5-9 — Requirements Traceability Matrix (RTM)

SOW/ Spec Para	Requirement	WBS Number	S/C SOW/ Spec Para	Unit Test Number	System Test Para	Monitor
SOW						
4.3.1	Security	06-03-02	N/A	T-0304	4.4.1	Smith
Spec						
3.2.1	System weight shall be less than 10,000 pounds	02-04-03	3.4.6	T-0045	3.4.1	Jones

RECOVERY

This situation results in either a duplicity of effort (overlaps) or a shortfall of effort (holes). Neither is acceptable. However, when evaluating purchase orders for holes and overlaps, consideration must be given to the fact that there will be some perceived overlaps with respect to required processes. For instance, if the "Buy America" clause is required of the overall program, it must be flowed down to each of the purchase orders. In this case, it might appear to be an overlap, but it is not. It is, in fact, an appropriate allocation of requirements.

Obviously, the first thing to be done is to identify the holes and the overlaps. You must have some idea that there are holes or overlaps or you wouldn't be here in the first place. Once again, create or review the Requirements Traceability Matrix, the Requirements Flow-Down Plan and the Design Plan.

If you do not have an RTM, you can use the Table 5-10 on the following page as a start. Modify the table for your own needs. Just be sure to not change the concepts of content and flow.

If you do not have a Requirements Flow-Down Matrix, you can use Table 5-11 on the following page as a start. Modify the table for your own needs. Just be sure to not change the concepts of content and flow.

57b (NO) Each Purchase Order is *not* complete.

Each purchase order is *not* complete unless it contains: reference number, order date, vendor, contact information, name of item, stock (catalog) number, number of units, price, delivery schedule, delivery location, and purchaser.

Note: Don't wait for a failure here. It is a good idea to create a list of all subcontracts and Purchase Orders and maintain a constant status of each. Post this list in a conspicuous place such as the Planning/Status Room (commonly called the War Room), available to all.

RECOVERY

Compile all purchases made and outstanding and update each to include all information listed above.

In future, create a Purchase Order form as a reminder. The Purchase Order is a simple transaction, and it's easy to create your own form for control. If you

Table 5-10 — Requirements Traceability Matrix (RTM)

SOW/ Spec Para	Requirement	WBS Number	S/C SOW/ Spec Para	Unit Test Number	System Test Para	Monitor
SOW						
4.3.1	Security	06-03-02	N/A	T-0304	4.4.1	Smith
Spec						
3.2.1	System weight shall be less than 10,000 pounds	02-04-03	3.4.6	T-0045	3.4.1	Jones

Table 5-11 — Requirements Flow-Down Matrix (RFM)

Spec Para	Company Reqt	WBS	Design Plan Para	S/C Plan Para	S/C A Para	S/C B Para
1.3.2		02-03-01	5.3.2	5.3.2	1.3.2	1.3.2
1.3.3		02-03-02	5.3.3	5.3.3	1.3.3	N/A
1.3.4		02-03-03	5.3.4	5.3.4	1.3.4	1.3.4
	QA Plan	04-01-01	8.2.6	8.2.6	4.3.6	4.3.6
	CM Plan	05-01-01	9.3.1	9.3.1	5.6.2	5.6.2

are creating your own form though, give consideration to status. Create the form so that the top line or some other single line contains: name of item, vendor, order date and delivery date, and other critical information (number of units, for instance). This one line will be carried forward to the Status List. Engineering, manufacturing, or anyone else should be able to look at the Status List and update their schedules from that one line.

Create a Subcontracts/Purchase Order Status List. Use the "one-liner" created above to establish a list for status.

58 PRODUCTION/MANUFACTURING

58a (NO) All production/manufacturing processes are *not* traceable to standard, customer, or enterprise processes (see glossary).

All production/manufacturing processes are *not* traceable to standard, customer, or enterprise processes when the heritage of the process is *not* clearly referenced in the process.

RECOVERY

Create a table similar to Table 5-12 below with your data inserted.

The purpose in creating the table is to determine where the "holes" exist in the trail. Of course, you should start with the references and work toward the appearances. If you work the other way, the table may be self-satisfying and of no use.

After you complete that part of the process, start with the production/manufacturing process itself and work backward. If a clear trail exists, the question will answer itself. If not, the questions to be asked are: "Why is this process here?" "What created the need for it?" If there is a need but no requirement, you should forward that need to the responsible department in the enterprise. If there is a requirement but no need, you should forward that comment also.

Table 5-12 — Standards Traceability Matrix (STM)

STANDARDS			APPEARANCE	
Industry	Customer	Enterprise	Project Plan	Technical Plan
ISO-9001	ISO-9001	Enterprise Quality Policy 09350	Para 4.6.8	Part I, Para 4.5.6
	MIL-STD-100	Enterprise Engineering Standards 06050	N/A	Part II, Para 1.2.3

You must seriously consider this situation. Is there really no need or do you just not recognize the need? Discuss the issue with the responsible department involved.

58b (NO) The line(s) were *not* properly designed and set up for this (these) product(s).

The line(s) were *not* properly designed and set up for this (these) product(s) if the line *does not* produce the product according to the requirements.

If the line design, the processes or the materials have not changed, chances are that the design of the line is okay. Changing either the processes (Cause Factor 58d/58d(NO)) or the materials (Cause Factor 58a/58a (NO)) can have an effect on production that was unanticipated. If the line design has changed, there has likely been an effect on the product that was unanticipated.

RECOVERY

Because line design, processes, and materials are interrelated, they must each be shown to be proper or improper to isolate the problem and fix it. This involves five steps:

First: Isolate line design by eliminating processes and materials.

Second: Isolate the part of the line that is contributing to the problem.

Third: Fix the problem.

Fourth: Research the processes and materials and ensure that they are still compatible.

Fifth: Make a trial run to ensure that all are compatible.

If necessary, iterate the process. When you are satisfied that the process is correct, return to full production

58c (NO) Shop Orders were *not* correct or thorough.

Shop Orders were *not* correct or thorough when the end product produced is *not* the product that was specified by the customer. (This statement is made on the assumption that input materials, labor processes, and the like are proper and correct.)

RECOVERY

Create a Shop Order that contains all the information necessary to produce the end product specified by the customer. If you do not have a Shop Order to use, consider the following information as a start:

- ❒ Product to be produced
- ❒ Station producing the product or a portion of the product specification reference for the product/portion
- ❒ Process reference for the product/portion
- ❒ Materials needed
- ❒ Tools needed
- ❒ Measurements required
- ❒ Tolerances required/allowed
- ❒ Time allowed
- ❒ Test/performance requirements

Introduce the new Shop Order into the system and carefully monitor the production of the first unit. If necessary, iterate the process. When you are satisfied that the process is correct, return to full production.

Additional Resources:

Shop/work order software from AyaNova
Contact: Support@ayanova

58d (NO) The materials were *not* proper for the processes and the product(s) and/or did *not* meet the requirements.

The materials were *not* proper for the product(s) when the product *did not* meet the requirements. This begins a process of "back tracing" the materials from the product to the source. The trail will, or should, lead from the product to the Shop Order to the process to the subcontract or Purchase Order to the original requirement or the derivative of that requirement.

RECOVERY

The first step that must be accomplished is to determine *what* materials were not proper. The next step is to determine *why* (in functional terms) they were not proper. While this sounds simple and straightforward, it is not always that way. The issue itself may well take analysis, not just observation. If this is the case, conduct or have someone conduct the analysis. It is absolutely essential to know what is not proper and why it is not proper. When you get to the why, it is likely you will need evidence as to exactly why. Certainly when you get to the next step, you will need this evidence.

After determining what and why, the next step is to go to the source that created the problem. Did the department, vendor, or subcontractor that created the errant element provide what was specified (either by the provider or by you)? If it did, the problem is yours. If it did not, absolute evidence is required to prove the point. If, at this point, there is disagreement regarding responsibility, it will be necessary to make a decision. The decision is whether to shut the process down until agreement can be achieved or to find alternative sources to resolve the problem. The answer to this problem is usually one of time and money. If the responsible party agrees to fix the problem quickly, then that is the solution. If not, you will likely be better off finding another source and letting the lawyers handle this one. It's sort of like being rear-ended in your car. You were absolutely in the right, but you still can't drive your car until it's fixed.

Back now to the other side of the problem. That is that the provider produced exactly what was supposed to be produced and the problem is yours. Once again, you have several options. First, you can change the specification in the subcontract or the Work Order and have the job redone. Second, you can find another source (if this is a purchased rather than a developed product), buy that part, and continue. A quick note here—you will likely be responsible for a thing called "liquidated damages" (see glossary) if you choose this route. In other words, you ordered 5,000 widgets against your incorrect requirement and caused a vendor to gear up for that production. You only bought one hundred, so the vendor has a bunch of these things (or at least the cost) already built. You are likely to be hit for the costs to make the vendor "whole" again. Is there any wonder it is so necessary to make absolutely sure the requirements are traceable and correct?

59 UNIT TEST

59a (NO) Each Unit[1] Test does *not* correctly reflect the requirement.

Each unit test *does not* correctly reflect the requirement when each element of the unit test is *not* directly traceable to each element of the unit requirement (Specification).

RECOVERY

Each testable unit should have its own requirement (Specification). This is true whether the unit will be built internally or by subcontract. The subcontract will contain procurement data in excess of the requirement (Specification) but will otherwise be the same.

The requirement (Specification) should be the basis of a Test Plan for the unit. The Unit Test Plan must define the:

- ❒ Test performance figures, standards, etc., that the unit must meet
- ❒ Conditions under which the test will be run
- ❒ Support equipment
- ❒ Test equipment
- ❒ Conditions for acceptance of the test
- ❒ Process for documenting and resolving test discrepancies
- ❒ The details and step-by-step process of the test itself

Test Plans vary widely in their composition and content, but the definitions above are consistent throughout all plans.

Additional Resources:

Hardware Plans	Software Plans
MIL-STD-1519/1	ISO/IEC 12207
MIL-STD-2076	MIL-STD-498
MIL-T-18303B	MIL-STD-2165
IEEE-STD 416	DI-ATTS-80002
MIL-STD-483	DOD-STD-2168
MIL-STD-499	
DI-ATTS-80005	
DI-ATTS-81270	
DI-ATTS-81273	
DI-NDTI-81284	
DI-NDTI-81307	
DI-SDMP-81475	

(continues)

DI-ATTS-80002
DI-ATTS-80005
DI-TMSS-80007
DI-QCIC-80204

59b (NO) Each design element that applies to the routine/module/ subsystem does *not* have its own test case.

Each design element that applies to the routine/module/subsystem *does not* have its own test case when there is *no* direct correlation between the requirement and the elements tested in the unit, subsystem, or system test.

RECOVERY

Return, once again, to the Requirements Traceability Matrix (RTM) and follow the columns to the right. There should be entries in the testing columns showing where the requirement is tested and proved. If this does not ring true or if you do not have an RTM, this is the time to build one. Refer to Attachment 7, Requirements Traceability Matrix.

In general, your RTM should look similar to Table 5-13.

Once the RTM is complete and the test reference data is appropriately entered, it should expose the holes in the test string.

Table 5-13 — Requirements Traceability Matrix (RTM)

SOW/ Spec Para	Requirement	WBS Number	S/C SOW/ Spec Para	Unit Test Number	System Test Para	Monitor
SOW						
4.3.1	Security	06-03-02	N/A	T-0304	4.4.1	Smith
Spec						
3.2.1	System weight shall be less than 10,000 pounds	02-04-03	3.4.6	T-0045	3.4.1	Jones

59c (NO) Unit Test findings were *not* reviewed for completeness and *not* forwarded to be incorporated into Subsystem Tests and the System Test.

If this is the condition with which you are faced at the subsystem or system level, you have a lot of work to do. The initial requirements must be proved somewhere in the test process.

RECOVERY

The quick and dirty method of recovery is to lay out the initial requirements as stipulated in the specification and then identify where the requirement was proved in the System Test. If you can prove that the requirements were incorporated and your customer accepts the process, you are in luck. If not, you will be relegated to the "complete documentation" method.

The complete documentation method requires starting with the Requirements Traceability Matrix (RTM) and flowing each requirement into the unit and subsystem that will be built as a part of the system. The requirements must first be flowed down from the requirements document (contract) to the specification for each unit and subsystem and then flowed up in the Unit Test Plan, the Subsystem Test Plan and the System Test Plan. This methodology is especially critical in the development of a secure system where security qualification must be proved and certified at every level of development. That philosophy really should ensure whether the system is secure or not; then, there is no question.

If you do not have an RTM, refer to Cause Description "51a All Critical Success Factors (CSFs) such as MTTR, MTBF, etc., have been documented and understood" and Attachment 7 for suggestions for how to develop your RTM.

If you do not have a Unit Test Plan (UTP), refer to Cause Description "59a Each Unit Test correctly reflects the requirement" for suggestions for how to develop your UTP.

If you do not have a System Test Plan (STP) refer to Cause Description "60c (NO) The System Test has *not* tested all elements of the system concurrently" for suggestions for how to develop your STP.

59d (NO) All Problem Test Reports (PTRs) were *not* captured, dispositioned, or worked off.

All (PTRs) were *not* captured, dispositioned, or worked off when there is *not* complete accountability for every error that occurred during test conduct.

Those errors were *not* assigned to responsible individuals for correction and the results were *not* worked into the system. The System Test as written was subsequently *not* run without error.

RECOVERY

Every test run should have PTR forms available to capture any anomalies that occur during the conduct of the test. Further, there must be a PTR log in which to record the PTRs and account for each and every one. Usually, a sequence number is assigned to a PTR preceded by a unique Alpha that relates to the test. For example, the first PTR for the System Test could be numbered as ST-001.

If you do not have a PTR system, consider using the information to create a form for your own use:

- ❒ PTR No.
- ❒ Priority
- ❒ System
- ❒ Subsystem
- ❒ Test Conductor
- ❒ Test Title Run No.
- ❒ Short Title of Problem
- ❒ Description of Problem
- ❒ Disposition: Responsibility
- ❒ Scheduled Correction Date
- ❒ Action Taken
- ❒ Completed By
- ❒ Date
- ❒ Accepted By
- ❒ Date

In addition to a PTR Form, you should have a PTR Log to collect the actions of all the PTRs opened. The PTR Log should contain:

- ❒ PTR No.
- ❒ Priority
- ❒ Short title of problem
- ❒ Name of person to whom assigned
- ❒ Date initiated
- ❒ Date to be completed
- ❒ Date actually completed
- ❒ Date accepted
- ❒ Name of person accepting the PTR closure

60 SYSTEM TEST

60a (NO) The System Test Plan/Procedure was *not* approved by the customer.

The System Test Plan was *not* approved by the customer when the System Test Plan/Procedure *has not* been provided to the customer with lead time adequate for customer review *or* the customer *does not* agree with or approve the final content *or* the customer returns the plan/procedure without review and/or approval *or* the customer has not been previously apprised of the content of the plan/procedure.

If the first time the customer sees the System Test Plan is when the customer arrives for the System Test, you can plan on a lot of stoppages, a lot of explanations, and possibly a disapproval of the entire System Test.

At this point, it should be clear that the System Test Plan should be finalized and forwarded to the customer with adequate time for review. If the customer does not review the plan or does not approve the plan, revise the schedule to ensure that the plan has been approved by the customer. Proceeding into test without customer approval of the Test Plan and Test Procedure is a sure way to ensure failure. Believe it or not, there are some customers around who will sandbag the process just to keep their options open. You cannot allow this to happen.

RECOVERY

The best solution to this problem is to not let it happen in the first place. That is achieved by scheduling the completion of the System Test Plan and

System Test Procedure as a part of the Data Plan. An understanding and agreement must be made that the documents will be reviewed and approved by the customer within a certain time period (two weeks to one month are usual). Your agreement and schedule can allow for iteration, if necessary, but the System Test should not be scheduled until final approval of the System Test Plan and the System Test Procedure are approved by the customer.

Your agreement with the customer should be such that nonapproval will result in a project stoppage. Due diligence will determine who is at fault for nonapproval and thus be the basis for compensation, if any.

If you did not get this approval early in the project and are now faced with going into System Test without approval, it is my recommendation that you stop and sit down with the customer and get approval before proceeding. Unless you have mutual understanding of all elements of the test, many issues will be unresolvable and must be run again and again. This will be extremely costly, probably to you.

For an outline of a System Test Plan, see Data Item Description DI-ATTS-80005.

60b (NO) The System Test is *not* traceable to the requirements.

The System Test is *not* traceable to the requirements when each requirement is *not* forward traceable through the unit and the subsystem to the system via the Requirement Traceability Matrix (RTM) or each requirement is *not* tested at least once at the appropriate level (i.e., at the unit level or at the subsystem level) or system level requirements are *not* visible and backward traceable to the requirement through the RTM. The exceptions to this statement are those requirements that are only visible at the system level. Your RTM should reflect this situation by showing the requirement in the leftmost column and the place where it is tested in the System Test. All columns in between will have no entries or dashes.

RECOVERY

At this point, you are in for a lot of work. It is not adequate to simply trace a single requirement back through the RTM; each and every requirement must be traced back through the RTM. The reason is that if a requirement is visible at the system level but has not been accommodated at the subsystem or unit level, there exists a potential point of failure buried within the system.

Return to Cause Description 60d and accomplish the tasks listed there. Then, repeat the testing advocated in Cause Descriptions 60a, 60b, and 60c.

60c (NO) The System Test has *not* tested all elements of the system concurrently.

The System Test *has not* tested all elements of the system concurrently when all elements of the system are *not* called into play as they will be whenever the system is operating in its normal mode.

The purpose of the System Test is to test the entire system together. This process tests the interfaces and the loadings of the system. In many systems, it is normal that all units or subsystems or modules are not operating at the same time but rather are operating at some predetermined or commanded sequence. This is the way the system should be tested, as if it were performing the tasks it is required to perform. If the system is not tested in its operating mode, it is not a system test at all but rather a series of subsystem or unit tests.

Generally, the customer will define the system test coverage and scenarios, and you will design the Test Plan around these criteria. The best way to design a System Test is to create and document the System Test as the system is being designed. This is not necessarily a day-to-day activity but should certainly be accomplished before each major review so that the design and the testing are concurrent. Using a documented Configuration Management Process, the test process should require revision of the test after each major revision and follow the same level of review as the system itself.

RECOVERY

If you are at this point and recovery is necessary, it is clear the System Test was not created concurrent with the system. You are probably the recovery project manager because the one that got the project to this point is somewhere else!

There are four steps that must be taken:

First, a lot of documentation must be reviewed. The original requirement and all changes to the baseline must be reviewed. The baseline must be updated (or, if you are really in trouble, created) to reflect the last documented baseline of the system. The baseline would now be established, but it must be validated. This is the tricky part. The only way to validate the current requirements baseline is to negotiate it with your customer. From the customer's standpoint, this could be an opportunity to add in all those things they wanted but couldn't afford. From your standpoint, you must insist that the customer provide documentation of the original baseline and each change afterward. Verbal changes must not be accepted.

Second, the system must be physically and functionally baselined. This will probably take a lot of time, but it must be done. Keep very close time records of this activity so the time can be properly allocated during negotiation.

Third, you must negotiate the differences with your customer, and responsibility must be assigned. If the customer has established and documented a valid baseline with changes and you (your company) has accepted these changes or, at least, not refused the changes, that's what you must work to, no mater how much it hurts. Any change to that statement must be a management decision because there are all kinds of legal ramifications.

Fourth, when the physical and functional baseline has been established and the requirements negotiated, they must be brought together. Usually, this requires changing the system. At this point, you can write (rewrite) the System Test with reasonable assurance it will be correct. Sometimes, at this point, there are other changes the customer sees he wants. This time, keep up with the changes in the System Test!

60d (NO) The System Test was *not* performed under appropriate load(s).[2]

The System Test was *not* performed under appropriate load(s) when the loads on the system are *not* the loads required by the specification.

RECOVERY

If the specification does not stipulate loads, it is best to create "reasonable" loads, as determined by engineering analyses, and perform the system tests under those loads. Those loads and that fact must be documented and presented to the customer/client prior to final acceptance. The best time to present these issues is in the first Design Review. If the customer/client has an issue with the loads, it is a point for negotiation.

60e (NO) The System Test was *not* performed using the same kind of personnel that will be used by the customer.

The System Test was *not* performed using the same kind of personnel that will be used by the customer with regard to training, education, experience, etc., *or* the personnel specified by the customer. To conduct a System Test with engineers instead of Level X technicians is an invalid test even when you follow all the procedures in the test. If the specification does not stipulate operating personnel level, it is best to assume reasonable operating levels, as determined by engineering analyses, and perform the system tests using those personnel. Those operating levels must be documented and presented to the customer/client prior to final acceptance. The best time to present these issues is in the first Design Review. If the customer/client has an issue with the created loads, that is a point for negotiation.

60f (NO) The System Test was *not* properly documented and did *not* incorporate the test results of all prior-level tests.

The System Test was *not* properly documented and *did not* incorporate the test results of all prior level tests when the results of the unit level tests and the subsystem level tests are *not* clearly visible in the construct and conduct of the system test.

RECOVERY

Assumption: The Unit Tests were properly constructed, and each associated group of units constituted an appropriate subsystem.

Pull together all the subsystem tests:

- ❒ Check the traceability of each unit and unit test to the appropriate subsystem.
- ❒ Check the inputs and outputs of each subsystem.
- ❒ Check the interfaces and interface compatibility of each interfacing subsystem.
- ❒ Check the loads of each subsystem.
- ❒ Make changes as necessary.
- ❒ Modify the system test as necessary and recheck the traceability to the requirements.

61 CONFIGURATION MANAGEMENT

61a (NO) The Configuration Management Plan (CMP) is *not* thorough, complete, *or* authorized.

The Configuration Management Plan (CMP) is *not* thorough, complete, *or* authorized unless it follows the required format and maintains the required content as specified in customer or company configuration management policy. Further, the CMP is *not* authorized unless it is signed by an authority that is authorized to sign such documents (usually the vice president or director of engineering or an equivalent position).

The Configuration Management process could easily be looked upon as the Janus process. Remember the Roman god Janus who looked both backward and forward? That's what the configuration management process does. It looks backward to the baseline, as established, and forward to the test process that will prove the viability of a change.

RECOVERY

If you do not have a CMP, consider the following outline. The detail of what should be contained in each section can be found in Attachment 5. Modify the outline as necessary for your purposes:

1. Introduction
2. Reference documents
3. Organization
4. Configuration management phasing and milestones
5. Data management
6. Configuration identification
7. Interface management
8. Configuration control
9. Configuration status accounting
10. Configuration audits
11. Subcontractor/vendor control

Configuration Management should be treated on at least at two levels. The generally accepted levels are, appropriately enough, Class I and Class II. Class I changes are those that affect form, fit, or function while Class II changes are those that affect only documentation. Class I changes require convening a full Configuration Management (or Control) Board, often called the CCB. Class II changes only require the concurrence of the head of the CCB.

The Configuration Management Plan should be prepared for specific project use and generally follow the requirements of MIL-STD-973, MIL-STD-483,

MIL-STD-61, EIA-649, or ISO 10007, as determined by the requirements document (contract).

The purpose of the Software Configuration Management (SCM) plan is to achieve the "Repeatable" level on the Software Engineering Institute's (SEI's) Capability Maturity Model (CMM) and meeting the ISO/IEC 12207/MIL-STD-498 and the additional MIL-STD-973 requirements.

Additional Resources:

The following may contribute to developing your plan:

Data Item Descriptions (DIDs)

DI-CMAN-81343

DI-CMAN-80858A

61b (NO) Change requests were *not* presented and approved by an appropriate level of the Review Board.

Change requests were *not* presented and approved by an appropriate level of the Review Board when the presentations and approvals *did not* follow the Configuration Management Plan (CMP).

RECOVERY

You should have a CMP (See Attachment 5) containing a Configuration Control Section. A Change Process should be part of the Configuration Control Section.

Additional Resources:

The following may contribute to developing your plan:

Data Item Descriptions (DIDs):

DI-CMAN-81343

DI-CMAN-80858A

Standards:

MIL-STD-973
MIL-STD-483
MIL-STD-61
EIA-649
ISO 10007
ISO/IEC 12207
MIL-STD-498

61c (NO) Version controls are *not* in place and are *not* reflected on (in) the product.

Version controls are *not* in place and are *not* reflected on (in) the product when the affected product is *not* appropriately marked with the version which describes it in the Version Description Document (VDD) (see glossary) and to which it has *not* been tested.

RECOVERY

Create a version system and a Version Description Document where:
The general convention for document versions is:

X.YZ

Where: X = Major issue or re-issue containing fundamental changes.
Y = Minor change containing use changes or additional modules.
Z = Minor use changes or documentation clarifications.

If you do not have a procedure for Version Description Documents, you can use DID DI-IPSC-81442 as a guideline. Its contents are as complete as any one document can get. The outline follows (the headings without content should be self-evident. If you need further direction, refer to the DID):

1. Scope
1.1 Identification
1.2 System overview

1.3 Document overview
2. Referenced documents
3. Version description
3.1 Inventory of materials released
3.2 Inventory of software contents
3.3 Changes installed
3.4 Adaptation data
3.5 Related documents
3.6 Installation instructions
3.7 Possible problems and known errors
4. Notes
A. Appendices

Additional Resources:

MIL-STD-973
DID DI-IPSC-81442

62 SYSTEM EFFECTIVENESS FACTORS

62a (NO) All required System Effectiveness Factors[3] have *not* been appropriately considered.

All required System Effectiveness Factors have *not* been appropriately considered unless all the necessary System Effectiveness Factors have been appropriately considered in both the product and the processes.

RECOVERY

Certainly, not all the System Effectiveness Factors are required for every project but they are often overlooked. Table 5-14 groups the System Effectiveness Factors into their usual primary organizations.

The larger a parent organization, the more likely the second listed organization will be a separate organizational element. This is important because, if System Effectiveness Factor is a distinct organizational element, its function is more likely to be addressed. When these functions are "buried" in engineering,

Table 5-14 — System Effectiveness Parent Organization

System Effectiveness Factor	Usual Parent Organization
Reliability	Engineering or Reliability & Maintainability
Maintainability	Engineering or Reliability & Maintainability
Vulnerability/Susceptability	Engineering or Electro Magnetic Interference
Transportability	Engineering[1] or Transportation[2]
Supportability	Engineering or Logistics
Producibility	Engineering or Manufacturing
Quality	Quality

[1] When transportability is a function of the product (i.e., a communications shelter).
[2] When transportability is a function of delivery of the product to its destination.

the likelihood is greater that they will be glossed over or even ignored. These functions must be addressed even in the smallest organizations. The most economical way to accomplish this task is to designate a person to be responsible for each of the applicable System Effectiveness Factors and to question or defend that function during reviews. The project manager must ensure that all the required System Effectiveness Factors are addressed in all processes. This is particularly true in Design Reviews.

Notes

1. Defined as the smallest stand-alone component that produces a definable output from a definable input. The unit may be hardware or software. In the case of hardware, power can be external (i.e., a separate unit).

2. Loads are stresses placed upon a system. Loads are those stresses in units typical for the product such as pounds, watts, ergs, number of subsystems, number of users, number of executions per second, I/O rates, number of queries per second, etc.

3. The System Effectiveness factors refer to Reliability, Availability, Maintainability, Supportability (including Logistics), Susceptibility, Producibility, Human Engineering, Safety, and Security.

EXPANDING THE CAUSE BASE FOR YOUR PROJECT

In developing this book, I had to take a "middle-of-the-road" position with regard to specific Cause Descriptions and then present a methodology or processes for deviating from that position. That's where you are right now.

You may well need to expand your cause database for any number of reasons. Most likely, you are dealing with an area that wasn't addressed in the creation of the Search Tables or Cause Descriptions presented in Chapter 1. Perhaps you are dealing with a product or service area such as health care or pharmaceuticals or construction. While the basic precepts presented in Chapter 1 are appropriate for most product and service areas, the specifics may well be different.

Expanding the cause database is fundamentally a problem-solving process. As such, it follows the traditional problem-solving steps. While there is any number of advocates of slightly different steps in the process, I find that Mary Ellen Guffey's[1] five steps are typical. These are:

1. Identify the problem. The first step in reaching a solution is pinpointing the problem area.

2. Gather information. Look for possible causes and solutions. Check files, call suppliers, or brainstorm with fellow workers.
3. Evaluate the evidence. How accurate is the information gathered? Is it fact or opinion?
4. Consider alternatives and implications. Weigh the advantages and disadvantages of each alternative. What solution best serves your goals and those of your organization?
5. Choose and implement the best alternative. Select an alternative and put it into action. Then, follow through on your decision by monitoring the results of implementing your plan.

6.1 General

The purpose of this chapter is to assist you in expanding your database by creating new causes and Cause Descriptions; these will usually be causes that are unique to your business area and your products.

The creation technique I recommend using to start the expansion process is brainstorming. The reason brainstorming is used before the other data collection and review techniques is so that you approach the issue with an open mind. That is, you are not biased in favor of the data you will uncover during the data collection techniques. After brainstorming, you review the processes that are unique to your market, your customer, your enterprise, and your products. These are normally referred to as "benchmarks." The basic Family of Causes can be expanded to include these business-unique causes. Likely, you will need the assistance of one or more of your staff organizations to get started on this task. Then you can research the processes that are standard to your business area, common to your customer(s), required by your company, and normal for your kind of project or program.

By following the precepts of this chapter, you will expand the basic Family of Causes that includes the Search Tables and the Cause Descriptions. You will eliminate holes and overlaps and you will have tailored the Family of Causes to your specific needs.

Table 6-1 is a listing of the Expansion Methodologies, together with their purposes, that you can expect in this chapter. You must be the judge of how many of these methodologies you need to use for your particular problem set. Base your choice on the purpose of each of the methodologies as shown in the table.

Table 6-1 — Expansion Methodologies

Process	Purpose
Brainstorming	To create a large body of related ideas
Benchmarking	To discover/research "Best Practices" or "Best-in-Class" for your industry or product
Standard Processes	To discover/research standard processes in your industry or in support of your industry
Customer Processes	To discover/research processes unique to your customers
Enterprise Processes	To discover/research processes characteristic of your enterprise to serve this (these) business areas
Project/Program Processes	To provide processes specifically for this project/program

6.2 Brainstorming

Ken Blanchard's notion that "None of us is as smart as all of us"[2] is synergy epitomized. If you try to come up with all the answers yourself, you'll end up with only a few of the potential answers and those will be from a single vector of thinking. I heartily recommend brainstorming as a technique to create a large list of potential solutions. The entries on that list can be evaluated later.

Brainstorming can be the function of a local group or it can be the function of a dispersed group using the distributed method. The advantage accrues by having a greater number of people, and thus ideas, involved in the process. The advantage of the distributed method is that more experts of a higher level or experts of more diversity (whatever that means to you) can be applied to the task. The main thing to remember when brainstorming is to include all inputs, no matter how unusual or inappropriate they may seem to be at the time. Rejecting any input will have the effect of throwing cold water on the process.

If your approach is to use a local group, you will need a room to accommodate the people involved. Experts suggest that the group be from two to twenty people. Seating in a circle or a "U" is preferred. Flipcharts or sticky notes can be used to capture the ideas offered by the group. These techniques have been updated by many companies through using overhead viewgraph projectors with blank slides to write on or by using computer projection techniques—that is, simply typing in the ideas as they come up and maintaining a permanent record of what went on. It is best to use a facilitator to moderate the activity. My suggestion is to use a professional (someone from your training department is appropriate) rather than trying to do it yourself. This is especially true if you are in charge of the program. The group will tend to defer to you, and you will miss a lot of good inputs. Write down all the inputs (even those that are repetitive). Keep the flow going . . . pump the participants for ideas . . . get the best from them. When everyone is totally exhausted, take a break. Come back and eliminate items and group the overall list by voting on the individual inputs. Sometimes changing a word or two will "commonize" the inputs, and they can be combined. The point is though, do it through a voting technique rather than by fiat.

Nowadays, the Internet makes distributed brainstorming an inexpensive alternative to a local group. This method is very good for very large companies spread across the nation or the world. You use the same techniques except you create a "chat group" with a moderator. This is extremely powerful when you can call upon the best minds in the business, no matter where they are. Using the "Track Changes" function of a word processing application also works very well for this process. In fact, the peer review of this book was conducted in exactly that way.

Software to provide brainstorming is listed in Table 6-2.

Table 6-2 — Brainstorming Software

Tool	Product	Vendor
Brainstorming		
	"Brainstorming"	Infinite Innovations, Ltd
	"PathMaker"	SkyMark

Following is contact information for the companies listed in Table 6-2:

Infinite Innovations Ltd.
Innovation House
71 Sheldon Road
Sheffield S7 1GU
U.K.
Phone/Fax: +44 114 2967546
Web site: www.brainstorming.co.uk
E-mail: info@brainstorming.co.uk

SkyMark
7300 Penn Avenue,
Pittsburgh, PA 15208
Order: 800-826-7284
Phone: 412-371-0680
Fax: 412-371-0681
Web site: www.skymark.com
E-mail: sales@skymark.com

For in-depth information on brainstorming, see Edward de Bono, *Serious Creativity*, New York: Harper Business, 1992.

6.3 Researching Appropriate Benchmarks

Webster defines Benchmark as "a point of reference from which measurements may be made; something that serves as a standard by which others may be measured."

Benchmarks, in the business world, are results achieved by enterprises, companies, corporations, etc., and are held up as standards for that particular application, function, etc. The use of the term "Benchmark" in industry means that benchmarks are the highest value achieved for that particular function in that particular business area. Therefore, that Benchmark is (or should be) a goal for others in the same business area to achieve. Reviewing benchmarks is akin to employing the old adage of "not reinventing the wheel." If another company in your business area has already solved a problem and created a process and a metric that indicates success, why not use it? Some companies hold their benchmarks (read successes) close to their chests, and discovering them may be difficult.

Several organizations have been created for the purpose of sharing benchmarks. One such organization is the Project Management Benchmarking Network. They can be reached at:

Project Management Benchmarking Network
4606 FM 1960 West
Suite 250
Houston, TX 77069
Phone: 281-440-5044
Fax: 281-440-6677
Web site: www.pmbn.org

According to their Web site, "The Project Management Benchmarking Network (PMBN) is currently a free association of Project Management organizations within major corporations. PMBN conducts benchmarking studies to identify practices that improve the overall operations of the members."

Additionally:

Best Practices, LLC
6320 Quadrangle Dr., Suite 200
Chapel Hill, NC 27514-7815
Phone: 919-403-0251
Fax: 919-403-0144
E-mail: best@best-in-class.com

Use these recommended methodologies as you see fit. You may or may not need them all. The point is to expand the constituents of your cause database so that it reflects the milieu in which you and your project or program operate.

One thing to remember though is that just because some company has created or holds claim to a "Benchmark" doesn't mean that is an absolute. It is entirely possible that another "Benchmark" of higher order or greater quality, etc., could be found . . . and you could find it!

6.4 Researching the Processes

It is imperative that you understand the processes that drive your projects and programs. The processes will likely drive the requirements and the metrics that evaluate the implementation of the project/program requirements. These processes fall into four categories: Standard Processes, Customer Processes, Enterprise Processes, and Project/Program Processes. They are placed in this order because Standard Processes cover an entire area of interest. Customer Processes cover the entire customer span of control and so on. The order of precedence is quite another matter. The customer may well modify a Standard Process, and that modification would take precedence over the Standard Process with regard to the contract you are bidding or performing.

6.4.1 STANDARD PROCESSES

The Standard Processes referred to here are those processes common to everyday problem solving and are probably *referred to* in Project/Program, Enterprise, or Customer Processes rather than being specifically rewritten. Such processes are Professional and Association general processes standardized by such organizations as IEEE, IATA, ISO, EIA, ASME, ASTM, CCITT, NEMA, UL, and a host of others. You can use these processes as standards during your problem analysis, or your customer can specifically invoke them as a part of your contract or requirements document.

6.4.2 CUSTOMER PROCESSES

Customer Processes are those processes established by the customer with which you are dealing for this specific project. Examples of such processes are: Military Standards, DOD Standards, Data Item Descriptions (DIDs), NASA Standards, FAA Standards, Municipal Government Standards, and so on. Sometimes standards are just that, standards and not processes at all. They are, however, just as appropriate.

6.4.3 ENTERPRISE PROCESSES

Enterprise Processes are those processes established by the enterprise, company or corporation as a whole and apply to all projects or programs run by that enterprise. Examples of such processes are: Customer Processes, Administration Processes, Finance Processes, Legal and Contracts Processes, Personnel/Human Resources Processes, Material Processes, Research and Development Processes, Quality Processes, Projects/Programs Processes, Engineering Processes, Manufacturing and Production Processes, Field Operations Processes, Warranty Processes, and Operations and Maintenance Processes. Within the enterprise, these processes usually begin as policies from the highest level in the enterprise. Processes, procedures, and plans are derived from and driven by policies (at least they should be).

6.4.4 PROJECT/PROGRAM PROCESSES

Project/Program Processes are, quite aptly, those processes you generate for your Project or Program. Usually, these are extensions of enterprise, company, or corporate processes and are written by those organizations and directed to be incorporated into your project or program plans. Usually, you extend and incorporate these processes or parts of these processes into your Program Plan or the plans that support the Program Plan. Examples of these kinds of processes are the specifics of Team Members and Alliance Processes, Subcontracts Processes, Materials Management Processes (including Make/Buy Decisions), Data Management Processes, Configuration Management Processes, Quality Assurance Processes, as well as Training Processes, Safety Processes, Security Processes, and Facilities Processes as they apply to your specific project or program.

On the technical side of the house, these processes frequently include: Technical Strategy, Functional Analyses, Requirements Allocation, Generation of Specifications, Generation and Control of Drawings, Alternative Designs, and Trade-Offs.

By way of example, Table 6-3, Policy-to-Program Plan Cross Reference,

Table 6-3 — Policy-to-Program Plan Cross Reference

Reference	Para	Title
M-M 11000 Series	5	Management
M-M 05010	5.1	Organization and Responsibilities
M-M 11010	5.1.1	General
M-M 12000 Series	5.1.2	System Management
M-M 06000 Series	5.1.3	Subcontracts and Materials
M-M 11050	5.1.4	Data Management
M-M 11030	5.1.5	Configuration Management
M-M 09000 Series	5.1.6	Quality Assurance
M-M 04020	5.1.7	Team Members and Alliances
M-M 06040	5.2	Make/Buy Decisions
M-M 02030	5.3	Safety
M-M 02040	5.4	Security
M-M 02020	5.5	Facilities
M-M 11060	5.6	Standardization
M-M 11028	5.7	Program Risks
M-M 11020	6	Program Controls
M-M 11022/3	6.1	Cost and Schedule Controls
M-M 11040	6.2	Communication Control
M-M 11041	6.3	Status Meetings
M-M 12010	6.4	Design Reviews
M-M 12090	6.5	Specification Control

shows which Enterprise Policies, Plans, and Processes should be referenced or "flowed into" which paragraph of the Program Plan. The references in the reference column are to Modern-Management Policies, Plans, and Processes, the details of which will be available in future books in my Strategy for Success series. For your use, however, you should enter your enterprise, company, or corporate policy reference. The paragraph (Para) number refers to the paragraphs in the Standard Program Plan which can be found in Attachment 1 in this book.

Notes

1. Mary Ellen Guffey, *Business Communication: Process and Product.* 2nd ed. (Cincinnati: South-Western College Publishing, 1997), chapter 1.

2. Kenneth Blanchard, "None of Us Is as Smart as All of Us" (first appeared in Kenneth Blanchard and Johnson Spencer, *The One Minute Manager* (New York: William Morrow and Co., Inc., 1982), and continues to be used in his High Performing Teams program, lectures, and workshops).

CHAPTER 7

GROUPING THE CAUSES FOR ACTION

7.1 General

Now that you have a pile of data, you need to turn it into information. You need to organize the data so that it is understandable by itself and in relation to other data items. This chapter will present four techniques to assist you in the organization of your data. These four were selected from the dozens, if not hundreds, of techniques available because they individually and collectively cover most of the ordering techniques that need to be covered.

7.2 Ordering Techniques

Ordering techniques are needed to make sense of the mound of data you have created by brainstorming, researching processes, and reviewing "Best Practices."

There are many, many ordering techniques available but I have chosen only a few (see Table 7-1). These few have either a primary and secondary purpose or lead directly to a secondary purpose. For example, the 85:15 Rule not only orders data but also places it into two primary categories. Cause and Effect Diagrams not only lay out the causes and reasons for the causes but provide a trail of sorts to the effect. Furthermore, the Cause and Effect Diagram leads directly to Failure Mode and Effect Analysis (FMEA). (You may or may not want to use FMEA depending on the issue with which you are dealing. It is more appropriate to technical issues than programmatic issues.)

Table 7-1 — Ordering Techniques

Ordering Technique	Purpose
85:15 Rule	To organize information into "process" or "people" categories.
Cause and Effect Diagrams	To show the relationship of reasons to causes and causes to effects
Affinity Diagrams	To organize large groups of information into meaningful categories
Relationship Diagrams	To show the relationship(s) between elements

7.2.1 85:15 RULE

The 85:15 Rule is used to separate causative data into process-related groups and people-related groups. The basis of the 85:15 Rule is that 85 percent of problems are process related while only 15 percent of problems are people related. Be careful when interpreting this rule, though. It does not mean that if you have rules, they will create 85 percent of your problems. It simply means that there is a significantly higher probability that an error was caused by a process than by a person.

There are some who say, "There are no good rules, just good sense." I believe that's half right. There are indeed good rules, but everything needs to be interpreted with good sense.

The 85:15 Rule is used extensively in the area of education. Brenda Barnes and James Van Wormer state:

> Deming and others have established that the potential to eliminate mistakes and errors in the workplace lies mostly in improving the systems through which work is done, not in changing the individual workers. Their observations have evolved

> into the rule of thumb that at least 85% of work problems can be corrected by changing the work system and less than 15% can be corrected by changing individual workers. Current research indicates that the split probably leans even more towards the system. The rule probably should be 95/5 or 97/3. In his famous Red Bead Experiment, Dr. Deming proved that the only way to improve a product or service is for management to improve the system that creates that product or service.[1]

The appropriateness of that statement here is that it not only confirms the ratio but also implies it is even greater than the 85:15 stated.

This rule is particularly appropriate for use in this process because our Program Plans and Technical Plans are directly driven by Standard, Customer, and Enterprise Processes.

The 85:15 Rule is used for separating process issues from people issues for the purpose of problem solution. I suggest using this technique first to orient your actions to the potentially most rewarding group of solutions. It is a simple way to put your data into two piles.

The 85:15 Rule is a very simple and highly effective technique to evaluate each issue you come up with. Look at the issue. What is the issue, what affects it, and what does it affect? If the answer to the questions is process, put it in Pile A. If the answer is people, put it in Pile B. If you follow the precepts of the 85:15 Rule, there is an 85 percent probability that the answer lies in Pile A and a 15 percent probability that the answer lies in Pile B. Which one would you address first?

7.2.2 CAUSE AND EFFECT DIAGRAM

The Cause and Effect Diagram shown in Figure 7-1 is used to create multiple pathways to find causes and then reasons for the causes that contribute to a problem.

The cause and effect process is a logical process and has been around for a long time. Cause and effect analysis is an effective tool that allows people to easily see the relationship between factors to study processes and situations and to use them for planning.

The Cause and Effect diagram is also called the Ishikawa Diagram (after its creator, Kaoru Ishikawa of Japan), or the Fishbone Diagram (due to its shape).

Figure 7-1 — Fishbone Diagram

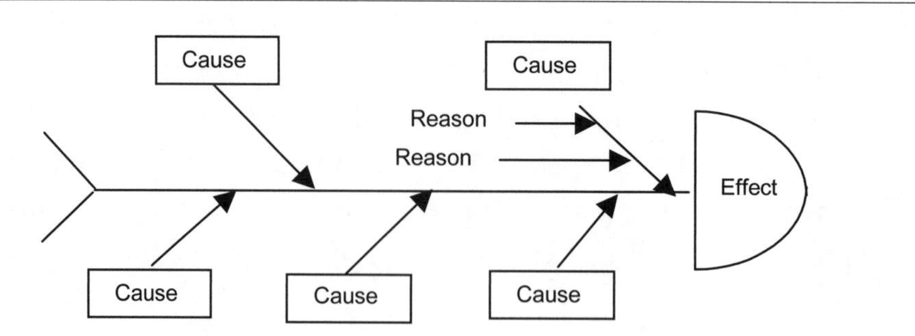

The Cause(s) in the diagram would be major contributors to the program or project such as Processes, People, Machinery, Materials, and Environment. You will need to adjust these Causes to fit your situation. In some cases, for instance, you may want to use elements of the organization as Causes. In other cases, you may want to use elements of your specific process as Causes. The Causes for your program could be similar to these but not necessarily the same. The Reasons are why the Cause is contributing to the problem. For instance, Reasons that contribute to Materials Cause could be: 1) The wrong materials were specified or 2) the SOW was incorrect or 3) the subcontractor or vendor did not perform properly. These Reasons will go on and on, and they will be specific to your project and to the product you are creating. Process Reasons could be an incorrect process that falls short of specifying some critical action necessary for this project. And so on.

Some time later, a modification to the classical fishbone diagram was created to make it into what is called a "Tree Diagram." A drawing of the Tree Diagram can be seen in Figure 7-2. If you use a drawing program to support your "Cause and Effect" analysis, your end product will resemble that figure.

An even simpler method than drawing the flow is to use a spreadsheet program to create an ordering of "Reasons," "Causes," and "Effects." For purposes of organization, the presentation is reversed: the Effect is on the left, the Cause in the middle, and the Reason on the right, as they appear in Table 7-2. The Effects are numbered as 1, 2, 3, and so on. The Causes are numbered 1a, 1b, and 2a, 2b, and so on. The reasons are numbered 1.a.1, 1.a.2, and 2.a.1, 2.a.2, and so on. Using this technique, you can develop your Causes and Reasons in a nonlinear or random fashion, so long as you maintain the relationships. A simple "sort" will place the Reasons, Causes, and Effects in their proper places.

Figure 7-2 — Tree Diagram

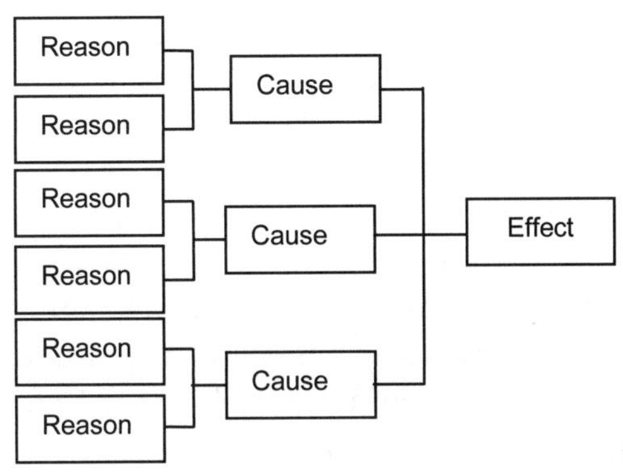

Table 7-2 — Cause and Effect Table

Sequence	Effect	Cause	Reason
1	XXXXXXX		
1a		YYYYYYYY	
1a1			ZZZZZZZZZZ
1a2			ZZZZZZZZZZ
1a3			ZZZZZZZZZZ
1b		YYYYYYYY	
1b1			ZZZZZZZZZZ
1b2			ZZZZZZZZZZ
1b3			ZZZZZZZZZZ
1b4			ZZZZZZZZZZ
1c		YYYYYYYY	
1c1			ZZZZZZZZZZ
1c2			ZZZZZZZZZZ

You can also use three columns of data and one column of sequencing as shown in Table 7-2. If necessary, another column can be added.

The Cause and Effect Diagram is used for listing the primary, secondary, and even tertiary causes that relate to some selected problem area and provides a visual display of a list in which you identify and organize possible causes of problems, or factors needed to ensure success of some effort. It was created so that all possible causes of a result could be listed in such a way as to allow a user to graphically show these possible causes. From this diagram, the user can define the most likely causes of a result. This diagram was adopted by Dr. W. Edwards Deming as a helpful tool in improving quality. Dr. Deming has taught Total Quality Management in Japan since World War II. He has also helped develop statistical tools to be used for the census and taught the military his methods of quality management. Both Ishikawa and Deming use the Fishbone Diagram as one of the first tools in the quality management process.

One limitation of the Cause and Effect Diagram, whatever presentation technique is used, is that the diagram does not show magnitude. One might say that it is "a good map but it lacks time and distance data."[2] Data Sheets, Histograms, Pareto Analysis, Failure Mode Effect Analysis (FMEA), and other data collection and analysis tools can be used to quantify the data.

For additional information on the Cause and Effect Process, see:

John F. Early, ed. *Quality Improvement Tools.* Wilton, Conn.: Juran Institute, 1989.

P.E. Plsek. "Tutorial: Management and Planning Tools of TQM." *Quality Management in Health Care* 1, no.3 (1993).

Peter Senge. *The Fifth Discipline.* New York: Doubleday, 1990.

Software used to support the Cause and Effect Process is listed in Table 7-3.

Table 7-3 — Cause and Effect Software

Tool	Product	Vendor
Cause and Effect		
	"REASON 4"	DECISION Systems, Inc.
	"Flowcharting Cause & Effect Module" for "Six Sigma Software Suite"	Quality America, Inc.
	"Root Cause Analysis (RCA)"	Root Cause Analyst
	"PathMaker"	SkyMark

Following is contact information for the companies listed in Table 7-3:

DECISION Systems, Inc.
802 N. High St. Ste. C
Longview, TX 75601
Phone: 903-236-9973
Fax: 903-236-3794
Web site: www.rootcause.com/
E-Mail: dsi@rootcause.com

Quality America, Inc.
P.O. Box 18896
Tucson, AZ 85731-8896
Order: 800-643-9889
Phone: 520-722-6154
Fax: 520-722-6705
Web site: www.qualityamerica.com/
E-mail: sales@qualityamerica.com

Root Cause Analyst
Orion Healthcare Technology
1823 Harney Street, Suite 101
Omaha, NE 68102
Phone: 800-324-7966
Fax: 402-341-8911
Web site: www.rcasoftware.com/
E-mail: info@casoftware.com

SkyMark
7300 Penn Avenue,
Pittsburgh, PA 15208
Phone: 800-826-7284
Fax: 412-371-0681
Web site: www.skymark.com
E-mail: info@skymark.com

7.2.3 AFFINITY DIAGRAMS

The purpose of the Affinity Diagram, shown in Figure 7-3, is to organize large groups of information into meaningful categories.

Figure 7-3 — Affinity Diagram

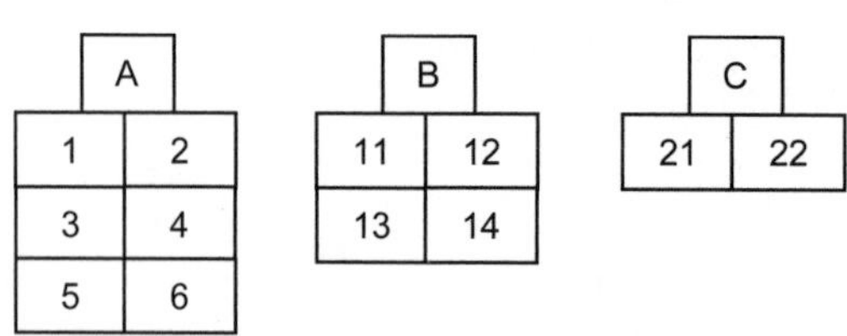

The Affinity Diagram or KJ Method (so named for Kwakita Jiro) helps break old patterns of thought, reveal new patterns, and generate more creative ways of thinking. The Affinity Diagram helps organize the team's thoughts most effectively when the families seem too large and complex; you need to break out of old, traditional ways of thinking; everything seems chaotic; or there are many requirements.

If you research this process, you will find there are two schools of thought. The first is to start at the top and work down. The second is to start at the bottom and work up. The following process is my favorite; that is, starting from the bottom and working up. The reason I choose this methodology is because it creates its own organization rather than being forced into some predetermined organization.

1. Convert the mound of data created earlier to 3 x 5 cards or to Post-it Notes.
2. Begin arranging these notes into related categories. These are the numerical squares shown in Figure 7-3. No doubt you will create a lot of categories and a lot of piles. As time goes on though, you will begin changing a word here and there and combining these piles into more closely related groups. Just don't lose the essence of the card entry.
3. At some point, it will make sense to create a "Header" card that describes the group. The "Header" cards become the Alpha cards shown in Figure 7-3. Iterate until the groupings and entries are, in your judgment, optimized. Your "gut" will tell you when you are through. The software shown in Table 7-4 is available to assist in this chore.

Table 7-4 — Affinity Diagram Software

Tool	Product	Vendor
Affinity Diagram		
	"EDGE Diagrammer"	Pacestar Software
	"SmartDraw"	SmartDraw.com
	"Six Sigma for Excel"	BaRaN Systems LLC

Following is contact information for the companies listed in Table 7-4:

BaRaN Systems, LLC
Phone: 780-449-6554
Web site: www.baran-systems.com

Pacestar Software
P.O. Box 51974
Phoenix, AZ 85076-1974
Phone: 480-893-3046
Fax: 413-480-0645
Web site: www.pacestar.com
E-mail: pacestar@compuserve.com

SmartDraw.com
10085 Carroll Canyon, Suite 220
San Diego, CA 92131
Phone: 800-501-0314
Fax: 858-549-2830

7.2.4 RELATIONSHIP DIAGRAMS

The next step is to evaluate and classify the data. One of the best tools to accomplish this task is a Relationship Diagram. The Relationship Diagram was reportedly invented by P. Chen and presented in his article in 1976.[3] The purpose of the Relationship Diagram is to show the interrelationships between causative factors that relate to a problem.

A Relationship Diagram, as shown in Figure 7-4, is one that shows connec-

Figure 7-4 — Relationship Diagram

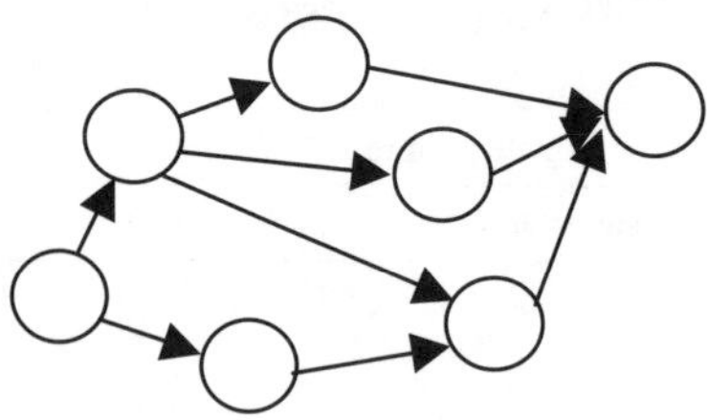

tions or relationships between the elements of the diagram. In this case, the elements are Issues.

The Relationship Diagram, in contrast to the Affinity Diagram, which only shows logical groupings, helps map the logical relationships between the related items uncovered in the Affinity Diagram. The Relationship Diagram shows cause and effect relationships among many key elements. It can be used to identify the causes of problems or to work backward from a desired outcome to identify all of the causal factors that would need to exist to ensure the achievement of an outcome. The Relationship Diagram doesn't necessarily need to follow the form of the "bubble" chart shown. A traditional organization chart and a flow diagram are examples of other presentations of Relationship Diagrams.

The process to be used is as follows:

1. State the problem or family under discussion—software defects, customer retention, process steps, whatever.
2. Capture that problem or issue in a box, bubble, or whatever.
3. Begin a process of looking for "drivers"; that is, functions or issues that drive the issue being considered. You can also use the rationale of the PERT Chart (see glossary) in considering "predecessors" for this part of the process. In other words, you are looking for items that drive or must be completed before the issue at hand.
4. Begin a process of looking for "drivens," that is, functions or issues that are being driven by the issue at hand. If you prefer, use the term "predecessors" for "drivers" and "successors" for "drivens."
5. When you have diagrammed the issue and have located all the "drivers" and "drivens" something will jump out at you. That bubble or square

that has "drivers" but no "drivens" is the primary issue whether that's the one you started with or not!

If you want or need to go beyond the simple relationships of one issue driving another, consider the following:

- ❒ The bubble is the issue.
- ❒ The lines (arrows) connecting the bubbles are the actions.
- ❒ The value of the line (arrow) is the magnitude.
- ❒ The characteristics of the bubble are its attributes.

A veritable glut of information exists on Relationship Diagrams. Much of it is Entity-Relationship Diagrams as a result of our software society. The source of a lot of the information is the use and application of relational databases such as Microsoft's Access. Most written information regarding Relationship Diagrams is in the form of articles rather than books.

Software used to support Relationship Diagrams is listed in Table 7-5.

Table 7-5 — Relationship Diagram Software

Tool	Product	Vendor
Relationship Diagrams		
	"EDGE Programmer"	Pacestar Software
	"SmartDraw"	SmartDraw.com

Following is contact information for the companies listed in Table 7-5:

Pacestar Software
P.O. Box 51974
Phoenix, AZ 85076-1974
Phone: 480-893-3046
Fax: 413-480-0645
Web site: www.pacestar.com
E-mail: mail@pacestar.com

SmartDraw.com
10085 Carroll Canyon Road, Suite 220
San Diego, CA 92131
Phone: 858-549-0314
Order: 800-501-0314
Fax: 858-549-2830
Web site: www.smartdraw.com
E-mail: mail@smartdraw.com

7.3 Interrelationships of Causes

Many causes will have interrelationships with other causes. That's not necessarily bad but what you must look for is duplication and overlapping. Duplication is a waste of time and money. Overlapping causes will tend to present an unclear picture of what the problem really is when you try to classify the problem.

When you have reached a stopping point or believe you have reached a plateau in your search and organization of causes and potential causes, step back for a moment and review what you have created, and take an objective view of your new cause package. If you have not reached Shangri-la, don't worry. Tomorrow is another day.

If you have solved the immediate problem, that's wonderful. If you are performing this process before you have a problem, congratulations. What you want to do now that you have a feel for the overall process is to look back at your business area standards, your customer references, and your enterprise policies and processes and make certain your new Search Table and Cause Descriptions reflect all these standards.

Notes

1. Brenda J. Barnes and James W. Van Wormer, "Process Thinking and the 85:15 Rule Applied to Education." Source: www.grand-blanc.k12.mi.us/qip/ProcessThinking.htm, last accessed August 5, 2002.

2. Robert Luttman and Associates Online Article, "Cause and Effect." Source: www.robertluttman.com/cause-effect.html, last accessed August 5, 2002.

3. P. Chen, "The Entity-Relationship Model: Toward a Unified View of Data," *ACM Transactions on Database Systems,* 1, no. 1 (1976): 9–36.

CHAPTER 8

SELECTING THE BEST OF THE BEST

8.1 General

In Chapter 6, you expanded the original causes to include additional causes necessary to solve the problem at hand. In addition, you probably expanded the causes to include those that are unique to your product area, customer, or product. Finally, you ordered the new causes into categories that are meaningful to you.

Now is the time to evaluate those causes you have chosen and ordered. The point of evaluation, of course, is to add a quantitative dimension to the causes that permits you to select the most important cause(s).

Table 8-1 summarizes the purpose of each of the techniques that will be talked about in this chapter.

You must be the judge of which and how many of these techniques you need to use for your particular problem set. Base your choice on the purpose of each of the techniques as shown in Table 8-1.

Table 8-1 — Analysis Techniques

Analysis Technique	Purpose
Pareto Analysis	To select the 20 percent of the issues that provide 80 percent of the results
Force Field Analysis	To understand restraining forces and driving forces
Failure Mode Effect Analysis (FMEA)	To predict potential failures
Monte Carlo Simulation	To refine estimates

8.2 Evaluation Techniques

There are numerous techniques available to assist you in evaluating your Causes. Some of the other techniques available are Blue Slipping, Consensus Gram, Flow Charting, Gallery Walking, Histograms, Light Voting, Lotus Flower Diagrams, Radar Diagrams, Run Charts, and Scattergrams. I have tried to select several that are the most appropriate for the general field of technical project management. Even at that, you will probably not use all of them to solve any one problem. Possibly, you may not use one or more of them ever. Still, you should know what is available to you.

8.2.1 PARETO ANALYSIS

The Italian economist Vilfredo Pareto (1848–1923), established a theory for the purpose of evaluating the sources of a society's wealth. His thesis was later confirmed by Juran, and the Pareto Principle was established as: "Not all of the causes of a particular phenomenon occur with the same frequency or with the same impact."

Pareto analysis is used to get a quick assessment of the most important factors involved in the data you are assessing.

To perform a Pareto analysis, you must first list all the issues. Next, you must determine the number of occurrences or the amount of deviation or apply whatever metric you use to determine "goodness" or "badness." Once you have achieved this evaluation, it is recommended that you create a bar chart. As the issues begin to unfold, you will see the relative sizes of the bars begin to take shape. The bar chart, similar to Figure 8-1, will give you a relative representation of the issues.

The next step is to reorder the bars of the chart so that the first bar is the tallest with the adjacent bar the next tallest and so on until you run out of bars.

Rearranged, the issues now look like Figure 8-2. Clearly Issue 2 and Issue 3 constitute the most number of occurrences. Pareto's Principle suggests focusing on identifying these key issues. Interestingly, Jay Arthur[1] has created what he calls his 4–50 rule. His principle suggests that 4 percent of the problems contribute to 50 percent of the losses. Or 4 percent of the zones contribute 50 percent

Figure 8-1 — Pareto Analysis: Raw Data

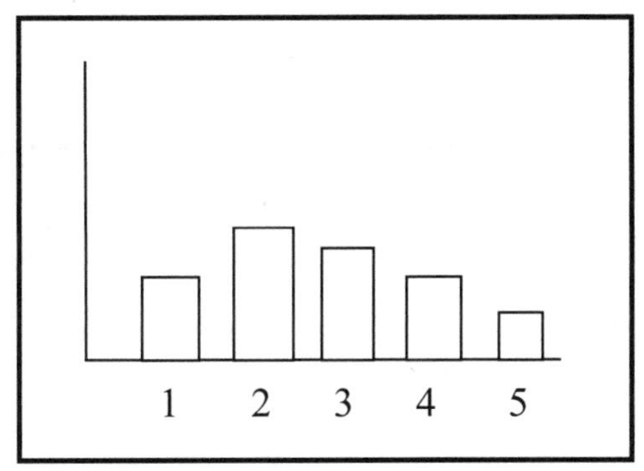

Figure 8-2 — Pareto Analysis: Ordered Data

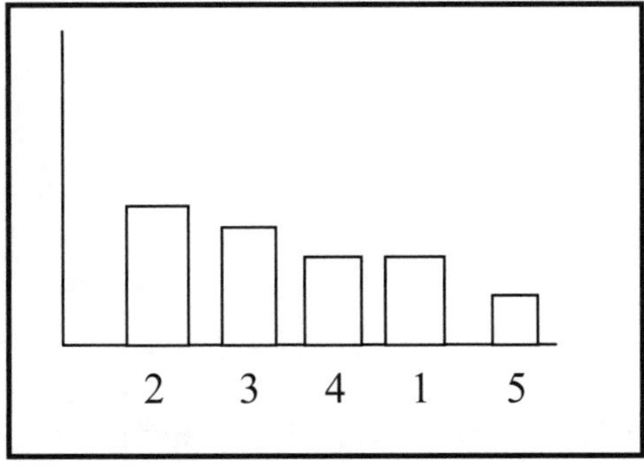

of the sales, and so on. I would not argue with either thesis. The principles are clearly the same in suggesting a few of the issues cost you the most money. Attack those few first to get the biggest "bang for the buck." Interestingly, the Arthur modification to Pareto Analysis is quite similar to the Barnes and Wormer modification of the 85:15 Rule (see paragraph 7.2.1).

Obviously, in order to invoke the 4–50 rule, one would need to have a significant number of issues to evaluate, certainly more than four.

There are many, many books that contain the Pareto Principle, but most are sociology books and economics books. The Pareto Principle, Pareto Analysis, etc., does not warrant a book per se. You will find all the information you need in articles and short references. If you want more detail, do an Internet search on Pareto and you will find more detail than you ever wanted.

See Table 8-2 for Pareto Analysis software.

Table 8-2 — Pareto Analysis Software

Tool	Product	Vendor
Pareto Analysis		
	"PathMaker"	SkyMark

Following is contact information for the company listed in Table 8-2:

SkyMark
7300 Penn Avenue,
Pittsburgh, PA 15208
Phone: 800-826-7284 or
412-371-0680
Fax: 412-371-0681
Web site: www.skymark.com
E-mail: info@skymark.com

8.2.2 FORCE FIELD ANALYSIS

The purpose of Force Field Analysis is to list the driving and the restraining forces of an issue so that you can take the next step—to neutralize the restraining causes and to amplify the driving causes.

The Force Field Analysis concept was developed by the American social psychologist Kurt Lewin based on the premise that any problem or situation is a result of the forces acting upon it. The forces acting upon a problem are issues of two kinds: driving forces and restraining forces. Driving forces are those that are trying to cause a change in a static condition. Restraining forces are those that are trying to maintain the static condition; not at all unlike Newton's First Law. When attempting change or improvement, if the restraining and driving forces can be understood, the process improvement team can look for ways to enhance the driving forces and moderate or eliminate the restraining forces.

Force field analysis uses a graphical technique to map the forces that are affecting the situation. All driving forces are shown on one side of the issue, and all restraining forces are shown on the other side, as in Figure 8-3.

An interesting, and frequently useful, modification to the basic approach assigns a number (value) to each of the forces, both positive and negative, affecting the issue. The value of the numbering system must be the same on both sides. By assigning values, one can add the total values and make an initial determination of the difficulty of changing the issue as well as the value of each force. This gives the project manager an idea of the magnitude of the problem and the power of the tool being used as well as the easiest and most difficult restraining forces with which to deal.

From a practical standpoint, Force Field Diagrams are generally constructed with two columns of data for each effect. The driving forces are listed in the

Figure 8-3 — Force Field Schematic

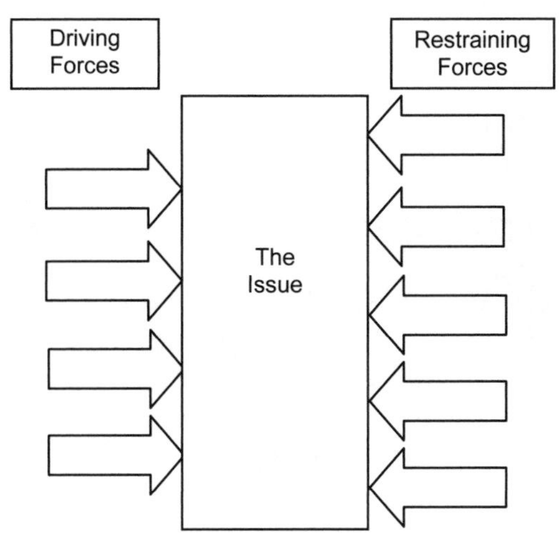

first column and the restraining forces are listed in the second column. The same technique can obviously be used to list strengths and weaknesses, pros and cons, and any other positive and negative influence that acts upon an effect. You can map these forces in a number of ways. The easiest way is to use a spreadsheet to list the forces.

Once all of the forces are mapped, it becomes possible to see how opposing forces line up and then look for ways to counter the forces against each other so that the current situation moves in the direction of the desired improvement. Additional columns can be added to the left and right of the two central columns to list factors that can emphasize (driving force) or neutralize (restraining force) the data in the center two columns. You can add columns outside the opposing forces to give each a Force Value. This will give you an idea of "How much of A" or "How much of B" you need to apply to counter its opposing force. You can use the sum function to balance or eliminate the forces.

Once the causes are known, cause and effect analysis can again be used to determine exactly what kind of incentive package (driving force) it would take to overcome this restraining force. There could be situations where you do not want to maintain the status quo or stop some activity. In those cases, simply reverse all the activities above. In other words, you want the restraining forces rather than the driving forces to "win."

Software used to support Force Field Analysis is called "PathMaker" from:

SkyMark
7300 Penn Avenue,
Pittsburgh, PA 15208
Phone: 800-826-7284 or
412-371-0680
Fax: 412-371-0681
Web site: www.skymark.com
E-mail: info@skymark.com

8.2.3 FAILURE MODE EFFECT ANALYSIS (FMEA)

Failure Mode Effect Analysis (FMEA), sometimes called Failure Mode, Effects, and Criticality Analysis (FMECA) is intended to result in preventive actions. FMEA and FMECA are "before-the-fact," exercises and you will most likely use this technique when evaluating technical, rather than programmatic, aspects of the system. A comprehensive FMEA will take a significant amount of time so be sure to allocate the time necessary.

An FMEA is performed from the bottom up by evaluating the lowest part of the system first. This involves the Lowest Replaceable Unit (LRU), the smallest or the least significant unit. In electronic systems, this "unit" is frequently a resistor or transistor or some such unit. After each unit is reviewed, it is used as a "building block" to ultimately re-create the entire system. The usual way to conduct an FMEA is to look at a "failed" unit and making a prediction by asking the question: "What happens when this unit fails?"

The purpose of the FMEA exercise is to identify critical components in a system and evaluate the impact of the failure of that component and then, if warranted, provide an alternate path, or back up or change the unit so that the impact of failure is removed. By way of example, we did an FMEA on two alternative data links from Cape Canaveral to Houston back before the first mission was run from Houston. The system was designed to have two completely diverse data paths. One route was completely land-line (telephone line) and the other was completely RF (microwave). We traced the design through the entire thousand miles from the Cape to the Mission Control Center (MSC) in Houston only to find that both diverse routes entered the Telco building just outside the Control Center, and both routes went through the same amplifier. Consider the effect of that failure!

Using reliability data is a good way to predict failure rates for components. For instance, if "X" fails, it will take the "Y" function with it. However, the probability of "X" not failing is 0.999999, so it's not likely "X" or "Y" will be a big contributor to overall system failure.

There are two kinds of failure, total and partial. In many systems, you will get a different result with a partial failure than with a total failure. Other than the obvious, a partial failure may affect the productivity of another unit in the system and that unit will change the direction of the failure. For instance, changing the bias on an electronic circuit will cause a different effect in a secondary circuit than if the circuit were completely dead.

Software to provide FMEA analyses is available as "Relex FMEA/FMECA" from:

Relex Corporation
40 Pellis Road
Greensburg, PA 15601
Phone: 724-836-8800
Fax: 724-836-8844

For additional information on FMEA, see:

McDermott, Robin E., et al. *The Basics of FMEA*. Portland, Ore.: Productivity Press, Inc., 1996.

Stamatis, Dean H. *Failure Mode and Effect Analysis: FMEA from Theory to Execution*. Milwaukee, Wis.: ASQ Quality Press, 1995.

8.2.4 MONTE CARLO SIMULATION

The real use of Monte Carlo Simulation in support of a project or program is risk control. You want to control schedule risk or cost risk and usually both. Monte Carlo Simulation almost demands the use of a computer because of the nature of the process. The utilization of an available software package that supports all these objectives is highly desirable. Fortunately, such things exist.

In times past, we made use of the "wet-finger-in-the-wind" technique to establish risk, and therefore contingency, in programs. If you have a small project and the overall risk is not perceived as great, you can still use this technique. Simply, the technique is to do a "bottom up" estimate of task cost and task schedule. Assign a value factor to your estimate. I have always used the value factors 10/90, 50/50, and 90/10. The factors go from more risk (10/90) to less risk (90/10). If you are involved in a proposal, the proposal manager will probably insist on a 50/50 (most likely) estimate based on the assumption that 10/90 is too risky and 90/10 is too costly. You can then estimate the variance of what it will take to get the task from 50/50 to 90/10. That estimate is the amount of risk money or time that should be included with your bid along with a statement of the task to be accomplished. *Note: When I say "Included with your bid," you need to follow the directions of your proposal manager. I insist that the time and money allocated to risk be kept separate so that it can be collected at the program level. Risk is then summarized, apportioned, and calculated at the program level. If you include risk money at the task level you will end up with a bid that will never win because of excessive cost.*

Even though Monte Carlo techniques have been around for centuries, they were not used extensively until the 1940s. History has it that Metropolis, associate of Stan Ulam, brought the technique to the fore during the Manhattan Project of World War II mainly to support Ulam's penchant for gambling—hence the name Monte Carlo. Ulam used the technique to solve mathematical problems using statistical sampling in the development of the hydrogen bomb.

Monte Carlo techniques were not used too often in project planning until the last ten or so years. There are two reasons for this: First, projects are more expensive today and profit and schedule sensitivities are critical. Second, software is now available to be used independently or in conjunction with other software that makes the job of planning much simpler and faster, not to mention more accurate.

The concept of the Monte Carlo technique is to assign Probability Density Functions (PDFs) to outcomes. For example: Assume you have established a task that is thirty days in duration. What is the probability that the task will be four days late? What is the probability that the task will be done on time? What is the probability that the task will be accomplished four days ahead of schedule? The probability figure is the traditional 0–1 where 1 is the equivalent of 100 percent. Note that each of the figures is independent and the sum of all the figures do not add up to one. Now, you don't have to run too many projects or programs to realize that, in the real world, the probability of schedule occurrence grows with time. In other words, the later the estimate, the more likely it is that the task will be completed. If the original estimate is anywhere near correct, you will get a distribution that looks something like:

−4 days	.1
0 days	.7
+4 days	.9

These are the PDFs that you run. It's clear that, even with all the objectivity of the computer and its processes, the basic data is subjective. In other words, you established the original thirty days and you established the PDFs that apply to each of the variances. That selection was, at least to some degree, subjective.

The computer will now select some random numbers and run the probabilities over and over. You will end up with a high probability that the task will be completed near the originally scheduled date but will be skewed slightly forward. The early/late probabilities will center on this highest probability and create a traditional bell curve or standard distribution curve. This foregoing has been an extremely simplified example of what you might encounter in the field.

As promised at the outset of this book, I will not go into the math involved in this process. If you are interested, I suggest you get a copy of any of the books dealing with the Monte Carlo method. There are many, many of them out there. You might consider the following books:

Rubenstein, Reuven Y. *Simulation and the Monte Carlo Method.* New York: John Wiley, 1981.

Fishman, George S. *Monte Carlo.* New York: Springer-Verlag, 1996.

Sobol, Ilya M. *A Primer for the Monte Carlo Method.* Boca Raton: CRC Press, 1994.

Software, compatible with Microsoft products to provide Monte Carlo Simulation, is available as "@RISK for Project" from:

Technology Associates
The Mansley Centre
Stratford-upon-Avon
Warwickshire CV37 9NQ
U.K.
Worldwide Sales Office:
Phone: +44 (0) 1789 297000
Fax +44 (0) 1789 292191
E-mail: info@techassoc.com
U.S. Office
Phone: 917-210-8120
Fax: 917-210-8182
Voice mail: 206-374-2154

8.3 Eliminating Holes and Overlaps

Holes exist when a requirement or issue is uncovered. Overlaps exist when requirements or issues are covered more than once, either totally or partially. The point in determining holes and overlaps is to make our processes more efficient by covering all the requirements or issues without unnecessary redundancy. One problem that overlaps will exhibit, if they are allowed to remain in the system, is to provide multiple answers to the same problem. If, in future, a change is necessary, it is possible that only one of the approaches will be changed, thereby leaving different answers to the same issue in the system. That creates, rather than solves, a problem.

Once all the approaches have been identified, they should be laid side-by-side, so to speak, and carefully analyzed for holes and overlaps. The best way to accomplish this task is to create yet another matrix with the requirement or issue across the top and the approaches up the side. Holes will be manifest by the lack of an intersect between a requirement or issue and an approach. Overlaps will be manifest by the existence of more than one intersect with a requirement or issue.

You should understand that it is possible that one approach can be used to resolve more than one requirement or issue, as in Approach A in Table 8-3. However, two approaches to the same requirement or issue create an overlap, as in Requirement 3.

Table 8-3 — Analyzing Holes and Overlaps

	Requirement 1	Requirement 2	Requirement 3	
Approach A	X		X	
Approach B		X		
Approach C				Hole
Approach D			X	
			Overlap	

8.4 Choosing the Causes

You should now have a pretty clear idea of the requirements and the answers. Looking at the matrix you just created should show which approaches to choose and where you have more work to do. You will want to choose approaches that give you the most "bang for the buck." As you continue to review the approaches, you may well want to combine the best of them into a single approach that applies to the greatest number of problems. As you read through the book and the Attachments, you will find that some approaches or forms or techniques apply to a great number of requirements or issues. The Requirements Traceability Matrix (RTM), presented in Chapter 1 and Attachment 7, is one such approach that is applied to many issues. Use this same applicability as you choose your causes.

Notes

1. Jay Arthur
   2244 S. Olive St.
   Denver, CO 80224
   Phone: 888-468-1537
   303-756-9144
   E-mail: jay@qimacros.com

IMPLEMENTING THE TAILORED CHANGES

9.1 General

This chapter presents three diverse techniques for implementing new Cause Descriptions and a process to assist you in selecting the technique or techniques you will use.

9.2 Implementation Techniques

There are undoubtedly many techniques you can use to implement these new causes you have developed. Naturally, you are free to use your own. I show three techniques in this chapter that will help greatly. In fact, I have already made accommodation in the existing Search Tables for two of the techniques.

First, you will find blanks in the Search Tables provided so that you can "slip in fixes" with subalphas that start where the filled-in Search Table subalphas leave off. When you review the Search Tables, you will find that each "family of causes" can accommodate seven potential causes (a through g) even though only two or three may have been used. The unused entry lines are designed to allow you to slip in new causes that relate to that family but may be unique to your product or company. You can simply fill in the new causes as they are identified.

Second, you will find additional blanks for the Search Tables that start at the end of the filled-in Cause Descriptions. These are provided as "On-Ramps" to allow you to add additional "families of causes" you discover that are unique to your product or company.

9.2.1 SLIPPING IN THE FIX

The process of "Slipping in the Fix" is one of putting the fix in where it belongs but not changing the basic ordering technique. This will put the fixes in approximately the right place for future use. Space has been left in the basic tables for you to make these entries. These rows have been left uncoded so you can type your entries directly into the tables. A representation of this technique is shown in Table 9-1.

Table 9-1 — Spaces for "Slipping in the Fix"

3	POLICIES, PLANS & PROCESSES			
3a	There is a clear trail between standard policies, plans, and program/project technical plans	Expand	No	Yes
3b	There is a clear trail between customer policies and the program/project and technical plans	Expand	No	Yes
3c	There is a clear trail between enterprise policies and the program/project and technical plans	Expand	No	Yes
		Expand	No	Yes
		Expand	No	Yes
		Expand	No	Yes

9.2.2 CREATING "ON-RAMPS"

The process of creating On-Ramps is a part of the planning process. When you are modifying the Search Tables and Cause Descriptions for your own use, simply accommodate changes that are sure to come. On-Ramps have been created for your data entry within the compact disk (CD) that accompanies this book. A representation of this technique is shown in Table 9-2.

The blank lines in the tables have been left uncoded so you can type your entries directly into the tables. The links however are coded and will work the same as they do in the provided tables.

Table 9-2 — Spaces for "On-Ramps"

TECHNICAL SEARCH TABLES (ADDED)				
70				
70a		Expand	No	Yes
70b		Expand	No	Yes
70c		Expand	No	Yes
70d		Expand	No	Yes
70e		Expand	No	Yes
70f		Expand	No	Yes
70g		Expand	No	Yes

9.2.3 "DUMPING" THE FIX

The process of "Dumping" the fix is simply a matter of dumping in the fix whenever it is discovered. This is a "quick and dirty" method of getting the job done and may be what you need because of time constraints. My suggestion is that you go back later and clean up the result of this technique by better organizing its incorporation when you have time.

9.3 Selecting Your Technique

The selection of your technique will probably be controlled by two things: the time available and your personality. If you have the time available, meaning you are in the Planning Phase, and if your personality is one of organization, you will probably use the technique of "Creating On-Ramps." If you are in the middle of your program and pressed for time but you have an organized personality, you will probably choose the technique of "Slipping in the Fix." If you are up to your hips in alligators and just want to get the job done and get on to the next issue, you will probably use the "Dumping" technique. Personally, I prefer the "On-Ramp" technique but I have "been there, done that" and have had to use the other techniques at times.

CHAPTER 10

CONCLUDING

10.1 General

As a project manager, you probably consider yourself through. After all, you found the problem, created a fix, invented new metrics, and incorporated the whole thing into your project that is now operating as it should. You've done your part so you're through, right? Wrong! Now is the time to follow through. Even though the program or project is temporary, by definition it has a beginning and an end, and you have a responsibility to the continuum, the enterprise. It was the enterprise that created the project or program in the first place, and it will be the enterprise that prevails after the project or program is completed.

Every company operates a little differently so you'll need to make your involvement consistent with how your company does business. Whatever it is, the findings you came up with must be incorporated back into how the company, the enterprise, the program, and the project do business. The "thing" that created the problem in the first place must be corrected. If you followed all the steps in this plan, you should know what the "thing" is. Now the issue is how to fix it.

10.2 The Concluding Process

Now that you have been through finding the causes of problems and expanding the cause base, you are in good position to carry the concept to the entire enterprise. Now is the time to gather together all the project managers, the quality manager, and the training manager and apply all this to the entire enterprise. It could well be that your enterprise wants you to continue with your project essentially unencumbered. After all, that's your primary task. In this case, hand off the findings to the person designated by the enterprise for follow-up. If you are an executive above the project level, ensure that the responsible project manager is involved in the conclusion process.

10.2.1 QUANTUM IMPROVEMENT

The principal thesis of Quantum Improvement (QI) is really just an extension of the 80/20 Rule by compounding the multipliers. Fundamentally, QI assumes that the top 20 percent of the 80/20 Rule is nonlinear and projects that one percent of the problems cost (or return) 50 percent of the money. What you want to do in this part of the process is to ensure that at least the most important findings are incorporated into the ongoing process.

Remember how the 85:15 Rule and the Pareto Principle and the Monte Carlo Simulation technique work? What was common to all of them? That just a few problems cause the most trouble or cost the most money, or both. That's the idea behind Quantum Improvement: To make a quantum leap with a minimum of effort.

This is the perfect place to implement or reimplement the concept of benchmarking. Pull together the benchmarks that represent your competition and evaluate your position with regard to them. Use Quantum Improvement techniques to select the best of the best of the best and make startling improvements.

There are many processes available that claim to do all things for all people: Total Quality Management (TQM), Total Quality Leadership (TQL), Quantum Improvement (QI), Quantum Process Improvement (QPI), Reengineering, Six Sigma, Business Process Redesign (BPR), Business Process Improvement (BPI) and a host of others. The truth is that each has something to offer but none is a panacea.

I can't recommend a company or consultant to perform this task for you. You need to do your own analysis based on your own needs. I do suggest you use a consultant or company that doesn't promise to solve all your problems. Your improvement process should be accomplished in stages. Until now, I have recommended using some technique, such as Pareto Analysis, that gives the greatest result first. Now however, you are dealing with people, with management, with employees. The approach in this instance is to attack the "lowest hanging fruit" first, so long as they represent important issues, and then evaluate the results. Early successes are important motivators to continue the effort. To try to change the entire culture of the enterprise is a sure path to failure.

Don't leave it all behind just because you made a breakthrough. Institute a program of "continuous improvement," but give it the resources that it will return to you. In other words, make your Continuing Improvement Process a series of Quantum Improvements. Above all, don't try to do it all at once.

Whatever process you choose, use a facilitator. Someone who is trained in facilitating and someone without "a dog in the fight." That is, someone who is independent and objective.

Back to the 85:15 Rule again. It says that 85 percent of the problems come from the processes (meaning documentation) and only 15 percent of the problems come from people. That rather suggests that you attack your documentation system first, doesn't it? Not only does that follow the 85:15 Rule but you can do it offline without involving the operating troops and thereby reducing efficiency.

10.2.2 DOCUMENTATION

Your documentation drives the actions of all the people in your corporation, company, enterprise, and project or program. If your documentation is incorrect, your process and actions are going to be incorrect. If your people are operating outside the established, documented policies, processes, and procedures, you've got a real problem.

If you are a medium or large company, you probably have a number of documents that drive your processes. In fact, the number of policies, processes, and procedures that exist in a company are usually a function of the size of the company. It follows then that if you are a small company, you have few, if any, policies, processes, and procedures. All that is understandable.

If you are part of an enterprise that deals in projects or programs, you must have more than just a few people in your company. To fit that profile, you must have executives, staff, and operations and that means you need centralized documentation, and that usually means a library. A library can take several forms. It can be a box of books, an organized place for filing documents, or a computer. The documents can be your own or they can be imported from other sources. Additionally, the documents can be hard—meaning books—or soft—meaning in a computer somewhere. Most likely, they are a combination of both.

When considering a library, consider the order of the documents shown in Figure 10-1. The order is important, particularly on the high end. If you are a very small company, you will have your own priorities. You will probably start at the Processes level or even the Reference Documents Level. The Policy level isn't particularly important because the guy who establishes policy is standing next to you. Normally, however, in a medium or large company, you need policies before you need processes, plans, and procedures. Reference documents and specifications will be a matter of doing business.

Let's assume that you are a medium or large company and already have a traditional library. It will be a huge step in the right direction to have all (or at least part) of that documentation in digital form. That form allows easy updating and follows the first rule of modern documentation: "Don't create, cut and paste." It allows the supervisor on the floor to have a copy of financial policies as well as copies of current work orders stored in the computer. It also allows you to control the documentation by ensuring a single master copy that is referenced by all users.

Figure 10-2 presents a schematic of an electronic library. The cylinder in the center is the central computer of the database that contains all the digitized documentation data. As you can see, that data is available to all personnel with computer access. In today's world, that usually means everybody. Further, all

Figure 10-1 — A Typical Traditional Library

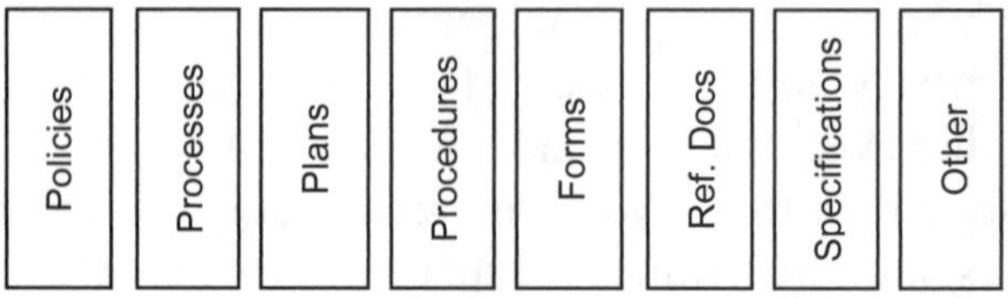

Policies	Processes	Plans	Procedures	Forms	Ref. Docs	Specifications	Other

Figure 10-2 — Schematic of an Electronic Library

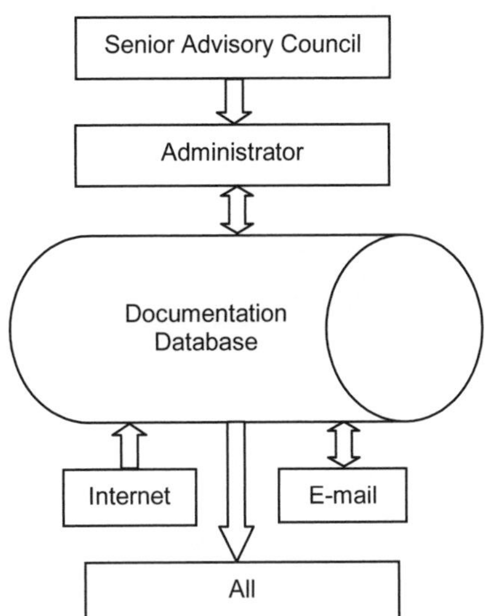

the employees could now have e-mail capability and Internet connectivity for communication. At the top of the diagram, you will see some terms that may or may not be familiar. Certainly, nearly everyone understands who the Administrator is. That's the person responsible for inputting and maintaining and controlling the database, as directed. The Senior Advisory Council is the authority for database content. The "Council" can indeed be a council, or it can be one person. Your company will decide on how large it should be and who should be a part of it. With the simple diagram shown in Figure 10-2, you can see the concept of the Electronic Library. I go into a considerable amount of detail in my Strategy for Success workshops regarding how to set up and control an electronic library for your scheme.

10.3 Data Trail

It is imperative that you have a data trail from the policy level to the implementation level and from the requirements to the sell-off test. In other words, throughout the system. To simply have a "bunch of books" is not a documentation system. In fact, it's not even a library. I spent a lot of time in this book encouraging a data trail from the requirement through the programmatics and the technical aspects of your project. The same is true of your administrative link. In my Strategy for Success workshops, I spend a lot of time going through the documentation to performance links and back again. Believe me, it's worth the effort.

10.4 Modifying Methods

Well, just how do you modify the information in (and not yet in) your database? The techniques will vary according to who is responsible for the data in the first place.

Project data as it applies to your project, there should be no problem at all. After all, it is you who are responsible for this data, and you have control of your Program and Technical Plans and all the other data generated by your project. As Nike says: "Just do it!"

Project data that will be applicable to other projects should be a part of the enterprise database. That data should be routed through the "Senior Advisory Council" or whoever else is responsible for commonizing and approving data to be used by all projects and incorporated into the database.

Corporate, company, or enterprise data that will be applicable to the entire enterprise should be a part of the enterprise database. That data should be routed through the "Senior Advisory Council" or whoever else is responsible for commonizing and approving data to be used by all projects. It should be clear at this point why an enterprise needs a "Senior Advisory Council."

Customer data takes a different route. Either the contracts manager or a senior enterprise executive should draft correspondence to the customer suggesting the change to the customer documentation and provide substantiating documentation as to why this needs to be done. This is a diplomatic issue and should be handled by someone in the organization capable of handling diplomatic correspondence. Incorrect handling of this issue could end up with a situation that could create far more harm than good.

Standard documentation, such at that written by a standards group, must be handled by an expert qualified to speak on the subject. After all, the standards group had a committee of experts that created that standards data—after much research and argument—in the first place. Be sure to substantiate your position clearly and thoroughly. Be absolutely certain that you are correct and have your correspondence drafted by an expert and cosigned by a senior enterprise executive. When everyone is satisfied, send your correspondence to the standards organization.

USING THE COMPACT DISK (CD)

11.1 General

The data on the Compact Disk (CD) complement the tables and Cause Descriptions in the book. The presentation, however, is slightly different. The add-on processes are unique to the book and are not repeated on the CD. It is best to read the book first and get a feel for how to use the tables and Cause Descriptions and for the add-on process.

If your project is failing or off-track, you can jump straight into the data on the CD. You will be guided by simple instructions. When you correct the problem, please, go back and read the book to preclude your project getting off-track again.

11.2 Loading

Insert the enclosed CD into the CD tray on your computer. The CD should open automatically but, if it does not, double click on the My Computer icon and then double click on Blueprint (D:). The CD will open. It is a native program and does not need installation.

11.3 Using the Tables

The tables on the CD are similar to the tables in the book except that they are designed to be continuous and interactive. As you click on each action—Explain, Yes or No —you will be taken automatically to the correct detail. Chapter 1 explains this action in more detail.

The tables are designed to allow you to enter your data into spaces provided and to create your own Cause Descriptions. These specific actions allow you to enter your own data into the blank spaces provided. However, you cannot change the existing table entries or existing Cause Descriptions. Chapter 9 explains this action in more detail.

You are allowed to print anything from the CD but you may not copy the CD.

11.4 Using the Attachments

The Attachments in the book are, by necessity, reduced to book size. The Attachment materials contained in the CD, however, are standard (8½ x 11) size. This means you can copy them onto your computer and change them to fit your project without a lot of retyping.

SUMMARY

At the outset, I introduced the Phoenix—a mythical bird that died and reconstituted itself and rose from the ashes. That was the theme of the book—to rise from the ashes created by a failure of the project or program somewhere in its lifetime.

In Chapter 1, you searched for a cause for the problem by defining the "Family of Causes" to which the problem or issue belonged and then using the Search Tables to find the Causes that contributed to the problem or issue. When you found the Cause, you turned to the Cause Description to discover a Recovery Plan to bring the project back into tolerance again. At the end of Chapter 1, it was recognized that the Search Tables and Cause Descriptions provided in the book would not be all-encompassing for every problem or issue that could possibly exist in any or all projects/programs. You recognized that you needed a process to expand the Search Tables and Cause Descriptions to tailor them to your particular situation.

To support Chapter 1 and to continue with the idea of creating new issues unique (or peculiar, if you prefer) to your product or company, I provided several techniques in Chapter 6 to broaden the scope of the Search Tables and the supporting Cause Descriptions. The techniques presented were: Brainstorming, Benchmarking, Standard Processes, Customer Processes, Enterprise Processes, and Project/Program Processes.

Now that you had this large amount of data, you needed to organize it. In Chapter 7, I presented four ordering techniques to quickly order the data. The techniques were: The 85:15 Rule, Cause and Effect Diagrams, Affinity Diagrams, and Relationship Diagrams.

It is good to have the data ordered, but now the data must be evaluated. In Chapter 8, I presented four analysis techniques to accomplish this end. Remember, these analytical techniques were: Pareto Analysis, Force Field Analysis, Failure Mode Effect Analysis (FMEA), and finally, Monte Carlo Simulation. At the end of the chapter you were able to select the causes you wanted to include in your expanded Search Tables and Cause Descriptions and the order in which you should incorporate them.

To review the overall process, consider Table 12-1. This table is a composition of the data originally presented as Table 6-1 Expansion Methodologies, Table 7-1 Ordering Techniques, and Table 8-1 Analysis Techniques.

Consider solving a typical problem. In the Process Table, use all the techniques to generate the largest pile of data you can. Then proceed to the Ordering Table, and first use the 85:15 technique to separate your data into a "process" pile and a "people" pile. Then create a Cause and Effect Diagram to organize your data (perhaps you chose to only use the "process" pile). Finally, go to the Analysis Table and perform a Pareto Analysis to get the "biggest bang for the buck." If you are solving a technical problem, you may want to continue on (using the dotted lines) to the Failure Mode Effect Analysis to predict the results before you implement the solution.

This is only one "data trail" you can choose through the tables. That's why I provided a number of alternatives to allow you to choose the ones that are right for you. In Chapter 9, you were confronted with how to incorporate the new causes into your project and indeed, into the other projects/programs of the enterprise. I presented three methods for incorporating these new causes. You will recall that those techniques were called Creating "On-Ramps," "Slipping in the Fix," and "Dumping" the Fix. You were then given methods for selecting your technique based on the needs of the project, the time available, and your own personality. And, to provide the tools to incorporate these changes, I left room in the Search Tables for you to "Slip in the Fixes" or to "Dump the Fixes."

Table 12-1 — Process Flow-Through Tables

Process	Purpose
Brainstorming	To create a large body of related data
Benchmarking	To discover/research "Best Practices" or "Best-in-Class" for your industry or product
Standard Processes	To discover/research standard processes in your industry or in support of your industry
Customer Processes	To discover/research processes unique to your customers
Enterprise Processes	To discover/research processes characteristic of your enterprise to serve this (these) business areas
Project/Program Processes	To provide processes specifically for this project/program

Ordering Technique	Purpose
85:15 Rule	To organize information into "process" or "people" categories.
Cause and Effect Diagrams	To show the relationship of reasons to causes and causes to effects
Affinity Diagrams	To organize large groups of information into meaningful categories
Relationship Diagrams	To show the relationship(s) between elements

Analysis Technique	Purpose
Pareto Analysis	To select the 20 percent of the issues that provide 80 percent of the results
Force Field Analysis	To understand restraining forces and driving forces
Failure Mode Effect Analysis (FMEA)	To predict potential failures
Monte Carlo Simulation	To refine estimates

Finally, the whole thing was concluded by recognizing that the "thing" that had allowed the project to be derailed in the first place needed to be corrected. It was suggested that you use Quantum Improvement methods and then update the documentation and that you provide a complete data trail back to the "offending" direction and the "how" of modifying. The technical aspects of modification as well as the diplomatic efforts were discussed.

Throughout the whole book, I have advocated using the Search Tables as a checklist and the Cause Descriptions as the detail for *planning* your project. Please, don't let your project get to the point of failure before looking ahead at what might happen and then building in processes, steps, and metrics to avoid the issue and determine when a problem is about to occur.

You all know this is what you should do, but for some reason it rarely gets done completely. When that occurs and a project element goes out-of-tolerance, you will find that this book is worth its weight in gold.

GLOSSARY

After Receipt of Order (ARO) – A number, usually expressed in days, weeks, or months, as a point after the official notification of the start of the project. Example: The PDR is due 90 days ARO. This technique allows the elements of a project schedule to move relative to the award or beginning of a project or program.

Alliance – A grouping of two or more companies for one project or program (a tactical alliance) or for all projects or programs (a strategic alliance) that require a particular combination of products or services.

Architecture – The structure established for the system as a whole or the structure established for a subsystem within the system.

Assertion – An affirmative statement.

Balanced Scorecard – A complex strategy-based process. The process involves researching the competitive environment, customers, stakeholders, employees, and company financial and growth objectives.

Benchmark – Also referred to as Best Practices, Exemplary Practices, and Business Excellence. Usually a series of studies regarding business processes and practices among businesses in the same or sometimes disparate business areas. You can use the benchmarks to compare your performance to others. The benchmarks may or may not be the best figure of excellence.

Best-of-Breed – A term applied to a system or process that has singular or limited application but is the best there is for that application. The highest level of achievement for that element.

Brassboard – Similar to Breadboard (below) but usually with hard parts that are soldered or welded together. Not a deliverable.

Breadboard – A table layout of the article being developed so that parts and wiring can be changed easily. Breadboards are usually many times the physical size of the final product. Not a deliverable.

Budget Review – A review of the budget associated with all or part of a task or contract. Usually, but not always, Budget Reviews are conducted concurrently with Schedule Reviews and Performance Reviews in Project, Program, or Division Reviews.

Business Process Improvement – A generalized term that includes such specific programs as Total Quality Management (TQM), Business Process Reengineering (BPR), Business Process Redesign (also referred to as BPR), Benchmarking, and Best Practices as well as other less well-known programs aimed at improving the process of a business.

Buying In – The act of bidding a project or program at cost or less than cost for any number of reasons.

Capability Matrix – A matrix consisting of tasks along the side and previous projects across the top. An intersect is acknowledged whenever the project contained the task and was successfully completed. The purpose of the capability matrix is to determine whether or not to bid a program or to identify those capabilities in inventory and those needed to approach a program or project.

Capability Maturity Model (CMM) – The Capability Maturity Model for Software (CMM or SW-CMM) is a model for judging the maturity of the software processes of an organization and for identifying the key practices that are required to increase the maturity of these processes. The SW-CMM has been developed by the software community with stewardship by the SEI. (From the SEI/Carnegie Mellon Web site.)

Challenge (Tasking) – A top-down application of budget and/or schedule and/or manpower that is less than requested. The challenge (tasking) imposed upon a work package leader by the project office (project manager).

Change Control Process (part of the Configuration Management Process) – A process to control the technical baseline of a project to ensure the baseline is always consistent with requirements and all changes are approved and documented by both parties (customer and contractor).

Change Order (CO) – A formal change introduced into a project controlled by a Change Control Process.

Company – A corporation or partnership.

Configuration Management Process – A process designed to maintain control of the technical baseline using formalized processes and consisting of a Control Board, a Chairman of the Control Board, and procedures for receiving, modifying, documenting, implementing, and verifying changes to the baseline.

Contract Data Requirements List (CDRL) – A list of documents that are contractually deliverable under the terms of a contract.

Contract Line Item Number (CLIN) – An ordering or sequencing number assigned to functional or physical deliverables that are contractually required on a program.

Corporation – A legal entity composed of a number of people joined together for a common purpose. Such legal entities are formed under local, state, or federal laws. Some corporations are public and some are private; some private corporations are organized for profit and some are organized for nonprofit. Private corporations often issue stock to their owners in return for the money they invest. [Modified from *The Plain-Language Law Dictionary* by Robert Rothenberg (see bibliography)].

Cost of Quality – A cost factor added to the basic bid cost by a subcontractor for labor and materials to bring the subcontractor's product up to the quality he should have produced but didn't. The Cost of Quality is a consideration when evaluating bids by subcontractors. The amount bid by a subcontractor plus the quantified Cost of Quality is the true bid of that subcontractor.

Cost Plus Contract – A contract that recognizes that profit is a necessary part of getting a job done. Cost plus contracts allow a profit over and above the cost involved.

Cost Review – A review of the cost associated with all or part of a task or contract. Usually, but not always, cost reviews are conducted concurrently with Schedule Reviews and Performance Reviews in Project, Program, or Division Reviews.

Cost Type Contract – A contract that includes cost plus provisions. The fee structure may be a percentage of cost, a fixed percentage or original bid cost, an award amount or an incentive amount. All structures are above the cost of getting the job done except that some Cost Plus Incentive Fee (CPIF) contracts have negative fee considerations as well as positive fee considerations.

Customer Meeting – A meeting with the customer, usually on a formal basis, where an agenda and minutes are a part of the meeting. May be scheduled and required by the requirements document (contract) or may be quickly called by the customer.

Customer Processes – Those processes established by a customer for use in performing that customer's programs or projects. Examples of such processes are: Mil Standards, DoD Standards, Data Item Descriptions (DIDs), NASA Standards, FAA Standards, Municipal Government Standards, and so on.

Customer Requirements – Specific requirements invoked in a requirement document (contract) to be a part of the task at hand. In this case, the requirement may be stated or referenced.

Data Item Description (DID) – A document consisting of a few sheets that outlines the format and requirements for a specific data report to be submitted as part of a contract. DIDs are assigned descriptive alphanumeric sequences. Originally issued to support federal government contracts but are now more widely used.

Design Review – A periodic review of the design and its requirements. Typically the performer (contractor) presents and defends the design together with all supporting data. Design Reviews are typically performed on an ever more detailed basis and frequently will be performed on an incremental basis.

DOD – The Department of Defense of the United States of America. Most other countries refer to this agency as the Ministry of Defense or MOD.

EIA – See Electronic Industries Alliance.

Electronic Industries Alliance (EIA) – An organization of over 2,300 member companies that, among other activities, mediates recommended standards by its members and publishes the results.

Enterprise – The "Today" term for an economic unit. An enterprise may be a corporation, a company, a profit center, or a cost center within a company or corporation.

Enterprise (Corporate/Company) Processes – Those policies, plans, processes, and procedures at the enterprise level that drive the content of project and technical plans and the conduct of project activities.

Enterprise Requirements – Specific requirements invoked by an enterprise on all or specific projects at the judgment of the enterprise.

Experience Window – A tool to quickly evaluate whether or not you should bid or can perform a certain task. The principal variables are customer experience and product experience.

Fast Track – A method of conducting elements of a project in parallel, rather than in series, or by deleting a task, or truncating the elements of a task in terms of time or by taking a risk on one or more elements of the project to shorten the overall time involved in that element and, ultimately, the project.

Firm Fixed Price (FFP) – A contract that is bid and awarded as a fixed amount. The customer pays a firm fixed price for some amount of work. The contractor's fee or profit is contained within that price.

First Article – The first article produced by the production process. The First Article is used not only to validate the design but to validate the production process as well. Sometimes the First Article is delivered first but, most often, its delivery is held in abeyance, and it is used to try out improvements in design and processes. Frequently, the First Article is delivered last.

Fixed Price Contract – A contract in which the basic price is fixed but the fee structure can be of several different types such as Fixed Price/Incentive Fee (FP/IF), Fixed Price/Award Fee (FP/AF), and Firm Fixed Price (FFP).

Force Majeure – From the French, generally meaning an act of God but now used as a legal term that allows recovery of costs or limits liability (depending on how written) when an act of war or superior force, such as a flood, fire, etc., impacts the performance of the task.

Functional Manager – A line manager in charge of a function such as software engineering, hardware engineering, etc.

General and Administrative (G&A) – An element of cost that generally includes the salaries of nonoperating personnel such as corporate management, human resources, finance, etc., as well as Bid and Proposal (B&P) costs. Some companies include these costs as overhead or burden. The breakout of costs into different categories is an accounting function and is usually standardized within the type of industry in which you operate.

IEEE – See Institute of Electrical and Electronic Engineers, Inc.

Independent Research and Development (IR&D) – Usually an in-house Research and Development (R&D) program funded by the company. When the company funds this research, all results are the property of the company and are usually patented.

In-Process Review – A review, frequently informal, that is conducted while a project is in process and before a major formal review.

Institute of Electrical and Electronic Engineers, Inc. (IEEE) – A nonprofit, technical professional association of more than 377,000 individual members in 150 countries. The IEEE is a leading authority in establishing and maintaining consensus-based standards in electrical and electronic industries.

International Standards Organization (ISO) – The ISO, established in 1947, is a worldwide federation of national standards bodies from some 140 countries, one from each country whose mission is to promote the development of standardization and related activities in the world resulting in international agreements that are published as International Standards. (Paraphrased from the ISO Web site.)

Lessons Learned – A conference, or simply a report, at the end of a project to review the situations that occurred during the project and their impact on the project and how the situations could be avoided or cured in the future.

Liquidated Damages – An amount stated in a contract, which the parties agree is an estimation of damages owed to one of the parties in the event there has been a breach by the other. (From the *Plain Law Dictionary* by Medbook Publications and Parsons Technology, Inc., 1997.)

Materials – Items where the Specification is determined by the vendor. You are buying to the vendor's Specification, not yours.

Milestone Review – A review of the milestones in the schedule against work accomplished.

MIL-HDBK – Military Handbook

MIL-SPEC – Military Specification

MIL-STD – Military Standard

Mission Statement – A statement of an action for the organization to take and a positive outcome of that action in one sentence. As an example, Abraham Lincoln's mission: To preserve the Union.

Myers-Briggs Type Indicator (MBTI) – A four-character designator derived from a four-pair, eight-character set resulting in sixteen combinations that represent a type of person (or later a company). Originated by Isabel Myers and Katherine Briggs. Example: An ENTJ is an **E**xtrovert (as opposed to an Introvert), **IN**tuitive (as opposed to Sensing), **T**hinking (as opposed to Feeling), **J**udgmental (as opposed to **P**erceiving) type of person.

NASA – National Aeronautics and Space Administration.

Negotiating Team – See Requirements Definition Team.

Negotiation Envelope – Predetermined limits to which the Negotiating Team can negotiate. Usually includes scope, schedule, cost, and manpower.

On the Job Training (OJT) – Informal training provided on the job by others involved in the same category of work.

Out-of-Tolerance – A measured parameter that is beyond its nominal value, plus or minus a percentage of that value that is the allowable range in which that parameter may operate.

PERT – See Program Evaluation Review Technique.

Profit and Loss (P&L) – The result of a contract beyond cost. A contract that returns money beyond all costs is a profit. A contract that costs more than its income is a loss.

Profit and Loss (P&L) Responsibility – Responsibility assigned to a program manager for operating the program and returning a profit to the company.

Program Advisory Council – A special-purpose management team that advises, but does not manage, the project or program team. The Program Advisory Council acts as a transparent link between the project team and management and the customer.

Program Evaluation Review Technique (PERT) – A scheduling system characterized by linking together the longest "string" of events to create a critical path.

Program Manager – The same as a project manager, except a program manager has P&L responsibility and manages a contract with a customer outside the parent organization.

Program Office – See Project Office.

Programmatic – Those issues associated with the management of a project or program. Such issues include budget, schedule, etc. Programmatic issues are separate and distinct from technical issues.

Project Manager – The individual responsible for managing the entire project internal to the parent company.

Project Meeting – Same as team meeting.

Project Office – The group of people and functions that surround the management of a project or program. These functions are usually those performed by the project manager, the administrator, and the scheduler, as well as the secretarial function. Sometimes the chief engineer is considered as a part of the Project Office.

Project Review – A review of project activities as defined by the Enterprise. Usually consists of a review of cost, schedule, and technical status at the project level and with project personnel in attendance. Usually held before a Division or higher level review to "iron out" issues.

Projectized – A project or program that essentially stands alone within an organization. The projectized organization contains all the line functions necessary to meet the requirements of the task or contract. Staff functions such as finance and human resources are usually not included although they may be in extremely large projects or programs.

Prototype – A nonproduction build of hardware or software generally used to test concepts and/or content and/or interfaces. Older terms, still in use in some places, are *Breadboard* and *Brassboard.* This term is sometimes extended to include the First Article (see above) of a production run. Prototypes should not be deliverable.

Purchase Order (PO) – A document used to commit project, program, or company funds to a certain purchase. The PO must contain the item, the vendor, the price, and the delivery date. Other contents are at the option of the company.

Reengineering – The common form of Business Process Management (BPM) used to establish standards for process design, deployment, execution, maintenance, and optimization.

Request for Proposal (RFP) – A request issued by a customer for a full response from companies. This usually means the response must include a Technical Section, a Management Section, and a Cost Section. RFPs are usually issued for complex requirements.

Request for Quotation (RFQ) – A request issued by a customer for a limited response from companies. This usually means a limited Technical Section (if any at all) and a cost for the item. RFQs sometimes require cost "back up" (the rationale for the cost).

Requirements – Webster defines requirements as something wanted or needed or something essential.

Requirements Definition Team – An ad hoc group formed to formalize the requirements for a project or program. For a project the group is a requirements definition team; for a program the group is a negotiating team.

Requirements Flow-Down Matrix (RFM) – A matrix created to track those requirements that must be flowed down and how they are flowed down to various Work Packages, subcontracts, and purchases. Example: Buy American Clause in a contract.

Requirements Traceability Matrix (RTM) – A matrix formed to track each requirement through the lifecycle of the project. The horizontal axis of the matrix begins at project start (program award) and ends with handover. The vertical axis lists each requirement.

Research and Development (R&D) – A project or program on the leading edge of technology. R&D projects can be performed in-house (see Independent Research and Development above) or for a customer as a Research and Development program.

Reverse Contract – To take a course of contractual action and advise your customer that you intend to incorporate this change unless otherwise directed. (Be careful—some customers take a dim view of this action.)

Reverse Engineer – To make a change in the Specification or design and advise the customer that you intend to incorporate this change unless otherwise directed. (Be careful—some customers take a dim view of this action.)

Risk Mitigation Plan – A plan to recognize, evaluate, and provide an approach to eliminating, mitigating, or neutralizing a risk, technical or programmatic.

Root Cause – The essential heart or underlying reason.

Schedule Review – A review of the schedule associated with all or part of a task or contract. Usually, but not always, Schedule Reviews are conducted concurrently with Cost Reviews and Performance Reviews in Project, Program, or Division Reviews.

Show Cause (Letter) – An order for a company (usually a contractor or subcontractor) to tell why it thinks the sender (usually the customer) should not take a certain action such as cancellation of the contract. Should the show cause not be answered, the letter will outline the next step that will be taken.

Software Engineering Institute (SEI) – The Software Engineering Institute (SEI) is a federally funded research and development center sponsored by the U.S. Department of Defense through the Office of the Under Secretary of Defense for Acquisition, Technology, and Logistics [OUSD (AT&L)]. The SEI's core purpose is to help others make measured improvements in their software engineering capabilities. (From the SEI/Carnegie Mellon Home Page.)

Specification (Spec) – That part of the requirements document (contract) that establishes how the system as a whole will perform.

Standard Processes – Those processes established and standardized by such organizations as IEEE, IATA, ISO, EIA, ASME, ASTM, CCITT, NEMA, UL, and a host of others. These processes are usually invoked by reference rather than by being restated.

Standard Requirements – Reference documents common to your business area or product such as IEEE Standards, SEI Standards, EIA Standards, etc., that are invoked by the requirements document (contract) or the enterprise policies, plans, processes, or procedures. These standards are usually referenced rather than being reprinted simply to save space.

Statement Of Work (SOW) – That part of the requirements document (contract) that describes what the task is and when the task will be accomplished.

Subcontract (S/C) – A contract that delegates work to a third party that contains a Statement Of Work (SOW) and usually a Specification.

Subcontract Requirements Traceability Matrix (SRTM) – A Requirements Traceability Matrix (RTM) used by a subcontractor (see Requirements Traceability Matrix above).

Sub-Program Office (SPO) – The SPO has the same responsibilities as the Program Office except that the SPO is responsible for only a portion of the overall system and usually does not have contractual responsibility and may not have P&L responsibility.

System Engineering Management Plan (SEMP) – A top-level plan that identifies and controls the overall engineering process. The SEMP is usually supported by a number of specialty engineering plans that contain much of the engineering detail.

Task (Challenge) – See Challenge (Tasking) above.

Team – A group of people, usually interdisciplinary, brought together to perform a task. A team is a casual relationship, as opposed to teaming, which is a legal relationship

Team Meeting – A meeting, usually somewhat informal, of the entire team where project issues are discussed.

Teaming – The legal association of two or more organizations (companies) to perform a specific task. Teaming (between companies) is separate and distinct from a team (individuals).

Technical Interchange Meeting (TIM) – A meeting wherein technical issues are discussed. Contractual issues are not discussed.

Tiger Team – An ad hoc group formed to pursue a specific problem or issue. Their charter may be to study the issue or to find a fix or to fix it.

Total Quality Management (TQM) – "A structured system for satisfying internal and external customers and suppliers by integrating the business environment, continuous improvement, and breakthroughs with development, improvement, and maintenance cycles while changing organizational culture." (From the Web site of Integrated Quality Dynamics, Inc.)

Vendor – A person or company that provides a product or line of products to a Specification that is usually his own.

Version Description Document (VDD) – A document that references and describes the changes included in this version of software.

Vision – The highest view of what a company is and where it wants to go.

Work Breakdown Structure (WBS) – A WBS is a description of the project/program in tree form. It is composed of the hardware, software, services, and data that completely define a project/program.

Work Package (WP) – The lowest level of the WBS that is the most efficient and cost-effective way of controlling schedule, cost, and technical performance consistent with the requirements of the customer and the performing agency (the company).

ATTACHMENTS

Attachment 1—Standard Program Plan Outline
Attachment 2—Standard Technical Plan Outline
Attachment 3—Risk Mitigation Plan
Attachment 4—Contract/Subcontract Outline
Attachment 5—Configuration Management Plan Outline
Attachment 6—Quality Assurance Plan Outline
Attachment 7—Requirements Traceability Matrix
Attachment 8—Requirements Flow-Down Matrix
Attachment 9—Data Delivery Matrix
Attachment 10—Capability Matrix
Attachment 11—Policy-to-Plan Trail
Attachment 12—Experience Window
Attachment 13—Standards Traceability Matrix
Attachment 14—Vendor Evaluation Process
Attachment 15—Design Review Approval Form
Attachment 16—In-Process Review Approval Form
Attachment 17—Negotiation Checklist
Attachment 18—Critical Success Factor (CSF) Matrix

STANDARD PROGRAM PLAN OUTLINE

The Program/Project Plan is one of the most important documents you will create to manage a project or program. The outline of the plan should be consistent from project to project. Obviously, the content of much of the plan will vary from project to project, but some of the content will also be consistent. Which is which should be a part of the enterprise policies that drive such plans.

Following is a suggested outline you can use to generate your first Project or Program Plan, even if you don't have an enterprise policy to drive it. Over time, you will find which parts of the plans are constant and which change. By using a word processing application you can create a new plan very quickly. This is particularly helpful in bidding new projects or programs. Start with the outline below and change it to fit your needs.

PROGRAM

STANDARD PROGRAM PLAN OUTLINE

TABLE OF CONTENTS

1 Introduction

2 Scope

2.1 Program Description

2.2 Deliverables

2.3 Schedule

2.4 Sell-Off Criteria

3 Applicable Documents

3.1 Contract

3.2 Customer Documents

4 Unusual Contract Clauses

5 Management

5.1 Organization and Responsibilities

5.1.1 General

5.1.2 System Management

5.1.3 Subcontracts and Materials

5.1.4 Data Management

5.1.5 Configuration Management

5.1.6 Quality Assurance

5.1.7 Team Members and Alliances

5.1.8 Training

5.2 Make/Buy Decisions

5.3 Safety

5.4 Security

5.5 Facilities

5.6 Standardization

5.7 Program Risks
6 Program Controls
6.1 Cost and Schedule Controls
6.2 Communication Control
6.3 Status Meetings
6.4 Design Reviews
6.5 Specification Control
6.6 Documentation Control
6.7 Customer Furnished Property Control
6.8 Action Items
6.9 War Room
7 Schedule
8 Requirements Flow-Down
9 Work Breakdown Structure (WBS)
10 Project Work Authorization
11 Technical Approach
12 Training
13 Packing and Shipping
14 Delivery
15 Field Operations
16 Operations and Maintenance
GLOSSARY
APPENDICES
A DEFINITIONS
B DELIVERABLES
C CONTRACT DATA REQUIREMENTS LIST (CDRL)
D CUSTOMER STANDARD REQUIREMENTS
E WORK BREAKDOWN STRUCTURE (WBS) AND WBS DICTIONARY
ATTACHMENTS
1 Capital Management Plan
2 Communication Control Plan

3 Configuration Management Plan
4 Data Management Plan
5 Delivery Plan
6 Facility Plan
7 Field Plan
8 Customer-Furnished Property Plan
9 Make or Buy Plan
10 Subcontract and Material Management Plan
11 Operations and Maintenance Plan
12 Packing and Shipping Plan
13 Project Work Authorizations
14 Quality Control Plan
15 Requirements Flow-Down Plan
16 Risk Mitigation Plan
17 Safety Plan
18 Schedule
19 Security Plan
20 Small Business Plan
21 Standardization Plan
22 Test Plan
23 Training Plan
24 Engineering Plan
25 Transition Plan
26 Manufacturing Plan
27 Sell-Off Plan

STANDARD TECHNICAL PLAN OUTLINE

Because the purposes of companies vary widely, their Technical Plans will vary widely as well. Once established within an enterprise however, the outline and purpose of the Technical Plan will be relatively constant. The content will, of course, change from project to project.

The basis of the following Technical Plan Outline is MIL-STD-490. It is purposely comprehensive. Start with this outline and modify it to your needs.

STANDARD TECHNICAL PLAN OUTLINE

TABLE OF CONTENTS

Part III—Specialty Engineering Plans

Plan	*Title*
1.0*	Concept of Operation
2.0*	Configuration Management Plan
3.0	Contamination and Corrosion Control Plan
4.0	EMI/EMC Plan
5.0*	Engineering Plan
6.0	Environmental Engineering Plan
7.0†	Hardware Development Plan
8.0	Human Engineering Plan
9.0	Logistic Support Analysis (LSA)
10.0	Mantainability Plan
11.0	Manufacturing Management Plan
12.0	Mass Properties Control Plan
13.0	Packaging, Handling, Storage, and Transportation Plan
14.0	Parts, Materials, and Process Control Plan
15.0	Producibility Plan
16.0	Production Engineering Plan
17.0*	Quality Plan
18.0*	RMA Plan
19.0	Requirements Plan
20.0	Safety Plan
21.0	Security Plan
22.0†	Software Development Plans and Standards
23.0†	Software Quality Plan
24.0	Standardization Plan

---

*Subplans, in addition to the Program Plan and Technical Plan, that should always be a part of the proposal or at least be completed at the time of the proposal. Other plans may also be a part of the proposal based on the nature of the requirement.
†Subplan to be included with the above dependent on the output product.

25.0* System Test Plan
26.0* Technical Data Management Plan
27.0* Technical Performance Measurement Plan
28.0* Technical Risk Management Plan
29.0 Value Engineering Plan
30.0 Vulnerability/Survivability Plan
31.0 Weight Control Plan

---

*Subplans, in addition to the Program Plan and Technical Plan, that should always be a part of the proposal or at least be completed at the time of the proposal. Other plans may also be a part of the proposal based on the nature of the requirement.

RISK MITIGATION PLAN

The Risk Mitigation Plan provides direction and control for the identification, documentation, correction methodology, and closure of risks on the program.

Risk Management is an organized, systematic decision-making process designed to identify, analyze, plan, track, control, and document each and all risks to increase the probability of achieving project goals. Risks are events that may or may not impact the cost, schedule, or technical quality of the project and product.

Risk management is the responsibility of everyone on the team. It implies control of possible future events and is proactive rather than reactive. There are four elements of the risk management process.

1. Risk Identification. Potential risks must be identified and managed. Once identified, risks are entered into a Risk Mitigation Form as in Figure A3-1

Figure A3-1 — Risk Mitigation Form

<PROGRAM> RISK MITIGATION FORM

Risk No. Priority Date Opened Date Closed

Risk Description

Source of Risk (i.e., SOW, Para X.X)

Mitigation Plan

Cost Exposure

Cost of Mitigation

Expected Date of Occurrence

Application of Mitigation Funds (dates & amounts)

Closure Authority:
Program Manager System Manager

M-M Form F-04028-1

and then into a Risk List as in Table A3-1. Risk identification is an element of the process that continues throughout the lifetime of the project.

2. Risk Assessment. Each risk must be characterized as to the likelihood (probability) of its occurrence (Po) and the severity of the potential consequences (So). When the assessments are made, the characteristics of the risk are documented in the Risk List.
3. Risk Disposition. Each risk must be assigned to an individual designated as the risk manager for that risk (this will likely involve a number of different people). Once a risk has been assessed, the project team must consider how to handle it. Alternatives include:

   Avoidance. Avoidance is best accomplished during the bid or negotiation process. Once the project has started, avoidance is difficult to accomplish.

Table A3-1 — Risk List

Risk No.	Risk	Resp	Po*	So*	Priority (Po × So)	Status
P-001	System Weight	Smith	.6	.8	.48	In Proc
P-002	Deceleration	Jones	.5	.5	.25	In Proc
P-003	Rxo BER	Nacker	.3	.4	.12	In Proc

Because this is the best method of risk mitigation, it should not be summarily dismissed, however. Consider alternative architecture, design, or project approaches that would avoid the incidence of this risk altogether.

Transfer. It may be possible to transfer a risk to a subcontractor or to a third party such as an insurance agency. In the final analysis, however, the program team is still ultimately responsible for the risk.

Sharing. When the risk cannot be appropriately transferred—and when it is not in the best interest of the program team to assume the risk—the risk may be shared with the customer, a subcontractor, or a third party. Such shared risks require extensive monitoring. Risk sharing with the customer is quite common in Research and Development (R&D) contracts. Sharing is implemented through both cost sharing, such as cost plus contracts or arrangements, and profit sharing, such as award fee or incentive fee provisions. Risk sharing with the subcontractor is accomplished in the same way. Risk sharing with a third party such as an insurance or bonding company is simply sharing of the cost outcome. These share situations are rare.

Assumption. When all the other alternatives have not been successful, the only option left is to assume the risk. Once the risk has been directly assumed, the issue of mitigation becomes your full responsibility. This statement means that the intensity of mitigation will increase significantly. The assumption of the entire risk will require a full plan to approach and neutralize or at least mitigate the risk.

4. Risk Tracking. Once a risk has been identified, as stated in Step 1, it must be entered into the Risk List. Every risk in the Risk List must be documented in a Risk Mitigation Form.

   The size, content, and intensity of Risk Mitigation will increase as you progress further down the process steps and as the Priority (Po × So) increases. Constant vigilance and status reporting must be maintained on each risk throughout its lifetime. Some risks will require monthly attention while others will require daily or even hourly attention.

Additional references that may contribute to developing your plan are:

SECNAVINST 4105.1
DoD Directive Dir 5000.2R, paragraph 3.3.3.

ATTACHMENT 4

CONTRACT/SUBCONTRACT OUTLINE

Every contract and subcontract should consider the same issues. The contents of each should be approximately the same. If you do not have an enterprise policy or procedure to cover this situation, consider the following outline. Order is not terribly important, but content is.

- ❒ Supplies/Services Prices/Costs
- ❒ Schedule
- ❒ Statement of Work containing:
  - Task Description
  - Deliverable Documents List (sometimes called Contract Data Requirements List or CDRL)
  - Period of Performance

- Schedule
- Reference Documents
- Modifying Factors (for instance, the number of labor hours of specific disciplines that must be provided)

❒ Specification containing:
- Scope of the Document
- Applicable Documents
- Requirements
- Item Definition
- Performance Characteristics
- Physical Characteristics
- The major components of the principal item and the primary interfaces between such major components and other items with which it must be compatible
- Qualification Requirements (for software) or Quality Assurance Provisions (for hardware)
- Process Requirements, if needed
- Materials Requirements, if needed

❒ Interface Control Document

❒ Packaging and Marking

❒ Inspection and Acceptance

❒ Delivery or Performance

❒ Contract Administration Data

❒ Special Contract Requirements

❒ Contract Clauses

❒ Representations and Certifications

❒ Attachments

❒ Contract/Subcontract Data Requirements List (CDRL or SDRL)

❒ Special Attachments

A properly defined SOW will contain (either incorporated or appended) the findings of the requirements discussions (negotiations). These findings are as much a part of the requirements document (contract) as the initial document.

Any item in or referenced by the SOW is a legal part of the SOW. Therefore, each of these items must be understood. It is a good idea to search the entire

SOW and find all the requirements and the modifiers and group them together for your own purposes.

There are several types of specifications. MIL-STD-490 has established and defined five major specification (Spec) types as well as a number of subtypes. The standard provides a great deal of good information regarding the content and purpose of each specification type. The specification types are shown in Table A4-1.

Table A4-1 — Specification Types

Type	Specification
A	System/Subsystem/Segment
B	Development
B1	Prime Item
B2	Critical Item
B3	Non-complex Item
B4	Facility of Ship
B5	Software
C	Product
C1a	Prime Item Function
C1b	Prime Item Fabrication
C2a	Critical Item Function
C2b	Critical Item Fabrication
C3	Non-complex Item fabrication
C4	Inventory Item
C5	Software
D	Process
E	Material

Additional Resources:

MIL-STD-245

ATTACHMENT 5

CONFIGURATION MANAGEMENT PLAN OUTLINE

1. INTRODUCTION

Purpose, scope, and a brief description of the system at top level, a description of the plan's major features and objectives, and a concise summary of your approach to CM (Configuration Management).

2. REFERENCE DOCUMENTS

Refers to specifications, standards, manuals, and other documents.

3. ORGANIZATION

The organization with emphasis on the CM activities including responsibility and authority for CM of all groups and organizations including their role in configuration control boards and the interfaces between the CM organization and outside organizations.

4. CONFIGURATION MANAGEMENT PHASING AND MILESTONES

The sequence of events and milestones for implementation of CM in phase with major program milestones and events. The establishment of configuration control boards and the conduct of configuration audits.

5. DATA MANAGEMENT

The methods for meeting the CM technical data requirements.

6. CONFIGURATION IDENTIFICATION

The identification of the Hardware Configuration Items (HWCIs) and Computer Software Configuration Item (CSCIs).

7. INTERFACE MANAGEMENT

The procedures for the establishment of interface agreements.

8. CONFIGURATION CONTROL

The responsibilities and authority of your configuration control board, the classification of changes, and the level of authority for change approval/concurrence.

9. CONFIGURATION STATUS ACCOUNTING

The procedures for collecting, recording, processing, and maintaining CM data.

10. CONFIGURATION AUDITS

The approach to plans, procedures, documentation, and schedules for functional and physical configuration audits and the format for reporting results of in-process configuration audits.

11. SUBCONTRACTOR/VENDOR CONTROL

The methods you will use to ensure subcontractor/vendor compliance with configuration management requirements.

The above outline is a condensed version of the table of contents advocated in MIL-STD-973. Source: www.edms.redstone.army.mil/edrd/973appa.html

Additional References:

MIL-STD-973

MIL-HDBK-61

EIA 649

ISO-10007

See: www.cmiiug.com/Standards.htm for additional information.

ATTACHMENT 6

QUALITY ASSURANCE PLAN OUTLINE

PROGRAM

QUALITY ASSURANCE PLAN

1. QUALITY MANAGEMENT

1.1 QUALITY POLICY

The purpose of this Quality Assurance Plan is to detail the quality assurance principles and to establish the structure of the <Program> quality assurance program consistent with <Company> Quality Assurance Policies and the <Company> Quality Assurance Plan.

1.2 QUALITY OBJECTIVES

The following quality principles are intended to be consistent with <Company> quality policies and plans.

- ❒ All measurements will include quantitative determinations.
- ❒ Methods will be consistent.
- ❒ Measurements will be linked to a standard value.

1.3 RESPONSIBILITIES AND AUTHORITY.

The <Program> Quality Assurance Representative is responsible for the day-to-day implementation of the <Program> Quality Assurance Program, including documenting all data and identifying out-of-tolerance situations.

2. STRUCTURE OF QUALITY SYSTEMS

2.1 QUALITY ORGANIZATIONAL STRUCTURE

The <Company> Quality Assurance Director reports directly to the Vice President/General Manager.

The <Program> Quality Assurance Representative reports operationally to the <Program> Program Manager and functionally to the <Company> Quality Assurance Director.

2.2 RESOURCES AND PERSONNEL

Each participant in <Company> shares responsibility for achieving the quality objectives. Therefore, portions of the program's budget are allocated to the quality assurance function as it relates to and supports the <Program>.

2.3 OPERATIONAL PROCEDURES

The <Program> Quality Assurance Plan will include a <Program> Quality Control Plan that outlines the specifics of controlling product quality on the <Program>.

2.4 QUALITY MANUAL AND RECORD KEEPING

The Quality Assurance Representative is responsible for maintaining quality assurance records during the conduct of all phases of the <Program>.

2.5 THE <PROGRAM> QUALITY ASSURANCE PLAN WILL BE UPDATED AS REQUIRED

Each update will be treated as an original plan and shall follow the same authorization path. The <Program> Quality Assurance Plan shall be updated as necessary to incorporate any new or updated changes found necessary to the <Company> Quality Assurance Policies, Plans, or Procedures.

QUALITY CONTROL PLAN

The Quality Control Plan, in conjunction with <Company> Policy (<M-M Policy 07000> Series), provides direction, control, and authorization for the overall quality control of equipment and data on the <Program> Program.

SUGGESTED OUTLINE

1. Introduction
2. Scope
3. Applicable Documents
4. Management Organization
5. Quality System Planning
6. Contract Review
7. Design Control
8. Document Control
9. Purchasing

A. Purchaser Supplied Products

B. Product Identification and Traceability

10. Process Control

A. Inspection and Testing

B. Inspection, Measuring, and Test Equipment

C. Inspection and Test Status

D. Control of Non-Conforming Product

E. Corrective Action

11. Handling, Storage, Packing, and Delivery

12. Quality Records

13. Quality Audits

14. Training

15. Servicing

16. Statistical Techniques

17. Quality System Effectiveness Factors

Additional Notes:

- ❐ There is usually considerable overlap between Configuration Management (CM) plans, Data Management (DM) plans, and Quality plans of all levels (i.e., Quality Assurance and Quality Control).
- ❐ The above Quality Assurance Plan and Quality Control Plan are excerpts from the Modern-Management Policies, Plans, and Processes presented in the Strategy for Success workshops. To that end, words that appear in angle brackets (< >) are part of a "global" update (i.e., "Find and Replace") process that allows the users to enter their specific data throughout the plans.

Additional references that may contribute to developing your plan are:

Data Item Description: DI-QCIC-81379

ANSI/ASQC Quality Standards Q91 and Q92

ISO 9001 and 9002

MIL-Q-9858 and MIL-I-45208 (both for reference only)

MIL-STD-2167 AND 2168

ATTACHMENT 7

REQUIREMENTS TRACEABILITY MATRIX

One of the best methods of generating entries for the Requirements Traceability Matrix (RTM) is to conduct a "shalls" review and use those results as requirement entries in the RTM. If you have not accomplished this task before, don't worry. It is rather simple nowadays with the "find" function on most word processing programs. There are, of course, applications dedicated to pulling "shalls" and "wills" from requirements documents and creating an RTM for you. If you use one of these programs, don't trust it completely. Although they are quite good, they do make mistakes in judgment. It's up to you to ensure that the RTM is complete and accurate.

The U.S. Army defines traceability as:

> The capability to track system requirements from a system function to all elements of the system which, collectively or in-

> dividually, perform the function; an element of the system to all functions which it performs; a specific requirement of the source analysis or contractual constraint which originated the requirement. Traceability includes tracking allocation design (and technical program) requirements through the work breakdown structure between the system level and the lowest level of assembly.*

Most requirements documents, including SOWs and specifications, contain statements that follow the general convention of "The system shall . . . . . ." These are referred to as "shalls" and, in some cases, "musts" that constitute the core requirements of the system. Care must be taken to evaluate the use of the words "will" and "should" by the document creator. In some cases, "wills" or even "shoulds" are treated the same as "shalls" while in other cases "shalls" are mandatory and "wills" are optional. If the word "goal" shows up, try to get it quantified. I assure you that your interpretation of a goal will be different than the customer's interpretation of it.

To ensure that your system or product is exactly what the customer has specified, conduct a "shalls" and "wills" search, and place the results in an RTM. The usual convention is to place the reference paragraph on the far left and the requirement in the next column. Further columns trace the requirement through your system following the way your company does business and the nature of the output product. The concept, however, is the same regardless of methodology or product.

You can create and print forms for this purpose or you can use a spreadsheet application such as Excel or Lotus to accomplish the same purpose. To start the process, use your word processing program such as MS Word or MS Works or MacWrite or a similar program to search for the "shalls" and "wills." When you find one, simply copy and paste and include the paragraph number. If your programs are compatible, such as MS Office, it is a simple matter to transfer the entries from the word processing program to the spreadsheet program.

Be cautious in the construction of your RTM. Don't necessarily limit it to "shalls" and "wills." If you customer has some other way of stating mandatory and lesser requirements, that is certainly the convention to follow.

The point and purpose of an RTM is to trace a requirement from its begin-

---

**U.S. Army Field Manual (FM)*, 770–778.

ning in the requirements document (contract) to its final proof, such as the System Test. There must be enough detail in the RTM to point immediately to the place, paragraph, table, etc., where the requirement is allocated.

You should assign each requirement to a monitor. The monitor should be listed in a column in the RTM. You may assign more than one requirement to a person but don't simply assign all requirements to the chief engineer. Show the actual person responsible for that requirement.

In general, your RTM should look similar to Table A7-1.

Table A7-1 — Requirements Traceability Matrix (RTM)

SOW/ Spec Para	Requirement	WBS Number	S/C SOW/ Spec Para	Unit Test Number	System Test Para	Monitor
SOW						
4.3.1	Security	06-03-02	N/A	T-0304	4.4.1	Smith
Spec						
3.2.1	System weight shall be less than 10,000 pounds	02-04-03	3.4.6	T-0045	3.4.1	Jones

The same concept and organization can be applied to a Subcontract Requirements Traceability Matrix (SRTM) and used by your subcontractor.

For a small project, you can use a spreadsheet program. For a larger program you can use a spreadsheet "workbook" with requirements in one sheet, WBS information on the second sheet, etc. You can then link the cells together with hyperlinks from a master sheet to form a thread of information for each requirement.

You can also do the same thing with a Relational Data Base (RDB). The RDB will require more up-front time but will result in a more cohesive product.

The current industry standard is a family of products titled DOORS (for large and enterprise wide projects) and DOORSrequireIT (for smaller projects). Both are commonly referred to as "Doors." Doors is available from:

Telelogic DOORS North America
400 Valley Road, Suite 200

Mt. Arlington, NJ 07856
Phone: 949-830-8022
Fax: 949-830-8023
To order: 877-275-4777
E-mail: doorssupport.us@telelogic.com
Web site: www.telelogic.com/doors

REQUIREMENTS FLOW-DOWN MATRIX

You can look at a Requirements Traceability Matrix (RTM) as a horizontal function and a Requirements Flow-Down Matrix (RFM) as a vertical function. The RTM traces where a requirement appears in the overall process while the RFM shows where a requirement has been allocated. Both apply to both prime and subcontractors. The subcontractor versions are usually preceded with an "S" for differentiating between the two.

If you do not have a Requirements Flow-Down Matrix (or Plan), you can use Table A8-1 as a start. Modify the table for your own needs. Just be sure to not change the concepts of content and flow.

In the case of the RFM, there are two levels or sets of requirements to be flowed down. The first is the requirement from the customer as contained in

Table A8-1 — Requirements Flow-Down Matrix (RFM)

Spec Para	Company Reqt	WBS	Design Plan Para	S/C Plan Para	S/C A Para	S/C B Para
1.3.2		02-03-01	5.3.2	5.3.2	1.3.2	1.3.2
1.3.3		02-03-02	5.3.3	5.3.3	1.3.3	N/A
1.3.4		02-03-03	5.3.4	5.3.4	1.3.4	1.3.4
	QA Plan	04-01-01	8.2.6	8.2.6	4.3.6	4.3.6
	CM Plan	05-01-01	9.3.1	9.3.1	5.6.2	5.6.2

the SOW or specification. The second is a requirement demanded by enterprise policy.

In some cases, a requirement may be flowed down to one subcontractor and not another. Observe Spec Para Requirement 1.3.3 in the table cross-referenced to Subcontractor B. Such requirements could be those that are product-specific; perhaps Subcontractor A provides that kind of product but Subcontractor B does not.

ATTACHMENT 9

DATA DELIVERY MATRIX

Some tool is necessary to compile data delivery requirements from the requirements document (contract), put them in a common place, and assign word dates and delivery dates and responsibilities. The Data Delivery Matrix is a simple and effective tool for accomplishing this overall purpose and providing a central location of past activities as well. A Data Delivery Matrix can be created by using a spreadsheet such as the one shown in Table A9-1. The columns can be extended to the right for multiple deliveries or the right column can be updated periodically as necessary.

If your data manager is so inclined and so talented, a Relational Data Base (RDB) such as Access can be used to do the same thing as the matrix in Table A9-1. The RDB takes more time to set up in the beginning but will save time and possibly mistakes in the long run. If the RDB is used, set the report format so that at least the "Data" column, the "Frequency" column, the "Next Due"

Table A9-1 — Data Delivery Matrix

Doc No	Title	Resp.	Format	First Del	Frequency
A-0001	Monthly Progress Report	Jones	DID 1234	30 days ARO[1]	Monthly
T-0001	System Test Package	Smith	DID 2345	System Test minus 30 days	One time
T-0002	System Test Results	Harris	DID 4567	System Test plus 30 days	One time

[1]ARO: After Receipt of Order.

column, and the "Responsibility" column are shown in the report format. Usually, the Data Delivery Matrix is routed frequently to all responsible individuals as well as being posted in a central location in a "paper" program. On a "paperless" program the Data Delivery Matrix is provided on the Program Web site.

It is also useful to identify a cognizant individual (project manager, chief engineer, engineer, etc.) associated with each "X." These people can act as internal experts (consultants) during the execution of your project.

CAPABILITY MATRIX

The purpose of the Capability Matrix is to evaluate your past experience against current requirements and thus reveal the level of capability you have to perform the current requirement. By default, the Capability Matrix will reveal those areas of requirements (tasks) where you do not have capability and must either buy the capability (includes hiring knowledgeable personnel), develop the capability, no-bid the task or requirement, or take a risk in performing the task or requirement.

The Capability Matrix either feeds or is fed by the Experience Window (see Attachment 12) and/or the Risk List (see Attachment 3).

Create a matrix similar to the one shown in Table A10-1 and list all the requirements or tasks (this includes the contents of referenced documents as well as explicitly included documents) along the side and the programs (including IR&D programs) that the enterprise has performed across the top. Every

Table A10-1 — Capability Matrix

	Project A	Project B	Project C	Project D	Project E	Project F
Task 1			X			
Task 2		X		X		X
Task 3						
Task 4			X			
Task 5	X				X	
Task 6				X		
Task 7						X
Task 8		X			X	
Task 9						

requirement or task should have an "X" at the intersect with at least one program. If not, continue with the process to try to bring the requirement to within your capabilities.

POLICY-TO-PLAN TRAIL

A Policy-to-Plan trail is necessary to ensure that the policies required by the enterprise are incorporated into the Project Plan and the Technical Plan. After the first use, this document can be set aside if you create your own Project Plans and Technical Plans. Incorporate the required policies into the respective plans, together with a reference back to the policy. Mark, in your own way, those paragraphs as standard and use them for all subsequent projects and programs.

If you do not have a Policy-to-Plan Process, you can use Table A11-1 to start your process.

Once developed, the Policy-to-Plan Table can be used as an input document to the Standards Traceability Matrix (STM) (see Attachment 13).

The numbers appearing in the policy column reflect the enterprise policy number. The numbers appearing in the plan columns reflect the paragraph number of the plan where the policy is invoked.

Table A11-1 — Policy-to-Plan Table

Policy	Project/Program Plan	Technical Plan
11011-Startup	4.1.1	2.1.1
11013-Funding	5.1.2	
11024-PWA	6.2.2	4.3.2
11025-Work Packages	6.2.3	4.3.3
11027-Performance Measurement	7.4.4	5.4.3
11041-Program Reviews	8.2.2	6.2.3
11044-Action Items	9.1.1	7.2.2
15012-In-Process Reviews		6.2.4
15026-Engineering Drawings		8.1.1
15033-Specifications		9.2.2

EXPERIENCE WINDOW

The purpose of the Experience Window is to provide a quick check of your experience and evaluate that experience against your capability to perform a particular task. This is particularly important if you are in the process of bidding a task. It can also be used as the first step in determining whether you should seek additional capability in order to perform a task you already have. Table A12-1 shows the inputs for the Experience Window.

If you determine you do not have the experience, the next step is to use the Capability Matrix to refine your needs. A sample Capability Matrix is shown in Table A12-2 and described in Attachment 10 with further information provided in Cause Description 1b and 1b (NO).

Table A12-1 — Experience Window

Condition	Have Customer Experience	Have Product Experience	Capability to Perform
1	Yes	Yes	High
2	No	Yes	Moderate
3	Yes	No	Low
4	No	No	Unknown

Table A12-2 — Capability Matrix

	Project A	Project B	Project C	Project D	Project E	Project F
Task 1			X			
Task 2		X		X		X
Task 3						
Task 4			X			
Task 5	X				X	
Task 6				X		
Task 7						X
Task 8		X			X	
Task 9						

ATTACHMENT 13

STANDARDS TRACEABILITY MATRIX

The first question you may ask is: "What is the relationship between a Requirements Traceability Matrix (RTM) and the Standards Traceability Matrix (STM)?" The fact is that they both accomplish the same purpose but for different kinds of requirements. The STM traces standards that are common to the industry, the customer, and the enterprise. The RTM tracks SOW and specification requirements that are unique (although some may be common) to this task.

The purpose of the STM is to "track" a standard that is common to the industry or required by the customer or the enterprise into the Program Plan and/or the Technical Plan. The matrix shown below is a typical and easy way of conducting this exercise. To develop this matrix, you can use a spreadsheet or a Relational Data Base (RDB). The spreadsheet method is easy and quick but can lead to some confusion because of duplication or overlap. The RDB is more difficult to create but always maintains the same relationships to other requirements.

The matrix in Table A13-1 is a multipurpose matrix in that the Industry, Customer, and Enterprise Standards Documents are all included in one chart. You can use this technique or separate them into three different charts. The advantage of using three charts is that Industry and Enterprise charts will probably remain constant for most, if not all, projects and only the Customer Chart needs to be researched. The advantage of using the multipurpose chart is that the relationships between all elements—and there will be many—are clearly presented in one place.

Before the project starts, you should have a Standards Appearance Matrix already established for all the known standards and enterprise documents that drive the Project and Technical Plans. This is frequently a staff function and might appear in one of your enterprise policies. If it does not, build your own. There should be plenty of blank rows in the standard to work with. Use the blank rows to enter the requirements specific to your task. Your requirements document (contract) will drive the entries in the customer column. Ensure that every necessary standard is covered. In the sample matrix above, notice that, in the second entry, a customer document and an enterprise document are side-by-side. That's because they are the same requirement. It is common for a company to absorb standard requirements for their areas of operation as standard policies within the company. If you use a multipurpose matrix and the standards are common, include them both on the same row. If any requirement exists in any column, ensure that it is covered.

You can clearly see the relationship between the Enterprise Policies, Plans, and Processes and the various paragraphs of the Program/Project Plan in Figure A13-1. Further, the figure shows the relationship between Attachments and Appendices to the Program/Project Plan and the paragraphs of the Program/Project Plan as well as the Enterprise Policies, Plans, and Processes.

Table A13-1 — Standards Traceability Matrix

STANDARDS			APPEARANCE	
Industry	**Customer**	**Enterprise**	**Project Plan**	**Technical Plan**
ISO-9001	ISO-9001	Enterprise Quality Policy 09350	Para 4.6.8	Part I, Para 4.5.6
	MIL-STD-100	Enterprise Engineering Standards 06050	N/A	Part II, Para 1.2.3

Figure A13-1 — Policy-to-Program Plan to Support Document Flow

Enterprise Policies, Plans, & Processes		Program Plan	Attachs & Appeds
	1	Introduction	
	2	Scope	
	2.1	Program Description	
	2.2	Deliverables	C
	2.3	Schedule	18
M-M 04018	2.4	Sell-off Criteria	27
	3	Reference Documents	
	3.1	Contract	
	3.2	Customer Documents	
	4	Unusual Contract Clauses	
	5	Responsibilities	
	5.1	Organization, Staffing, and Responsibilities	
	5.1.1	General	
M-M 05000	5.1.2	System Management	
M-M 06000	5.1.3	Subcontracts and Materials	20
M-M 04050	5.1.4	Data Management	4
M-M 04030	5.1.5	Configuration Management	3
M-M 07000	5.1.6	Quality Assurance	14
M-M 10050	5.1.7	Team Members and Alliances	15
M-M 11000	5.1.8	Training	23

This matrix should be built for the entirety of the Program/Project Plan and another should be constructed for the Technical Plan.

The symbol M-M refers to my company Modern-Management and is a part of the file database for all writings, workshops, and seminars. You need to enter your company policies, processes, etc., in this column.

I sincerely hope you are reading this Cause Description before your program starts rather than trying to recover from a problem. This is a time-consuming process, but is necessary for a smooth-running program.

If you have built your Project or Program plan according to the recommendations of this book, all but the left-most column will be apparent. It should then be a simple matter to insert your company plans into the left-most column.

If you have your own outline for a Project or Program Plan, you will need to start from scratch. The mechanics, however, are the same.

Once you receive your contract, you can begin referencing the elements of the contract to the outline of the Project Plan and the Technical Plan.

ATTACHMENT 14

VENDOR EVALUATION PROCESS

Several things need to be said about vendors. First, they are very important to a lot of businesses. Perhaps they are important to your business as well. Second, you should have a broad and deep supply of vendors you can rely upon to provide products for your projects. Third, a central file should be kept on all vendors who deal with your company. The central file should contain performance histories of each vendor and, hopefully, a quality process to quantify the vendor's performance. Fourth, you should have an evaluation process to evaluate and reevaluate each vendor for each procurement for each project. It is the fourth item that this process is all about.

For each procurement, establish an evaluation scheme before the Request for Proposal (RFP) or Request for Quotation (RFQ) is released. Decide on what is most important: cost, schedule, technical, etc. Then weight the evaluation scheme so that it will evaluate each vendor's response fairly and equally. Create an evaluation team with specialists in each of the areas to be evaluated (management, engineering, materials, quality, etc.). When the vendor's proposals are received, begin the evaluation process.

Each specialty area—management, engineering, materials, quality, etc.—should have a sheet for each similar to the Vendor Evaluation Sheet shown in Figure A14-1 on page 260. The factors in each sheet will change with the specialty area and will be consistent with the overall evaluation scheme devised before the RFP/RFQ was issued and documented by the materials or subcontracts manager in a cover letter to all evaluators.

The materials or subcontracts manager will order and stack the Vendor Evaluation Forms as they come in and enter the results for each vendor in the Vendor Evaluation Summary Form as shown in Figure A14-2 on page 261.

Finally, the results from the Vendor Evaluation Summary Form will be transferred to the appropriate lines on the Vendor Selection Summary Score Sheet as in Figure A14-3 on page 262. The winner is determined from the Vendor Selection Summary Score Sheet.

Figure A14-1 — Vendor Evaluation Sheet

VENDOR EVALUATION

Date	4-Jul-02
Program	High-Flyer
Subcontractor/Vendor	National Software
Equipment/Software	Analog Selction Algorithm
Evaluator	G. Smith
Scale Factor	0-5

Item	Consideration	Rating*
1	Organization	3
2	Management	4
3	Manpower	5
4	Access to Management	5
5	Processes	3
6	Procedures	2
7		
8		
9		
10		
	Subtotal**	22
	No. of items rated**	6
	Average of ratings (Subtotal/No of items)**	3.7

*An evaluated number within the Scale Factor.
**Calculated number.

M-M Form

Figure A14-2 — Vendor Evaluation Summary

VENDOR EVALUATION SUMMARY

Date	
Program	
Subcontractor/Vendor	
Equipment/Software	

Item	Consideration	Scale	Rating*
1	Technical	0–25	10
2	Management	0–5	2
3	Quality	0–15	7
4	Procurement	0–5	3
5	Financial	0–10	5
6	Delivery	0–20	10
7	Cost	0–20	10
8			
9			
10			
	Subtotal		47
	No. of items rated		7
	Average of ratings (Subtotal/No of items)		6.7

Current Quality Vendor survey on file?	Yes
D&B on file?	Yes

*From Vendor Evaluation Sheets

Figure A14-3 — Vendor Selection Summary Score Sheet

VENDOR SELECTION SUMMARY SCORE SHEET

SCORE SHEET FOR: *

Date Item

EVALUATION CONSIDERATIONS (POINT ALLOCATION = 100)

Vendor	Name	Score
1.		
2.		
3.		
4.		
5.		

Total (Sum of Points Given)

Score (Total/No. of Entries)

Comments:

Comments:

You should have a Vendor Evaluation Summary Score Sheet for each of the operating elements of the team (Engineering, Management, QA, etc.) and each of the factors of the procurement (cost, delivery, etc.). This form is the summary, by evaluator, of all the previous forms.

This form can be modified and used to evaluate subcontractor and vendor proposals. In that case, establish a "weighting" for each of the factors based on your program (e.g., Is technical more important than cost?)

*Operating element or factor, such as: Technical, Management, QA, Procurement, Cost, Delivery, etc.

M-M Form F-06013A

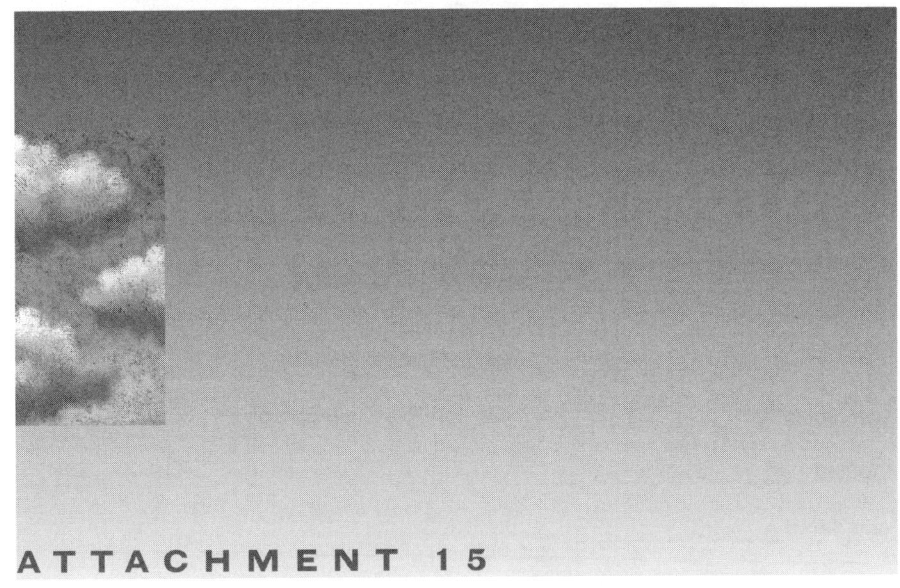

ATTACHMENT 15

DESIGN REVIEW APPROVAL FORM

The Design Review Approval Form in Figure A15-1 is used to document the completion of all the elements of a design review. While you may have documented each of the elements (i.e., Design Review Package, Design Review, etc.) individually, it is a good idea to have one form where all the elements are recognized and approved. This will come in handy when you are assembling all the data for sell-off.

Figure A15-1 — Design Review Approval Form

DESIGN REVIEW APPROVAL

The ________(1)_____________ Design Review Minutes

containing the ______(1)_________Design Review Package

labeled _______(2)____________

and dated _____(3)________

and

The _________(1)___________Design Review

conducted on _____(3)__________ together with the Design Review Action Items are

hereby approved

therefore

__________(4)____________________ is hereby directed to proceed to the next stage

of the program.

Signed _____(5)________ of __________(6)_____________ Date _______________

Where:

(1) The Design Review—PDR, CDR, etc.
(2) Modification or issue
(3) Date of package or event
(4) The Contractor
(5) The Customer's Representative
(6) The Contracting Authority

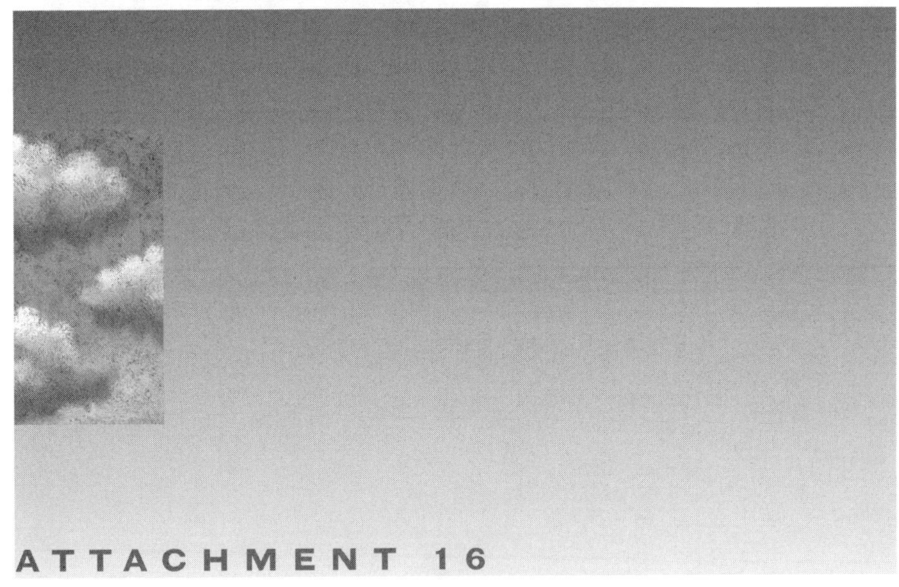

ATTACHMENT 16

IN-PROCESS REVIEW APPROVAL FORM

The In-Process Review Form shown in Figure A16-1 can be used by you to document the In-Process Reviews you have conducted in-house, or it can be initiated by you and signed by your customer, or it can be initiated by your subcontractor or team mate (probably by you) and acknowledged by you for the purpose of documentation. The point is: Document the activity!

Figure A16-1 — In-Process Review Approval Form

IN-PROCESS REVIEW APPROVAL FORM

The ___(1)____ In-Process Review Minutes containing

the __(1)_____In-Process Review Package

labeled ___(2)_______ and

dated ____(3)_______

and

The __(1)___In-Process Review

conducted on ___(3)_______ together with the In-Process Review Action Items are

hereby approved

therefore

____(4)____ is hereby directed to proceed to the next stage of the program.

Signed ___(5)_____ of ______(6)________ Date _______________

Where:

(1) The In-Process Review (Step 1, Step 2, etc.)
(2) Modification or issue
(3) Date of package or event
(4) The contractor or lead engineer
(5) The appropriate authority
(6) The organization of the appropriate authority

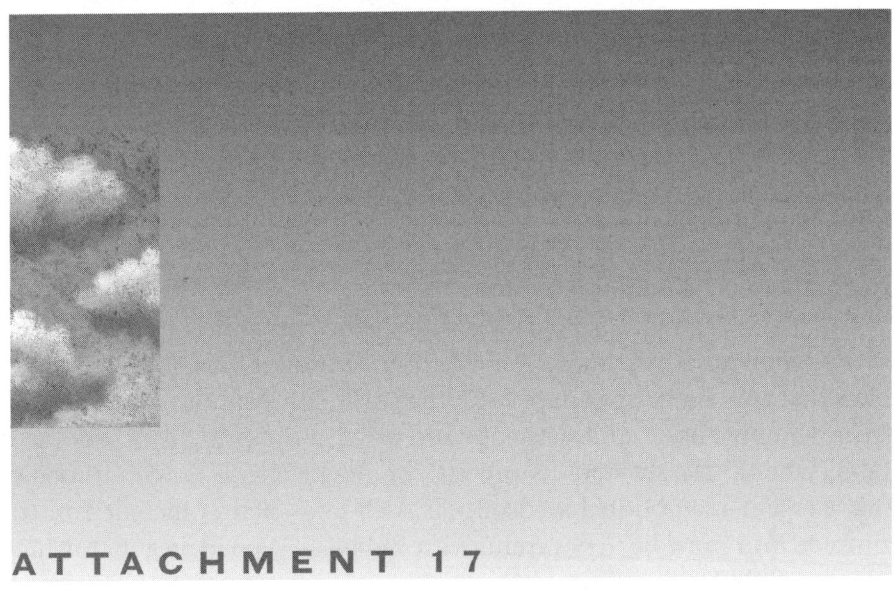

ATTACHMENT 17

NEGOTIATION CHECKLIST

Before entering *any* negotiation, you should outline your needs and wants and then seriously consider the list. Ensure that *needs* are indeed needs and *wants* are indeed wants and that they are not intermixed. Wants and needs include all items except price.

The next element to define is the price you are willing to pay or be paid (depending on which side of the table you are sitting on). Usually, this price is not necessarily a single number but a range of numbers. Because of the complexity of most negotiations, you need to outline what this number or range of numbers represents. This is your basic "Negotiation Envelope." In other words, if you get the scope you want or need within the price you are willing to accept or pay, everything is okay. Usually, your Negotiation Envelope must be approved by someone with contractual and Profit and Loss (P&L) responsibility.

If, during negotiations, the Negotiation Envelope is about to be exceeded or is not being achieved, you must either ask for—or declare—a recess and return to the approval authority to get additional authority, or you must conclude the negotiations as being unsuccessful.

The basic Negotiation Envelope is frequently modified by additional scope/ price arguments sometimes referred to as "Bubbles." Bubbles are single-issue items that contain their own price. Usually, Bubbles are not stand-alone but are dependent on a basic contract scope and price in order to be incorporated. Each Bubble should clearly state its precedence requirements or conditions such as: This element may be included only if such-and-such is included in the basic contract. You must be very careful with Bubbles. A smart negotiator may try to get your Bubbles included without including the necessary precedents/conditions or cost.

Your Negotiation Checklist should containing headings like:

- ❐ Program
- ❐ Scope
- ❐ Objective Price
- ❐ Acceptable Price Range
- ❐ Negotiator
- ❐ Authority

Each Bubble should have its own Negotiation Checklist that contains headings like:

- ❐ Program
- ❐ Addition
- ❐ Scope
- ❐ Precedence/Conditions
- ❐ Objective Price
- ❐ Acceptable Price Range
- ❐ Negotiator
- ❐ Authority

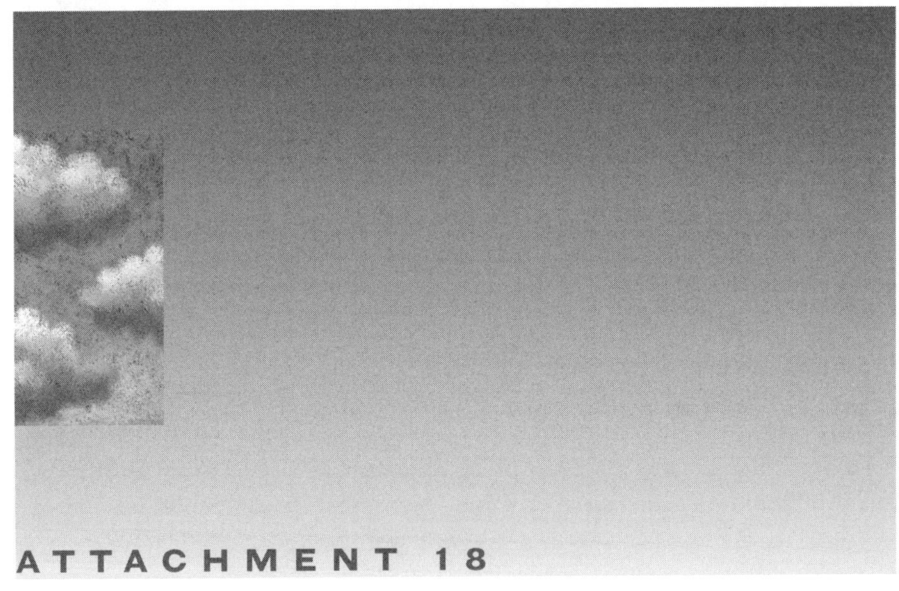

CRITICAL SUCCESS FACTOR (CSF) MATRIX

It is necessary to track each Critical Success Factor (CSF) from requirement to implementation. The tracking of CSFs is a little more complex in that each CSF must be tracked into each unit to which it should be applied. Further, proof must be supplied along the way and in the final system test that each CSF is being met.

If you do not have such a checklist, an outline follows that you can employ. Modify Table A18-1 for your own needs.

Table A18-1 — Critical Success Factor (CSF) Matrix

CSF	Unit A	Unit B	Unit C	Unit D	Final Proof
MTTR 0.5 hrs	0.5 hrs	0.5 hrs	0.5 hrs	0.5 hrs	RMA Analysis Para 3.2.1
MTBF 30,000 hrs	30,000 hrs	30,000 hrs	30,000 hrs	30,000 hrs	RMA Analysis Para 3.2.2

BIBLIOGRAPHY

Books

Blanchard, Kenneth and Spencer Johnson. *The One Minute Manager.* New York: William Morrow and Co., Inc., 1982.

de Bono, Edward. *Serious Creativity.* New York: Harper Business, 1992.

Fishman, George S. *Monte Carlo: Concepts, Algorithms, and Applications.* New York: Springer-Verlag, 1996.

Guffey, Mary Ellen. *Business Communication: Process and Product.* 2nd ed. Cincinnati: South-Western College Publishing, 1997.

McDermott, Robin E., et al. *The Basics of FMEA.* Portland, Ore.: Productivity Press, Inc., 1996.

Rothenberg, Robert. *The Plain-Language Law Dictionary.* New York: Penguin, 1996.

Rubenstein, Reuven Y. *Simulation and the Monte Carlo Method.* New York: John Wiley, 1981.

Senge, Peter. *The Fifth Discipline: The Art and Practice of the Learning Organization.* New York: Doubleday, 1990.

Sobol, Ilya M. *A Primer for the Monte Carlo Method.* Boca Raton, Fla.: CRC Press, LLC, 1994.

Stamatis, Dean H. *Failure Mode and Effect Analysis: FMEA from Theory to Execution.* Milwaukee, Wis.: ASQ Quality Press, 1995.

U.S. Army Field Manual (FM) 770-78. Available from the Superintendent of Documents, Government Printing Office (GPO), Washington, D.C., or the Consumer Information Center, Pueblo, Colo., and in digital form, online at: www.incose.org/stc/fm77078.htm.

Articles

Barnes, Brenda J., and James W. Van Wormer, Ph.D. "Process Thinking and the 85:15 Rule Applied to Education." Source: www.grandblancommunityschools.com/qip/processthinking.htm (last accessed Aug. 5, 2002).

Chen, P. "The Entity-Relationship Model: Toward a Unified View of Data." *ACM Transactions on Database Systems*, 1, no. 1 (1976): 9–36.

Luttman, Robert & Associates Online Articles, "Cause and Effect." Source: www.robertluttman.com/cause-effect.html (last accessed Aug. 5, 2002).

Patrick, Francis S. "Program Management—Turning Many Projects into Few Priorities with TOC." Newtown Square, Pa.: Project Management Institute, 1999. (Project Management Institute Seminar/Symposium [30th : 1999 : Philadelphia, Pa.], PMI 1999 Annual Seminars & Symposium Proceedings.)

Plsek, P.E. "Management and Planning Tools of TQM." *Quality Management in Health Care* 1, no. 3 (Spring 1993): 59–72.

Private Documents

Early, John F., ed. "Cause-Effect Diagrams." *Quality Improvement Tools.* Wilton, Conn.: Juran Institute, 1989. The training kit entitled *Quality Improvement Tools* is produced by the Juran Institute, and is a part of their inventoried items.

Systems Application Architecture—Common User Access Guide to User Interface Design. IBM Corporation, 1991. IBM Document Number SC34-4289. Available through IBM field offices.

The Windows Interface Guidelines for Software Design. Redmond, Wash.: Microsoft Press, 1995. ISBN 1556156790. Available from Best Buy Books.

TRADEMARKS

Brainstorming™ is a trademark of Infinite Innovations, Ltd.
DOORSrequireIT™ is a trademark of Telelogic DOORS, North America

EDGE Diagrammer™ and EDGE Programmer™ are trademarks of Pacestar Software

Flowcharting Cause & Effect Module for Six Sigma Software Suite™ is a trademark of Quality America, Inc.

MacWrite™ is a trademark of Apple Corporation

MBTI™ is a trademark of Consulting Psychologists, Inc.

Microsoft™, Microsoft Word™, MS Word™, Microsoft Excel™, MS Excel™, Microsoft Access™, MS Access™, Microsoft Office™, MS Office™, Microsoft Works™, MS Works™ are trademarks of Microsoft Corporation

PathMaker™ is a trademark of SkyMark

PMBN™ is a trademark of Best Practices, LLC.

Post-it™ is a trademark of 3M Company

REASON 4™ is a trademark of DECISION Systems, Inc.

Root Cause Analysis (RCA)™ is a trademark of Root Cause Analyst

Six Sigma for Excel™ is a trademark of BaRaN Systems LLC.

SmartDraw™ is a trademark of SmartDraw.com

INDEX